PURITAN PAPERS

A Symposium of Papers Read at Four Annual
Puritan and Reformed Studies Conferences,
Westminster Chapel, London

PURITAN PAPERS

Volume 1
1956–1959

EDITED BY
D. Martyn Lloyd-Jones

FOREWORD BY
W. Robert Godfrey

P&R
PUBLISHING
P.O.BOX 817 • PHILLIPSBURG • NEW JERSEY 08865-0817

Previously published as separate annual volumes by Tentmaker Publications.
Compiled and reformatted by the den Dulk Christian Foundation.

Published by the den Dulk Christian Foundation, Kingsburg, California,
and by P&R Publishing Company, Phillipsburg, New Jersey, on behalf of the
Committee of the Westminster Conference.

Page design by Tobias Design
Typesetting by Michelle Feaster

Printed in the United States of America

ISBN: 0-87552-466-4

CONTENTS

Part 4: How Shall They Hear? (1959)

FOREWORD

W. Robert Godfrey

Puritanism has been controversial from its beginning. The principles and passions of the Puritans, along with the powerful attraction of their movement in the seventeenth century, made them profoundly influential in church and society. Their convictions and impact also made them very unpopular with many in their own day and ever since. The Puritans have had severe critics from the beginning. William Shakespeare, for example, disparaged them in *Twelfth Night*:

> MARIA: Marry, sir, sometimes he is a kind of puritan.
> SIR ANDREW: O, if I thought that, I'd beat him like a dog.

A popular song of the early seventeenth century accused them of hypocrisy:

> Pure in show, an upright holy man,
> Corrupt within—and called a Puritan.

Lord Macaulay, in a famous statement, caricatured them as kill-joys: "The Puritan hated bear-baiting, not because it gave pain to the bear, but because it gave pleasure to the spectators."

Yet even Macaulay had grudgingly to recognize the fortitude and commitment of the Puritan: "The Puritan was made up of two different men, the one all self-abasement, penitence, gratitude, passion, the other proud, calm, inflexible, sagacious. He prostrated himself in the dust before his Maker; but he set his foot on the neck of the king."

Scholarship in recent decades has recognized the vitality and power of the Puritan movement for its lasting impact not only in religion, but also in politics, education, economics, and science. The great increase in knowledge about the Puritans and the recognition of their influence has done little, however, to change the widespread perception of the Puritans as busybodies who sought to eliminate pleasure from life, by force if necessary, in the service of their arbitrary and unattractive God.

In the light of these attitudes it is truly remarkable that about fifty years ago two young scholars conceived the idea of holding a conference on Puritanism as a practical help for pastors and Christians generally. Surely a modern conference largely devoted to the study of Puritan thought as a vital resource for the contemporary church would not commend itself to many. But O. Raymond Johnston and James I. Packer had an advantage over many: they had actually read the Puritans. They had so profited spiritually from their own study of the Puritans that they wanted others to share in the rich spiritual blessing that had been theirs. In the late 1940s they consulted with D. Martyn Lloyd-Jones, minister at Westminster Chapel, London, who enthusiastically embraced the idea and offered the chapel as a meeting place for what became known as "The Puritan Conference."

The first conference took place in December 1950. Six papers, each about an hour in length, were read over the course of two days, one in the morning and two in the afternoon. After each paper a discussion followed of about one hour, often a very vigorous exchange of ideas. The basic form of the conference has remained the same over the years. For nearly thirty years Dr. Lloyd-Jones chaired the sessions of the conference and from 1959 contributed an annual paper and led the discussions. His commitment to the conference reflected his conviction: "As I see things, it is of supreme importance for the future of the Christian faith in this country that we should experience a revival of interest in the literature of the great Puritans of the seventeenth century."[1]

James I. Packer organized the conference for many years and contributed regularly for the first twenty years. His keen study and analysis helped set a very high standard for the papers. His presentations, along with those of Dr. Lloyd-Jones, ensure that the volumes of the conference papers from those years are of great value.

No conference was held in 1970. Dr. Lloyd-Jones objected strongly to some of the ecumenical positions taken by Dr. Packer. Dr. Lloyd-Jones was approached by several men who asked him to chair a reconvened conference of the same character as the earlier ones. He agreed to do this, and so the Westminster Conference was held in 1971 and has continued to operate under that name.

The basic purpose of the conference has remained the same for the fifty years of its existence. As Dr. Packer wrote in a foreword to the 1958 conference papers,

> [the conference] exists because its organisers believe that historic Reformed theology in general, and the teaching of the great Puritans in particular, does justice to certain neglected Biblical truths and emphases which the church today urgently needs to re-learn. This is not, of course, to imply that Puritan expositions of Scripture are infallible and final, or that the Puritans always succeeded in balancing truth in exactly the right proportions; nor is it suggested (forsooth!) that the way to solve the problems which face Christians of the twentieth century is to teach them to walk and talk as if they were living in the seventeenth. What is meant is simply that the Puritans were strongest just where Protestants today are weakest, and their writings can give us more real help than those of any other body of Christian teachers, past or present, since the days of the apostles.

The pursuit of that "real help" from the Puritans was very much the purpose of the conference. Again, Dr. Packer: "The interests of the Conference, therefore, are practical and constructive, not merely academic. . . . the aim of the Conference is to make a constructive application of what is learned to our own situation."

The conference played a vital role in reinvigorating evangelicalism with a strong Reformed influence in Great Britain and beyond. The decision to publish the conference papers annually in 1956 further extended its influence. God used this conference—along with the work of great preachers and scholars, the Evangelical Library, the Banner of Truth Trust, and other agencies—to renew British evangelicalism.

The historical importance of the Puritan Conference and its papers is clear. For that reason alone the decision of the den Dulk Christian Foundation to reprint these papers is sound and proper. But these papers are much more than historical documents, and the foundation—dedicated primarily to the publication and dissemination of Reformed literature—has seen that. The republication of these studies will continue their original purpose: to furnish Christians today with insight into the rich heritage of Puritan thought. In the shallowness, pragmatism, and confusion of much current evangelicalism, the depth, conviction, and steadiness of the Puritans can again help renew the churches.

[1] Iain Murray, *D. Martyn Lloyd-Jones, The Fight of Faith 1939–1981* (Edinburgh Banner of Truth, 1990), 2:352.

Part 1

The Wisdom of
Our Fathers

❧

1956

1

THE PURITANS AND THE
DOCTRINE OF ELECTION

Iain Murray

It would be foolish to ignore the very wide difference which lies between our days and those of our seventeenth-century forefathers. Their times were characterized by the powerful operations of the Spirit of God. The observance of secret prayer and family worship, the hearing of sermons of two hours' duration, the keeping of days for thanksgiving or for fasting, were all pleasant duties to a great many of the people. Macaulay truly wrote of the Puritans, "To know Him, to serve Him, to enjoy Him, was with them the great end of existence." It was not uncommon in their days for such a demonstration of the Spirit to accompany the word preached that multitudes were converted—five hundred people traced their conversion to one sermon preached by John Livingstone at Kirk O' Shotts in 1630—and believers overwhelmed with the force of the truth.

Thomas Goodwin, after hearing Rogers of Dedham preach,

hung "a quarter of an hour upon the neck of his horse weeping, before he had power to mount." From the Houses of Parliament to the homes of lowly cottagers godliness was known and loved. One historian writing of seventeenth-century Scotland, says, "There was the atmosphere of a paradise of communion with God." But an even clearer difference between their times and ours is in matters of doctrine, and no doctrine so unquestionably proves this as the doctrine of election. Of all the doctrines of the gospel, the one about which Christians today have become must unlike the Puritans in their view of it, is the doctrine of election.

It is the place which the Puritans gave to this doctrine, and the value which they set upon it, which supplies the real explanation why their memory and writings have fallen into such neglect and even disrepute in the last hundred years. The enlightened nineteenth century outgrew the Calvinistic faith of their forefathers. Matthew Arnold could write of the Puritan movement, with its doctrine of election, as extinct, save for some backward corners of the land. Professor Froude of Oxford, addressing the students of St. Andrews in 1871, declared, "Every one here present must have become familiar in late years with the change of tone throughout Europe and America on the subject of Calvinism. After being accepted for two centuries in all Protestant countries it has come to be regarded by liberal thinkers as a system of belief incredible in itself, dishonouring to its object, and as intolerable as it has been itself intolerant" *(Short Studies on Great Subjects,* J. A. Froude, vol. 2, Ch. Calvinism). In 1873 even such an alleged leader of evangelical thought as Dr. Dale of Birmingham described Calvinism as obsolete. Spurgeon had few to stand by him when he replied to Dale, "Those who labour to smother 'Calvinism' will find that it dies hard, and, it may be, they will come, after many defeats, to perceive the certain fact that it will outlive its opponents. Its funeral oration has been pronounced many times before now, but the performance has been premature. It will live when the present phase of religious misbelief has gone down to eternal execration amid the groans of those whom it has undone. Today it may be sneered at; nevertheless, it is but yesterday that it numbered among its adherents the ablest men of the age, and tomorrow it may be, when once again there shall be giants in theology, it will come to the front, and ask in vain for its adversaries" *(The Sword and Trowel,* Feb. 1874). Any superficial consideration of the Puritans which overlooks the great gulf which lies between their doctrine, and the doctrine commonly accepted by most evangelicals today, merely obscures the real issues. The doctrine of election was vital to the Puritans, they believed with Zanchius that it "is the golden thread that runs through the whole Christian system," and they asserted that a departure from this truth would bring a visible church under God's judgment and indignation. No subject could have a more direct reference to us and to our times.

In taking up this subject it is essential to remind ourselves of the manner and spirit in which the Puritans approached the doctrine of election. "This truth," writes Anthony Burgess, "may be handled either sinfully or profitably; sinfully as when it is treated on only to satisfy curiosity, and to keep up a mere barren speculative dispute . . . This point of election . . . is not to be agitated in a verbal and contentious way, but in a saving way, to make us tremble and to set us upon a more diligent and close striving with God in prayer, and all other duties . . . This doctrine, if any other, should produce sobriety, holy fear, and trembling" (folio entitled *"Spiritual Refinings,"* Sermon 111, 1658). The Puritans were men whose deep concern was to feel the power of the truth in their hearts.

Let us then proceed to the doctrine itself. The following statement from the Westminster Confession of Faith, declares their united belief: *"By the decree of God, for the manifestation of His glory, some men and angels are predestinated unto everlasting life, and others foreordained to everlasting death . . . Those of mankind that are predestinated unto life, God, before the foundation of the world was laid, according to His eternal and immutable purpose, and the secret counsel and good pleasure of His will, hath chosen in Christ, unto everlasting glory, out of His mere free grace and love, without any foresight of faith or good works"* (Confession 3.3, 5).

From this tremendous statement we can extract the principal points of their doctrine of election.

(1) Election Is an Act of God's Eternal Will and Sovereign Pleasure

All the Puritan divines were agreed in this, writes Sibbes, "that there was an eternal separation of men in God's purpose; secondly, that this first decree of severing man to his ends, is an act of sovereignty over his creature, and altogether independent of anything in the creature as a cause of it" (Sibbes's Preface to Baynes on Ephesians, Nichols ed., p. 3). "The purpose of God," writes Thomas Brooks, "is the sovereign cause of all that good that is in man, and of all that external, internal and eternal good that comes to man. Not works past, for men are chosen from everlasting, not works present, for Jacob was loved and chosen before he was born; nor works forseen, for men were all corrupt in Adam. All a believer's present happiness, and all his future happiness, springs from the eternal purpose of God" (Brooks's Works, Nichols, 5:317). "God dealeth not equally with all," asserts Thomas Manton, "that are of equal merit . . . That grace is given to some and not to others, floweth from God's eternal decree. This eternal decree is a free election, or the mere pleasure of God, giving faith to some and not to others" (Manton's Works, 20:361–62, Nichols). Burgess expounding John 17:2, "That to as many as thou hast given him, he should give eternal life," says, "We see here that God the Father hath power to appoint and determine concerning the everlasting salvation and damnation of men: It's plain, for you see it is as the Father wills, whom He chooses He gives to Christ . . . This disparity of God's grace choosing some and leaving others, is plainly asserted by Scripture, Matthew 11, where Christ makes a solemn acknowledging of it . . . Take we then this Truth for a foundation, it is in the sovereign power of God to choose when He pleases to Salvation and to leave the rest in their damnable estate: *Neither is this any cruelty or injustice in God,* for He might have forsaken all mankind, and not recovered one of them" (A. Burgess, Expository Sermons on John 17, Folio 1656).

(2) Election Is an Unchangeable Act

It is according to God's "immutable purpose." Which means, as the Confession states (3.4) that the number of the elect "cannot be either increased or diminished," and that therefore God infallibly gives them in time all things necessary for their eternal salvation. "The doctrine of election," says Elisha Coles, "containeth the whole sum and scope of the gospel," all the other parts are but the carrying out of God's first intention. Listen to Thomas Goodwin giving a comment on this marvellous truth. "All the ways and acts that God doth to eternity are but mere expressions of that love which he at first took up," when He elected us. "Christ, and heaven, and whatever else God shews you of love and mercy in this world, or in the world to come, they all lay in the womb of that first act. God was not drawn on to love us, as a man is, who first begins to love one, and to set his heart upon him, and then his heart being engaged, he is drawn on beyond what he thought, and is enticed to do this and thus beyond what he first intended. No, God is not as a man herein, but as 'known unto God are all his works, from the beginning of the world,' so is all his love that he meant to bestow. There is no new thing to God, his love at the very first dash, when he began to love us, was as perfect as it will be when we are in heaven . . . My brethren, when God first began to love you, he gave you all that he ever meant to give you in the lump, and eternity of time is that in which he is retailing of it out" (Goodwin's Works, Nichols, 2: 166–67). Brooks drives home the same truth in these words: "The love of God is unchangeable; 'whom he loves he loves to the end,' John 13:3; whom God loves once he will love for ever. He is not as man, soon in and soon off again, Malachi 3:6, James 1:17; Oh no! His love is like himself, lasting, yea, everlasting; 'I have loved thee with an everlasting love,' Jeremiah 31:3" (Brooks, Nichols, 5:316).

It is this "immutable purpose" of God which makes the conversion (effectual calling), justification, and perseverance of the elect certain. "Whom he did predestinate, them he also called: and whom he called, them he also justified; and whom he justified, them he also glorified" (Romans 8:30). Thomas Horton

mightily expounds that verse—"It is clear from the text that
God's Election and Predestination is necessarily and infallibly followed with other acts in the *execution* of it, as calling and justification etc." There is an "indissoluble connection and conjunc-
tion of the means with the end. These rings and links in this
golden chain here before us are so involved one in another, as
that they cannot possibly be disjoined or severed one from the
other . . . predestination is not only the antecedent, but also the
cause of effectual vocation. And the same grace, and good pleasure of God, that ordains us to eternal life, makes us also to embrace the means which tend to this life . . . Those who were
elected shall be glorified, God Himself cannot be deceived, nor
his purpose be intercepted, nor his calling be revoked" (Horton's
Sermons on Romans 8, folio 1674, pp. 500–507. See also Westminster Confession 3.6).

(3) Election Is in Relation to Christ

Now this truth lay at the very heart of their doctrine of election and determined every other part of gospel truth. God, says
the apostle Paul, "hath chosen us in Him [in Christ] before the
foundation of the world" (Ephesians 1:4). "His first choice of us
was a founding us on Christ," comments Goodwin on this verse,
"and in and together with choosing us, a setting us into him, so
as then to be represented by him. So that now we are to run the
same fortune, if I may so speak, with Christ himself for ever, our
persons being made mystically one with his, and he a Common
Person to us in election. Other men, as likewise the angels that
fell, were ordained to be *in themselves,*—to stand or fall by themselves . . . But we were considered in Christ from the first, and
therefore, though we fall, we shall rise again in him and by him
for he is a Common Person for us, and to stand for us, and is for
ever to look to us, to bring us to all that God ordained us unto,
and so this foundation remains sure. We are chosen in Christ,
and therefore are in as sure a condition, as for final perishing, as
Christ himself . . . Remember election is unto this great privilege,
to be in Christ, and one with him, (of all the highest, and fundamental to all other)" (Goodwin's Works, 1:76–77, Nichols).

It is not until we understand this point that we will see why the Puritans regarded a denial of the doctrine of election as an overthrow of the whole nature of the gospel. The great glory of the New Covenant is that God should carry out both His part and ours, and He does this by committing the elect to the care of Christ, by whom they are given all saving graces. "Christ, as mediator," says Brooks, "had a command from his Father to die, and he observes it: 'I lay down my life for my sheep; this commandment have I received of my Father,' John 10:11, 15 . . . Jesus Christ has not only leave to save the elect, but a charge to save the elect: 'All that the Father giveth me, shall come to me, and him that cometh to me, I will in no wise cast out, for I came down from heaven, not to do mine own will but the will of him that sent me. And this is the Father's will which hath sent me, that of all which he hath given me, I should lose nothing, but should raise it up again at the last day . . .' Christ is to be answerable for all those that are given to him; at the last day, and therefore we need not doubt but that he will certainly employ all the power of his Godhead to secure and save all those that he must be accountable for. Christ's Charge and care of these that are given to him, extends even to the very day of their resurrection, that he may not so much as lose their dust, but gather it together again, and raise it up in glory, to be a proof of his fidelity, for, saith he, 'I should lose nothing, but raise it up again at the last day'" (Brooks, 5:368–69).

We find this truth affirmed throughout the writings of the Puritans. Thomas Manton says, "If the elect should not be saved, Christ should neither do his work nor receive his wages" (Manton's Works, 5:213). Likewise Christopher Love, "If the elect could perish then Jesus Christ should be very unfaithful to his Father, because God the Father hath given this charge to Christ, that whomsoever he elected, Christ should preserve them safe, to bring them to heaven. Now should not this be accomplished, Christ would be unfaithful to his Father, John 6:39" (A Treatise of Effectual Calling and Election, p. 187, 1658 ed.). The whole of the work of Christ is therefore to be understood in relation to the doctrine of election, and indeed they asserted it cannot be understood without it. "Christ's blood-shedding was special blood-shedding, not for all, but for you many, Matthew 26:28. Sanctification is a special sanctification, not for all, but of you, John 17:9. Justification is a special justification, not of all, but of you only, his elect, Romans 8:33. Christ's purchasing was a special purchasing, not of all, but of you his church, Acts 20:28. Christ's prayer is a special prayer, not for all, but for you, John 17:9" (William Fenner, Sermon on The Mystery of Saving Grace, 1626).

We have thus considered the three principal points which characterize the Puritan doctrine of election. Before we proceed to hear them answer objections, *we will consider a few reasons why they considered this truth to be of such tremendous importance.*

(1) It is neglect of the doctrine of election which leads to the Arminian error of supposing that Christ purchased redemption for some to whom it shall never be *applied. This is a direct denial of Christ's office.* "We are reconciled by his merit, but saved by his life," writes Manton. "He liveth in heaven, and procureth influences of his grace . . . In heaven he accomplisheth the other part of his priesthood. He doth not work out a part of man's salvation, and leave the rest of our freewill: the sacrificing part is ended, and by his intercession, we get the merit applied to us" (10:167). If we should say that Christ died for some who now are in hell, it is "blasphemous against Christ: it is as much as to say, that Christ died for some, and after that, was not able to bring them to life and salvation" (Elton's Commentary on Colossians 1:4, 1620).

(2) A neglect or denial of the doctrine of election *destroys the perfect unity and agreement of the Trinity in their will and intention of salvation.* Manton writes, "Our spiritual estate standeth upon a sure bottom, the beginning is from God the Father, the dispensation from the Son, and the application from the Holy Ghost . . . It is free in the Father, sure in the Son, ours in the Spirit; the Father purposeth, the Son ratifieth, the Spirit giveth us the enjoyment of all . . . Election is ascribed to God the Father, sanctification to the Spirit, and reconciliation to Jesus Christ . . . This is the chain of salvation and never a link of this chain must be broken. The Son

cannot die for them whom the Father never elected, and the Spirit will never sanctify them whom the Father hath not elected nor the Son redeemed." Then Manton solemnly charges the Arminians, "which put asunder those operations which God hath joined together, by dividing Christ from election, or election from Christ, as if Christ were to die for those that were never elected and chosen to life, equally as for those that were" (10:161, 256–57).

(3) The denial of the doctrine of absolute election leads to the dishonouring and destroying *errors of universalism.* Dishonouring to God, in that, says Burgess, "by the doctrine of those universalists, notwithstanding Universal grace, and Christ's dying for all, not one man may be saved, God may lose all the glory of his mercy, and Christ all the fruit of his sufferings." Destroying to men, in that, says Perkins, it leads to "universal atheim. For it pulls down the pale of the church, and lays it waste as every common field: it breeds a carelessness in the use of the means of grace, the word and sacraments" (Perkins's Works, 1:302, 1608 ed.).

We will now briefly consider the Puritan's answers to objections that are ever raised against these truths.

(1) Listen to Anthony Burgess clearing God from the charge of injustice. "Howsoever it be God's Sovereign good pleasure to choose some and not others, yet a man's damnation is wholly of himself in respect of the meritorious cause; for no man is damned precisely because God hath not chosen him, because he is not elected, but because he is a sinner, and doth willfully refuse the means of grace offered, insomuch that there is no sinner but he doth as willingly and readily sin with as much choice and delight, as if he were not at all left by God; and therefore the Scripture doth wholly attribute a man's destruction to his own self. Let no man think then to evade God's justice under this pretence. No, God will be justified, and every man will be found to be a sinner. Neither may this be thought injustice in God; for if he had not saved one man, none could have blamed him: we see he did not spare one of the apostate angels. Thus also might he have done with all mankind. Let us therefore admire the goodness of

God that chooses and to eternal life" (Sermons on Spiritual Refining, p. 646).

(2) A further objection is that this doctrine leads to carelessness. The Puritans would answer that the great cause of carelessness is presumption, self-confidence, and the lack of the fear of God, and that nothing more breaks down these things than this very doctrine.

But they would moreover make this reply. God has not only ordained the persons who shall be saved, but He has also ordained the means—namely faith, sanctification, and holiness. Now the only way any soul may know God's secret will, namely his election, is by so diligently applying himself to the means of grace and striving after holiness. Only by obedience to the duties of God's revealed will may anyone know his election. "As Dr. Preston says, if a man does not use those means that may evidence to his soul that he is elected, it is an argument he is not elected. If thou say, if God hath determined it, he will save me, whether I am holy or profane, and therefore I will never hear sermon, never pray in my family, never use holy duties; says Preston, if thou neglect these means, it is an argument thou art not elected . . . At that very instant wherein God did decree or determine to bring a man to life, at that very instant God did decree *that that man would be holy before he died;* he shall use all holy and sanctified means conducible to his salvation. Romans 8:29. Whom he did predestinate, them he did predestinate to be comfortable to the image of his Son" (Christopher Love, Treatise on Calling & Election, pp. 197–98). So that rather than making men careless nothing could make men more serious and earnest than this doctrine. "Oh then search, and again search and try your ways! Oh enquire, whether thou art in the number of those chosen ones or no! For the thing may be known. The Scripture gives many characters of those chosen, do thou then fall upon this study . . . If God appoint thee to eternal life, he doth *here in this world* appoint thee to a gracious and heavenly life. This is a sure argument, no Sanctification, no Election; no choice grace, no choice glory. Thou art to be a precious jewel here, ere God will make thee up at that great day" (Burgess, Sermons, Spiritual Refining, p. 648).

The Practical Use of the Doctrine of Election

(1) Knowing that nothing was more humbling and alarming, they used this doctrine in preaching to the unconverted. A remarkable illustration of this occurs in a sermon of David Dickson's. Dickson was one of the most prominent ministers in a widespread revival which occurred in Scotland between 1625 and1630, and great numbers were saved under his ministry. In a sermon on 2 Timothy 2:19 Dickson speaks as follows: "The doctrine of election and reprobation is a doctrine which may be safely taught and propounded unto people, albeit men say it should not be meddled with, because (say they) it makes some men despair, and others become careless what they do. I answer, let God make an answer for his own doctrine, who has commanded us to teach it . . . The apostle says boldly, the election obtained it, and the rest were blinded. Would Christ have propounded this doctrine if it had been dangerous? Therefore we oppose to such carnal men, secure sleepers in sin, this doctrine of Christ and his apostles, clearly set down in scripture. Let none take offence at this doctrine, for Christ's sheep will hear his voice, and if any will startle away, let them go . . . This doctrine is a strong attractive to draw back those who are fallen in error or vice, that they lie not in it, for this doctrine forces such men to turn to God, or else, to take on the name of reprobates . . . It is a doctrine meet for this age, wherein God is mocked and blasphemed by the lewd lives of those who are called Christians, to tell them, that they must either turn to God, or take home with them these black tidings, that they are vessels of dishonour, fitted for destruction. *This doctrine is very needful to put men to their decisions;* and yet it condemns not a man to hell presently, who is lying in sin; but it tells him, that there are some elect, who will come home, and some reprobate, who will not come home. Therefore, if a man be elect, albeit for the time he be a deboshed villain, this doctrine will serve him for the third and last summons: for when he hears that he must either quit his sinful courses, or have no portion with God, presently he must resolve, I will renounce my old lovers, my uncleanness, worldliness, and turn in to God, and seek a covering

to hide my vileness. *This effect will this doctrine work in the elect"* (Select Practical Writings of David Dickson, 1:95–96, 1845 ed.). Owen defends this use of the doctrine of election; it is not only to be preached to believers, he says, but "it hath its proper benefit and advantage toward others also" (3:603).

(2) The Puritans further used this doctrine in comforting awakened and distressed souls. "This doctrine" (of election), says Thomas Horton, "is a doctrine of comfort, as it takes all out of ourselves, and our own deservings. Doctrines of arrogance and presumption, they are for the most part doctrines of despair, because indeed they are such as will not hold out, nor support a man when he stands in greatest need of them. But doctrines of free-grace and favour, they are doctrines of special comfort and encouragement, because they reduce all to God, who is able to perform what he promises, and to do all that he undertakes." Likewise Elnathan Parr, in his commentary on Romans, "This doctrine affords comfort: the unworthiness may dismay thee, but remember that thy election depends not upon thy worthiness but upon the will of God." "Oh despise not election! therein lies all your hope, that there is a remnant who shall infallibly be saved" (Goodwin, 9:6).

(3) The pre-eminent use they made of this truth was in teaching believers their privilege and safety, and in instructing them in it as a foremost motive to holiness. "God maketh the consideration of his electing love, as free and undeserved, his principal argument to stir up the people unto holy obedience, Deuteronomy 7:6–8,11. And a supposition hereof lies at the bottom of that blessed exhortation of our apostle, Colossians 3:12–13, 'Put on therefore, as the elect of God, holy and beloved, bowels of mercies, kindness, humbleness of mind . . .' These things are required of them on the account of their interest in electing love and grace. Men may frame a holiness to themselves, and be stirred up unto it by motives of their own . . . , but that which the gospel requires is promoted on the grounds and by the motives that are peculiar unto it, whereof this of God's free electing love and grace is among the principal" (Owen, 3:598). Not only is election a motive, it is also an indispensable encouragement to holiness. "The difficulties we meet withal in a course of holiness

are great and many. Here Satan, the world, and sin, do put forth and try their utmost strength. Ofttimes the best are foiled, ofttimes discouraged, sometimes weary and ready to give over. It is no small relief herein, no small encouragement to continue in our progress, that the fountain of electing grace will never fail us, but continually give out supplies of spiritual strength and refreshment. Hence may we take heart and courage to rise again when we have been foiled . . . And *they are unacquainted with a course of holy obedience* who know not how needful this consideration is unto a comfortable continuance therein" (Owen, 3:601).

In conclusion it is necessary for us to note what relevance this great subject has to us and to the times in which we live. There can be few better ways of finding an explanation of the present low state of the visible church than reconsidering what was taught by God's servants when this land enjoyed His favour three hundred years ago. When we make a study of the Puritans with this in mind, we cane to the startling and solemn conclusion that this doctrine of election which they considered to be vital and essential to the very existence of the gospel, has almost wholly disappeared in the past century. The denial and disappearance of this truth has been accompanied by a decay in godliness, and a decline in powerful preaching. Men and women no longer hearing that apostolic command to give all diligence to make their calling and election sure by observing all the holy duties recorded in God's word (2 Peter 1:10), are content with a mere profession of faith. Carelessness has replaced seriousness, and carnal presumption a well-grounded assurance. A lack of the fear of God is betrayed by the neglect of those duties, such as secret prayer and family worship, which He has enjoined. These errors which the Puritans so faithfully and scripturally opposed have become almost universally accepted. Free-will teaching is dishonouring to Christ, whose office it is to teach His people and make them willing (John 17:6, Psalm 110:3), and offensive to the Spirit to whom is entrusted the application of the work of redemption. In the latter part of the seventeenth century some of the Puritans lived to see a similar withdrawal of the Spirit as we have experienced. John Owen accounted for the causes in one of his last and most important treatises, "The Nature and Causes of Apostasy from the Gospel." Among the foremost causes he lists the denial of the sovereignty of God, and all that involves. For "the sovereignty of God," writes Owen, "is the sole foundation of the covenant of grace and runs through the whole mystery of the Gospel. Thence proceedeth the incarnation of the Son of God . . . Thence was His substitution as the surety of the covenant in our stead. Eternal election flows from thence, and is regulated thereby, Romans 9:11,18; so doth effectual vocation, Matthew 11:25–26, and justification by faith. The like may be said of all other mysteries of the gospel. Love, grace, goodness, dispensed in a way of sovereign, unaccountable pleasure, are in them all proposed as the objects of our faith" (Works, 7:157). Surely such considerations as these must make it clear to us that we are living in days of apostasy from the truth, that this is the cause of the controversy which God has with us, and that our only hope of escaping those judgments which have swept many visible churches from the pages of history is the performance of that duty recorded in 2 Chronicles 15:12: "They entered into a covenant to seek the Lord God of their fathers with all their heart, and with all their soul."

2

THE WITNESS OF THE SPIRIT:
THE PURITAN TEACHING

J. I. Packer

"The Spirit itself beareth witness with our spirit, that we are the children of God," wrote Paul (Romans 8:16). Our aim is to discover what the Puritans taught about the Spirit's work in assuring believers of their salvation. The work of the Holy Spirit is the field in which the Puritans' most valuable contributions to the church's theological heritage were made, and the subject of assurance in particular is treated with great fullness and profundity by some of the finest Puritan minds—notably Richard Sibbes, the "sweet dropper," in his exposition of 2 Corinthians 1 (on v. 22, *Works,* vol. 3), in "A Fountain Sealed" on Ephesians 4:30 (*Works,* vol. 5) and elsewhere; Thomas Brooks, one of the greatest of the later Puritans, in "Heaven on Earth. Or, a Serious Discourse touching a well-grounded Assurance" (1654; *Works,* vol. 2); and Thomas Goodwin, in his three sermons on Ephesians 1:13 and in the second book of the second part of his great trea-

17

tise "Of the Object and Acts of Justifying Faith" (*Works,* vols. 1, 8).
Alexander Whyte called Goodwin "the greatest pulpit exegete of
Paul that has ever lived," and perhaps justly. Goodwin's biblical
expositions are quite unique, even among the Puritans, in the
degree to which they combine theological breadth with experimental depth. John Owen saw into the mind of Paul as clearly as
Goodwin—sometimes, on points of detail, more clearly—but not
even Owen ever saw so deep into Paul's heart. Goodwin, Sibbes,
and Brooks will be our main guides in this study. We shall find
them in substantial agreement (especially Sibbes and Goodwin,
between whose thought on this subject there is an evident ge-
nealogical connection); and they represent the main current of
Puritan thinking. Let us see what they have to say.

The Puritans speak of assurance, sometimes as a fruit of faith,
sometimes as a quality of faith; they talk both of assurance growing out of faith and of faith growing into assurance. Assurance is
to them faith full grown and come of age; there can be faith without assurance, but where assurance is present, it is present as an
aspect of faith, organically related to it, not as something distinct
and separable from it. This being so, we must begin this study by
reviewing what the Puritans taught about the nature of faith in
general.

Faith, said the Puritans, begins in the mind, with belief of the
truth of the gospel message. It results from spiritual illumination.
In illumination, the Spirit both enlightens the mind, making it
capable of receiving spiritual things, and impresses on the mind
the objective reality of those things of which the word of God
bears witness. The knowledge of spiritual realities thus given is as
immediate and direct in its way as the knowledge of material
things which we gain by sense, and it brings with it a quality of immediate conviction analogous to that which sense perception
brings. Scripture refers to the process in terms borrowed from
the senses—seeing, hearing, tasting (John 6:40; Ephesians 4:21;
Hebrews 6:5)—and tells us that it yields *full assurance of understanding* (Colossians 2:2). This spiritual appreciation of spiritual
things is mediated to man, as a thinking being, by reasoned exposition of Scripture and rational reflection upon it; man cannot

come to know any spiritual object except through the use of his mind; but the knowledge itself goes beyond reason. It is not a mere logical or imaginative construction, nor is its certainty the derived certainty of an inference drawn from more certain premises; its certainty springs from an immediate awareness of and contact with the thing known. It is not a "notional, swimming knowledge," second-hand and unstable; it is "real" and "solid" knowledge, the product of a direct cognizance by spiritual sense f the things known. The divine operation whereby it is given is what Calvin and his successors called the *testimonium internum Spiritus Sancti*—the inner witness of the Holy Ghost. Paul refers to it in 1 Corinthians 2:4 as the "demonstration of the Spirit." Goodwin puts it thus: "The Holy Ghost, when he doth work faith in us . . . doth two things: *First,* He doth . . . give us a new understanding . . . 1 John 5:20 . . . a new eye to see Christ with . . . *Secondly,* himself cometh with a light upon this new understanding," thus bestowing a spiritual "sight" of spiritual realities (8:260). This spiritual knowledge is in fact more certain than anything else. It may be obscured by temptations; one who has it may for long doubt and deny it, but it will prove dominant in the end, and in the long run the effect of his lapses from it will be to make him realise how utterly and unshameably he is in his heart convinced of it. Such is the knowledge of all true believers, and it is the quality of certainty attaching to it which guarantees them against finally falling away. This witness of the Spirit to the objective truth of the gospel is the fundamental factor in personal faith. Full assurance of understanding is prerequisite for personal assurance of salvation.

Faith is, of course, more than mental enlightenment. It extends from the head to the heart, and expresses itself in what Baxter calls a "practical trust" in God through Christ. Man turns from self-reliance and sin to rest his soul on Christ and the promises. Hereby he both expresses and establishes the habit of faith in his soul, and faith, once established, asserts itself as the dynamic of a new life. It begets hope; it works by love; it steels itself to patience; it lays itself out in well-doing; it causes joy and peace to arise naturally and spontaneously in the heart. "Faith is the master-wheel; it sets all the other graces running" (T. Watson, *Body of Divinity*, 1869 ed., 151). "Faith is the spring in the watch that sets all the golden wheels of love, joy, comfort and peace a-going" (Brooks, 2:359). Faith is thus regarded as containing a measure of assurance within itself from the outset; the believer hopes, loves, serves, and rejoices because he believes that God has had mercy on him.

But this is not the "settled, well-grounded" assurance which the Puritans regarded as alone worthy of the name. The young convert may in exceptional cases enjoy continual strong consolation, but usually such assurance is not given till faith has been tried and seasoned, ripened and strengthened, by conflict with doubt and fluctuations of feeling. The Puritans were somewhat suspicious when transports of rapture accompanied the first profession of faith; they never forgot that it was the stonyground hearers who received the word with such notable joy. True, sound, thorough converts, they held, do not usually start like that. "Full assurance" is a rare blessing, even among adults it is a great and precious privilege, not indiscriminately bestowed. "Assurance is a mercy too good for most men's hearts . . . God will only give it to his best and dearest friends." "Assurance is the beauty and top of a Christian's glory in this life. It is usually attended with the strongest joy, with the sweetest comforts, and with the greatest peace. It is a . . . crown that few wear . . . " "Assurance is meat for strong men; few babes, if any, are able to bear it, and digest it" (Brooks, 2:335, 316f., 371). Assurance is not normally enjoyed except by those who have first laboured for it and sought it, and served God faithfully and patiently without it. "Assurance comes in as a reward of faith . . . A man's faith must fight first, and have a conquest, and then assurance is the crown, the triumph of faith . . . and what tries faith more than temptation, and fears, and doubts, and reasonings against a man's own estate? That triumphing assurance, Romans 8:37–38 . . . comes after a trial, as none are crowned till they have striven" (Goodwin, 8:346). Assurance of this kind is not essential to faith; as Brooks puts it, it is of faith's *bene esse*, not of its *esse* (p. 317). It is, in fact, an aspect of faith which normally appears only when faith has reached a high degree of development, far beyond its minimal saving exercise. Goodwin speaks of assurance as both "a branch and appendix of faith, an addition or complement to faith" and "faith elevated and raised up above its ordinary rate"; "the Scripture speaks of it," he says, "as a thing distinct from faith (though it doth coalesce with it, and they both make one)" (8:346, 352; 1:236). This was the general Puritan conception of assurance.

It is evident that "assurance" to the Puritan was something quite other than the "assurance" commonly given to the convert of five minutes' standing in the enquiry room. ("You believe that John 1:12 is true? You have 'received Him'? Then you are a son of God.") The Puritans would not have called mere assent to such an inference, *assurance* at all. Professions of faith must be tested before they may be trusted, even by those who make them, and assurance, to the Puritan, was in any case more than a bare human inference; it was a God-given conviction of one's standing in grace, stamped on the mind and heart by the Spirit in just the same way as the truth of the gospel facts was stamped on the mind when faith was born, and carrying with it the same immediate certainty. "Assurance," says Brooks, "is the reflex act of a gracious soul, whereby he clearly and evidently sees himself in a gracious, blessed and happy state; it is a sensible feeling and an experimental discerning of a man's being in a state of grace" (p. 316). The operative words here are *sensible* and *experimental.* Assurance is an experimental, conscious fruit of supernatural enlightenment, and cannot exist till it pleases God to give it. The young convert's position is really this: As he believes and obeys, he will know a measure of peace and joy, for real believing at once brings real comfort ("no man looks upon Christ but cometh off more cheerily" [Goodwin, 1:233]; "there is a voice of God's Spirit speaking peace to his people upon their believing" [Sibbes, 3:456]); he may *think* and *hope,* and with some warrant, that he is a child of God, but he cannot say, in the unqualified sense of John's first Epistle, that he *knows* his sonship until the Spirit sets this certainty home on his heart. Till the Spirit does so, in the Puritan sense, at any rate, he lacks assurance; which, said the Puritans, seems to be the case of most Christian people.

When this supernatural assurance dawns, it transforms a man's entire Christian life. "It is a new conversion," says Goodwin; "it will make a man differ from himself in what he was before in that manner almost as conversion doth before he was converted. There is a new edition of all a man's graces" (1:251). This sounds startling, but Goodwin means what he says, and works the idea out. Assurance, he tells us, increases faith (faith "receives a new degree" [8:355]), and this invigoration of faith results in a new release of energy at every point in one's Christian life. In the first place, it deepens one's communion with the Triune God in meditation on the "plot" of redeeming love. "In assurance . . . a man's communion and converse is . . . sometimes with the Father, then with the Son, and then with the Holy Ghost; sometimes his heart is drawn out to consider the Father's love in choosing, and then the love of Christ in redeeming, and so the love of the Holy Ghost, that searcheth the deep things of God, and revealeth them to us, and taketh all the pains with us . . . And we should never be satisfied till we have attained it, and till all three persons . . . make their abode with us, and we sit as it were in the midst of them, while they all manifest their love to us; this is John's communion (1 John 1:4), and this is the highest that ever Christ promised in this life (in his last sermon, John 14)" (8:379). (John 14 is a favourite passage with Goodwin; he often develops the thought of the distinct knowledge of all three persons of the Trinity, and of their love, which is there promised to the disciples through the coming of the Comforter.) Nor is this all. The coming of assurance quickens the spiritual understanding: by it "the eye of the soul is strengthened to see further into truths; all truths are more clearly known by this" (Sibbes, 5:442). It makes a man bold and powerful in prayer. It makes him holier, though he was holy before: "all assurance that is true assurance . . . maketh a man holy" (Goodwin, 1:250), "nothing makes the heart more in the love, study, practice, and growth of holiness, than the glorious testimony of the Holy Spirit" (Brooks, 2:522). Assurance makes a man tireless in Christian service: "When once . . . the love of God is shed abroad in a man's heart, it makes a man work for God ten times more than before" (Goodwin, 1:251); "assurance will strongly put men upon the winning of others . . . A soul under assurance is unwilling to go to heaven without company" (Brooks, 2:515f.). Finally, assurance brings with it the "joy unspeakable and full of glory" of 1 Peter 1:8, which is one of Goodwin's favourite texts in this connection. Such assurance as this, so far from encouraging presumption and laziness, is in fact the strongest possible incentive against sin, for its possessor knows that by sinning he will jeopardize his assurance, prompting God to withdraw it, and there is nothing that he is more anxious to avoid than that. These, then, are the chief fruits of assurance.

How does the Spirit assure? The answer to this question turns on the sense given to Romans 8:16, which speaks of two witnesses giving evidence together, the Holy Spirit corroborating the testimony of our spirit. The Puritans identified "our spirit" with the Christian's conscience, which, with the Spirit's aid, is able to discern in his heart the marks which Scripture lays down as tokens of the new birth and to conclude from them that he is a child of God. The Spirit "writes first all graces in us, and then teaches our consciences to read his handwriting" (Goodwin, 6:27). Without the Spirit's aid, man can never recognise the Spirit's handiwork in himself: "if he do not give in his testimony with them, your graces will give no witness at all" (I. 306). Sometimes the Spirit's help here is given in full measure; sometimes, however, to chasten us for sin, or to try our faith for a time, this help is partly or wholly withdrawn, and because the Spirit is not always active to enable us to know ourselves to the same degree, the witness of our spirit inevitably fluctuates: "a man shall find the same signs sometimes witness to him, and sometimes not, as the Spirit irradiates them" (8:366f.). We must recognise that God is sovereign here, to give more or less assurance in this way as He pleases. Thus far, all the Puritans are agreed.

But what is meant by "the Spirit beareth witness"? Here, there is a difference. Some of the Puritans equate the witness of the Spirit to which Paul refers with the work of the Spirit in enabling our spirits to bear witness, as described above. John Goodwin, the free-lance Puritan, writes, "The expression of witnessing with our spirits plainly implies that it is but one and the same act of wit-

nessing . . . jointly in common ascribed unto the Spirit of God
and the spirit of man, and that the Spirit of God doth not hear
any such witness . . . apart from the spirit of man . . . from whence
it appears, that the witness, or joint-witnessing, of the Spirit here
spoken of, is only a fortifying, strengthening, raising and enrich-
ing of the witness or testimony of a man's own spirit" (*A being
filled with the Spirit,* p. 449; so also Watson, p. 174; Thomas Manton, *Works* 12:1299; and others). On this view, the Spirit bears witness when the believer finds himself able to infer with confidence
from the evidence of his heart and life that he is a child of God.
But Sibbes, Brooks, and Goodwin, among others, take a different
view. They take the text as referring to two distinct modes of witness, the first being inferential, as described above, but the second being that of the Spirit testifying, no longer indirectly, but
immediately and intuitively; not merely by prompting us to infer
our adoption, but by what Goodwin calls an "overpowering light"
whereby He bears direct witness to the Christian man of God's
everlasting love to him, of his election, and sonship, and inheritance. Sibbes says: "The Spirit . . . witnesses . . . by . . . whatsoever
of Christ's is applied to us by the Spirit. But, besides witnessing
with these witnesses, the Spirit hath a distinct witness by way of
enlarging the soul; which is joy in the apprehension of God's fatherly love . . . The Spirit doth not always witness . . . by force of
argument from sanctification, but sometimes immediately by way
of presence; as the sight of a friend comforts without help of discourse" (5:440). There is a twofold assurance of salvation, says
Goodwin; "the one way is discoursive; a man gathereth that God
loves him from the effects (i.e., marks of regeneration), as we
gather that there is fire because there is smoke. But the other is
intuitive . . . it is such a knowledge as whereby we know that the
whole is greater than the part . . . There is light that cometh and
overpowereth a man's soul, and assureth him that God is his, and
he is God's, and that God loveth him from everlasting" (1:233).

Goodwin analyses this direct witness in much detail. It is, he
tells us, self-evidencing, and self-authenticating; and it is analogous in character to the Spirit's witness to the objective truth of
the gospel. In each case, the Spirit witnesses to the truth of the

word of God and its application to the individual. In creating
faith, He convinces the sinner that the conditional promises of
the gospel are held out by God to him (e. g. "come unto me, all
ye that labour . . . and I will give you rest") and prompts him to
make the appropriate response, i.e. to trust. In giving assurance,
He convinces the Christian that the absolute promises of Scripture include him in their scope (e.g. "my sheep . . . shall never
perish"), and moves him to make the appropriate response, i.e.
to rejoice. "When we say that (assurance) is an immediate testimony," Goodwin explains, "the meaning is not that it is without
the Word; no, it is by a promise; but the meaning is, it is immediate in respect of using your own graces as an evidence or witness but he bringeth home a promise to the heart some absolute
promise . . . We do not speak for enthusiasms; it is the Spirit applying the Word to the heart that we speak of" (1:250). What happens is that "God says unto a man's soul (as David desires), 'I am
thy salvation,' and as Christ said on earth to some few, 'Thy sins
are forgiven thee,' so from Heaven is it spoken by his Spirit: that
a man's sins are forgiven him, and he is owned by the whole Trinity to be God's child" (8:366). The Spirit applies words and
thoughts of Scripture to the heart so powerfully and authorita-
tively that the believer is left in no doubt that they are being spoken by God to him. This direct testimony does not normally begin to be given until a man has first gained assurance by the lower
road of Spirit-guided inference; our spirit is the first to witness,
and God's Spirit joins His witness with it later, but when the direct testimony is experienced, it creates a degree of joy to which
the other could never give rise. "It works that joy in the heart
which the saints shall have in heaven . . . It is not a bare conviction that a man shall go to heaven; but God telleth him in part
what heaven is, and lets him feel it" (1:260). It is pre-eminently as
thus witnessing to our adoption that the Spirit is the "earnest of
our inheritance" (Ephesians 1:14), Goodwin thinks. His immediate testimony takes a man's mind off himself, and centres him
wholly upon God; he foretastes heaven on earth. Goodwin insists
that Christians do not enjoy the full riches of assurance till they
know, not merely the Spirit's indirect witness through con-

science, but His direct witness also; those who lack it, therefore, should stir themselves up to seek it from God.

Goodwin, in part following Sibbes, expounds the phrase in Ephesians 1:13, "sealed with the Holy Spirit of promise," of this direct testimony. He suggests that it is a part of the ministry of the Spirit promised by Christ in John 14, and calls attention to the words "in that day ye shall *know* that I am in my Father, and ye *in me and I in* you," and to the promise that Christ Himself would manifest Himself to the disciples (vv. 20–21). These promises, he holds, are fulfilled in the Spirit's direct witnessing; and whenever the New Testament mentions the receiving of the Spirit at some point subsequent to believing, the reference is to a conscious experiencing of the Spirit's direct witness. This, he suggests, is the inner, experimental aspect of the charismatic outpourings of the Spirit recorded in Acts and such passages as Galatians 3:2.

In his capacity as a "sealer," the Spirit was not given before Jesus was glorified (John 7:38f.); full assurance is a specifically New Testament blessing. Clearly, Christ had to be glorified before the Spirit could witness to believers of their union with Him in His glory.

Then Goodwin proceeds to a remarkable piece of sacramental theology. This "sealing," he says, "is the great fruit of your baptism." Here he develops a line of thought peculiar to himself. Its basis is the scriptural and Reformed conception of baptism as a sign and a seal. As a sign, it signifies God's reception and appropriation of man into saving union with Himself: man is "baptized into the name of the Father, Son and Holy Ghost" (Matthew 28:19). As a seal, it assures man, as did circumcision in Old Testament times, that God has entered into covenant with him, pardoning his sins and making him an heir of the promised inheritance. It is a sign and seal proclaiming that the candidate is God's and God is his. God has taken the man to Himself and given Himself to the man. Prof. G. W. H. Lampe has recently shown that Paul's references to the New Testament gift of the Spirit as a "seal" (Ephesians 1:13; 4:30; 2 Corinthians 1:21) have a direct connection with the rite of baptism. Goodwin sees this clearly, and attempts to pin down the point of connection. "The seal of

the Spirit is the proper work that answereth to baptism. Therefore . . . it is called "baptizing with the Holy Ghost" (Acts 1:5,
11–16), because it is that which is the fruit of baptism, it answereth that outward seal . . . Peter biddeth them be baptized,
and they should receive the promise, Acts 2:38" (1:248). The gift
of the Spirit thus witnessing brings home to the believer what his
baptism symbolically proclaimed to him: an assurance that he is
now God's, and God is henceforth his. In the early church, says
Goodwin, "baptism was the ordinance to the newly converted,
which conveyed the Spirit as sealing" (8:264), the outward and
inward seals were commonly received together, as Acts shows,
and the epistles suggest that "almost all the saints in the primitive
times (were) sealed" (1:248). The position for later ages, however, is that the two are normally not conjoined, most of God's
people being baptized in infancy; but believers who have received
the outward seal of baptism are thereby authorised and encouraged to seek from God in faith the complementary inward seal of
the Spirit. When, or whether, God will give it to them they cannot
know in advance; they must bow to His sovereignty here, but they
can be sure that they will not find it unless they seek it, and that
it is supremely worth seeking.

To confirm his view of the connection between baptism and
the "seal" as he conceived it, Goodwin makes a striking appeal to
the baptism of Christ, the representative head of God's elect. He
lays down the principle that, since it is of Christ's fullness that we
receive, "whatsoever work God doth upon us, he doth upon
Christ first." Now, Christ was *sealed* (John 6:27) at his baptism,
when the Spirit descended on him and he heard His Father say:
"this is my beloved Son." This, says Goodwin, was a giving of direct
assurance analogous to that which the "seal" brings to believers.
"Though (Christ) had the assurance of faith that he was the Son
of God . . . out of the Scriptures, by reading all the prophets . . .
yet to have it sealed to him with joy unspeakable . . . this was de-
ferred to the time of his baptism. He was then anointed with the
Holy Ghost (Acts 10:38) . . . Answerably (compare 2 Corinthians
1:22) (God) hath sealed and anointed us, just as he sealed and
anointed Christ in his baptism" (1:245). And the mode of the seal-

ing of Christ conformed precisely to the mode of the sealing of Christians. "It is always, I say, by a promise . . . Jesus Christ was sealed . . . by a promise . . . What was it? 'This is my beloved Son, in whom I am well pleased.' This is a Scripture promise . . . Isaiah 42:1 . . . That which had been spoken before of the Messiah was brought home to his heart" (p. 249).

How much of this line of exposition is acceptable? Certain facts are clear. The reception of the Spirit after believing certainly had experimental repercussions for New Testament Christians, as Acts and Galatians 3:2, etc., make plain; it produced, not merely charismatic action (prophecy, tongues, miracles) but also great joy, boldness, and vigour in Christian life and service. John 14–16, as Goodwin points out, certainly links the coming of the Comforter with a new depth of assurance and a new intimacy of communion with God. Romans 8:16 certainly admits, grammatically, of either of the exegeses reviewed above, and certainly refers on any view to a strong, God-created and God-sustained conviction of one's standing in grace, which Paul and his readers shared. It seems certain that the Puritans are in fact directing our attention to one of the experimental dimensions of New Testament faith of which we know too little today, whichever mode of conceiving of the twofold witness we adopt. But it seems incorrect to equate the dawning of assurance, direct or indirect, with the "seal of the Spirit" in Ephesians 1:13; 4:30; 2 Corinthians 1:21. Goodwin's interpretation, that the Spirit is the sealer, the "efficient cause" of the sealing operation, and that the sense of assurance is the seal, is not what the Greek means. John Owen, discussing these texts, rightly dissents from this exposition: "it is not said that the Holy Spirit seals us, but that we are sealed with him. He is God's seal to us," (*Works*, Russell, 4:215). Christ's baptism was certainly the prototype of our sealing; but the seal given to Him was the gift of the Holy Spirit in all fullness, anointing Him for His Messianic public ministry, and the word of assurance given with it was something distinct from it. Correspondingly, "God's sealing of believers . . . is his gracious communication of the Holy Ghost unto them . . . to enable them unto all the duties of their holy calling, evidencing them to be accepted with him . . . and as-

serting their preservation unto eternal salvation." Assurance may
come with the gift, but is not to be equated with it. The seal is not
any particular operation of the Spirit, but the gift of the Spirit
Himself. "It hath been generally conceived that the sealing with
the Spirit . . . gives assurance . . . and so indeed it doth, although
the way whereby it doth it, hath not been rightly apprehended."
It is the presence of the Spirit, as manifested by His total action
in the life, and not any single element in that action, which is the
ground of the believer's assurance that he is God's (1 John 3:24;
4:13; Romans 8:9). Scripture forbids us to postulate an interval of
time between believing and being sealed. All who believe have
the Spirit; moreover all who have the Spirit have been sealed with
the Spirit; and those who have not been thus sealed are not Christians at all. However, the doctrine of the Spirit's witness through
the awakening of joy in the light of the knowledge of God's love
has a much broader scriptural basis than a particular exegesis of
the "seal" texts. Owen recognised the reality of this witness by sovereign gift of supernatural joy though he would not identify it
with the "seal." "Of this joy," he wrote, "there is no account to be
given, but that the Spirit worketh it when and how he will; he secretly infuseth and distils it into the soul, prevailing against all
fears and sorrows, filling it with gladness, exultations, and sometimes with unspeakable raptures of mind" (Russell 10:310).
Owen's statement would, I think, have been subscribed by all the
Puritans. Whether or not they regarded such experiences as experiences of assurance in the strict sense, whether or not they believed that Romans 8:16, or the "seal" texts, referred to them,
they none of them doubted that such things happened, and that
it was supremely desirable for every Christian that such things
should happen to him. This is the central fact to fasten on in our
assessment of the Puritan teaching on this whole subject.

3

THE PURITANS' DEALINGS
WITH TROUBLED SOULS

G. A. Hemming

In this paper we are concerned with the principles which the Puritans followed in their dealings with those who came to them complaining that all was not well with them spiritually. The Puritans realised that the child of God does not walk in a state of unbroken joy: there come times when clouds intervene and the Christian loses the sense of God's favour. The Puritan pastor encouraged his people to come to him and disclose the state of their hearts so that counsel and advice could be given. In this way he built up an amazing stock of knowledge not only of God's dealings with His children but also of the Christian's experience of those dealings.

The complaint of the church member who came to his pastor might be more, or less, serious. He might complain simply that he has an indefinable sense that all is not well with him spiritually; he might have lost all his joy; he might have fallen back into some obvious sin which he thought he had put behind him for ever—as when Peter cursed and swore; he might have lost his assurance of salvation; he might even have found assurance of damnation! He might be finding in his heart doubtings of the gospel, of the goodness of God, of the very existence of God. Troubled that such terrible things should enter and temporarily, at any rate, possess his mind, he turns to his pastor in distress of soul.

In such a case the Puritan pastor worked along well defined lines.

1. He Considered the Possibility That the Man Coming to Him Is Not Truly Converted

To this end he looked for two things. First, a true and deep sense of sin. The Puritans seldom concerned themselves with the moment, real or imagined, of a man's turning to God; they were much more concerned with a man's present state. This does not mean, of course, that they were indifferent to the question of conversion, it means rather that they realised clearly that a true conversion will be shown by its fruit, and they looked for that fruit as evidence that a work of grace had taken place in the man's heart. If this work of grace had taken place then, they said, one great overriding result would follow, that is, the man would have a deep and continually deepening sense of sin. And they resolutely refused to offer any comfort unless they were convinced that a real sense of sin was present. Thus "the conscience is not to be healed if it be not wounded. Thou preachest and pressest the law, comminations, the judgment to come, and that with much earnestness and importunity. He which hears, if he be not terrified, if he be not troubled, is not to be comforted. Another hears, is stirred, is stung, takes on extremely; cure his contritions, because he is cast down and confounded in himself." Or again, says Perkins, "First of all a man must have knowledge of four things, of the law of God, of sin against the law, of the guilt of sin, and of the judgment of God against sin, which is eternal wrath." Or again "never any of God's children," says Greenham, "were comforted thoroughly, but they were first humbled for their sins."

These quotations give a brief indication of the Puritans' attitude to this all-important question, and they resolutely declined to apply any comfort to a troubled soul until they were first sure that the soul had indeed been troubled as it should be troubled by a sense of sin.

The second thing for which they looked was a genuine love toward God. This will be evidenced by a genuine desire to please God, out of love, not fear. Baxter puts it in this way: "Are you heartily willing to take God for your portions and had you rather live with Him in Glory, in His favour and fullest love, with a soul perfectly cleansed from all sin, and never more to offend Him, rejoicing with His Saints in His everlasting praises, than to enjoy the delights of the flesh on earth in a way of sin and without the favour of God? Are you heartily willing to take Jesus Christ as He is offered in the Gospel, that is to be your only Saviour and Lord, and to give you pardon by His blood shed and to sanctify you by His Work and Spirit and to govern you by His laws? Note that to be willing to be ruled by His laws in general and utterly unwilling when it comes to particulars is no true willingness or subjection. You must know that His laws reach both to heart and outward actions, that they command a Holy, Spiritual, Heavenly life, that they command things so cross and unpleasing to the flesh that the flesh will be ever murmuring and striving against obedience; particularly, they command things quite cross to the inclinations of the flesh as to forgive wrongs, to love enemies, to forbear malice and revenge, to restrain and mortify lust and passion, to abhor and mortify pride and to be low in our own eyes, and humble and meek in spirit. These are the laws of Christ which you must know before you can determine whether you are indeed unfeignedly willing to obey them."

Perkins sees five characteristics of saving faith. The man that has it, he says, will know what it is "to feel his extreme need of Christ and His merits: to hunger and thirst after Him as after meat and drink: to be nothing in himself: to be able to say that he liveth not, but Christ liveth in him by faith: to loathe his own sins with a vehement hatred, and to prize and value Christ and the least drop of His blood above a thousand worlds."

Much more could be said under this heading but it is not the main purpose of this paper to deal with this branch of the subject. Suffice it to say that the Puritans were very thorough in their probing of a man's state, and they realised the great seriousness of allowing any man to rest in a false sense of security when in point of fact he is not truly a child of God. Bolton refers to those who too readily administer the comfort of the gospel as "dawbing ministers, a generation of vilest men, excellent idiots in the mystery of Christ, and merciful cut-throats of many miserable, deluded souls, to whom they promise life and peace; when there is no peace towards, but terrible things at hand, tumblings of garments in blood, noise of damned souls and tormenting in hell for ever."

Let us now assume that the pastor is satisfied that the distressed soul who has turned to him for help is truly regenerate. How next did he proceed?

2. He Considered the Possibility That the Man's Distress Might Be Due to Non-spiritual Causes

The Puritans recognised that a man might be deeply distressed through what we should call psychological troubles, but which they termed "Melancholy." They recognised that it was no good seeking to apply spiritual remedies to psychological maladies. Thus says Baxter, "Expect not that rational spiritual remedies should suffice for this cure, for you may as well expect that a good sermon or comfortable words should cure the falling sickness, or palsy, or a broken head, as to be a sufficient cure to your melancholy fears: for this is as real a bodily disease as the other." It is at this point that the Puritans display that shrewdness and robust common sense which are ever needed as a complement to spiritual understanding. They are prepared to give good advice as far as good advice is worth while in such cases. Thus they would counsel a man to watch his prayers. They recognised that some men needed to spend most of their prayer time in praise and thanksgiving and recollections of God's mercies, and that a minimum of time should be spent in confession and expressions of penitence. They recognised too that some Christians should not be over-encouraged to spend much time in solitary prayer and meditations. Rather, they should seek the company of cheerful Christians, for, said they, "There is no mirth like the mirth of believers." They should pray in the company of cheerful saints, and they should converse with men of strongest faith that have this heavenly mirth and can speak experimentally of the joy of the Holy Ghost. These things, said the Puritans, would be great help in lifting a man out of melancholy and depression and establishing him on the pathway of normal and peaceful Christian experience. They recognised that while every man must examine himself, yet there are those who need to observe restraint even in this excellent practice. "Spend more time in doing your duty than in trying your estate" is the Puritan advice to the unduly introspective Christian.

Here again much more could be said, but this must suffice for our present purpose.

Let us now assume that the Puritan pastor is satisfied that the man who has approached him in distress is neither unregenerate nor melancholic. He now considered

3. The Genuine Spiritual Distress of the Genuine Child of God

This is the main theme of our present study, and we examine it under four headings:

A. Its Reality

It is impossible to read any of the Puritans, better or lesser known, without coming across some reference to this subject. A few quotations will illustrate: thus "Among all the works of God's eternal counsel there is none more wonderful than His Desertion: which is nothing else but an action of God forsaking His creature—that is, by taking away the grace and operation of His Spirit from His creature." Or again "The blessings that God bestoweth on His own elect children are of two sorts, positive and privative. Positive are real graces wrought in the heart by the Spirit of God. Privative are such means whereby God preserves men from falling into sin, as crosses and desertions: and these in number exceed the first as long as men live in the world." Or again "the man Christ is the blessed channel betwixt the fountain and the cistern through which grace, life, peace, strength, glory come by a gracious and glorious convoy; every vessel shall have its fullness to all eternity; sometimes indeed the streams come fuller, and sometimes slower; sometimes Christ stayeth the current that we may thirst, that, after thirsting, we may drink again with re-doubled pleasure." Or, yet again, "This is the main of a godly man's unhappiness—that he neither has a full nor a fixed state of comfortable communion with God in the world. After sweet meetings come sad partings." These quotations are given because it is so necessary to insist on this point. Nowadays the Christian is taught often that he should look forward to a life of unbroken victory, joy, and happiness, as not merely desirable, not only at-tainable, but actually obligatory for him in this life; not so the Pu-ritans. They recognised that quite the reverse is the Christian's portion, and quoted such verses as Isaiah 49:14, "And Zion said, 'the Lord has forsaken me and my God has forgotten me,'" in support of their views: and lest it should be argued that Zion merely feels forsaken but is not actually so, they quote such verses as Isaiah 54:7, where God Himself is the speaker and says, "For a small moment have I forsaken Thee." i.e., God confirms that we do not merely feel deserted: we are deserted.

Yet, said the Puritans, "though God deserts His people really, yet He does not desert them totally. "The Lord will forsake His People for His great name's sake," 1 Samuel 12:22; and the Puri-tans interpolated the word "totally" or "finally" between "not" and "forsake." Thus, they argued, desertions are not the interruptions of God's love, they are rather the acts of God's love. God's love of benevolence or intention remains ever unchanged, but God's love of benificence or execution does change. It is these consid-erations which give rise to the complaints of the saints, either that God does not carry on the spiritual life as He was wont, or that He gives not that peace, joy, comfort, assurance as he was wont; or that He brings them into outward straits and does not deliver them. The Christian finds that the tenure of grace and peace is not the same.

B. Its Seriousness

The Puritan recognised that few worse things could befall a child of God than to lose the sense of God's gracious presence. Thus, says one, "And when it's thus with you, that you have declined in your acquaintance with God, and in your apprehension of the sinfulness of sin, the beauty of holiness, the excellency of Christ, the preciousness of the Covenant, you have cause to sit down and weep, for you have not so much of God in you as you have had." Or again, "This unbelief and atheism is a rock which the Saints, the most part of them, do strike upon at one time or another, but it's a dreadful evil." They recognised that God does not merely withhold His light from His children when they are turning away from Him and trifling with sin. When a child of God is truly walking in God's ways, and when his witness is wholly pleasing unto God, yet still God may withhold His light from His child: and that, they felt, was a most serious and dreadful thing to experience. One of the Puritans gives this most moving illustration: "Robert Glover, martyr at Coventry, being condemned by his Bishop and now at point to be delivered out of this world, it so happened that two or three days before his death, his heart being lumpish and desolate of all spiritual consolation, felt in himself no aptness or willingness to lay down his life, but rather a heaviness and dullness of spirit. Whereupon he feared in himself that the Lord had withdrawn His wonted favour from him. He confided to his friend Austin, who counselled patience and assured him that the Lord would indeed return in all His brightness. Glover continued, therefore, in meekness and patience, and on the day of his death, as he was going to the place of martyrdom, he was so replenished with the Holy Ghost that he cried out, clapping his hands to Austin and saying with these words, 'Austin, He is come, He is come,' and that with such joy and alacrity as one seeming to be risen from some deadly danger to liberty of life than as one passing out of the world by any pains of death."

To illustrate God's withdrawing of Himself in sin the Puritans turn to such examples as Noah's drunkenness, David's adultery, and Peter's denial of His Lord; incidentally, on the last incident

Sibbes has a pungent comment; he refers to Peter as a bruised reed, and he adds, "Peter was bruised when he wept bitterly. This reed, till he met with this bruise, had more wind in him than pith."

All this springs out of the basic Puritan theme of the complete sovereignty of God; no man, even though he be regenerate, can keep himself from sin, and if God for any reason withholds is supporting grace, then that man immediately falls.

C. Its Causes

The Puritans realised that this withdrawing of the realised presence of God could arise from a number of different causes which may, for our convenience, be grouped under three subheadings.

(a) *Sin unrealised or unconfessed.* It is at this point that the Puritans show two things, first their own view of the seriousness and extent of sin and second their understanding of the strange and tortuous workings of the human mind. The Puritan pastor was not merely content that his people should reject sin in a general sense, he was always ready to particularise, and he found, as men have always found, that there is vast difference between a general acceptance of a principle and an acceptance of the detailed application of that principle. The Puritan pastors therefore made a point of detailing the ways in which their people might be falling into sin and did not hesitate to approach them and point out their failings. Not that they found this an easy task, nor did they find a ready acceptance of their reproofs or probings. Baxter comments ruefully that however gently and graciously a pastor admonishes or reproves an individual member of his flock, yet frequently his reproof is met with resentment rather than with amendment of life. Furthermore, the Puritan approach to this matter was never negative only; they recognised the seriousness of sins of omission as well as sins of commission, and they were quick to point out that failure to perform duty and failure to obey, in detail, the commandments of God was just as much sin as the more obvious forms. Here then was one of the most common causes of the loss of God's favour and gracious presence— unrealised sin.

The Puritans recognised further that sin might be realised yet not confessed. Says Guernall, "Thou mayest, though a child of God, be under fresh guilt and defilement as yet unrepented of. Now in this case—God can shut His door upon His own child. As a saint, thou hast a right to all the promises of the covenant: but as a saint under guilt or the defilement of any sin that thou hast not yet repented of, thou art not fit to enjoy what thou hast a right to as a saint. God doth not disinherit thee indeed, but He sequesters the promise from thee, and the rents of it shall not be paid to thee till thou renewest thy repentance and faith on the Lord Jesus for the pardon of it. Thy God will choose a fitter time than this to signify His love to thee."

For this reason they laid much stress on the keeping of short accounts with God; let a man, they said, make his peace with God at the close of each day. Let him search his heart and conscience in the light of God's word, and let him be quick not only to recognise, but to confess and mourn for his sin. They saw, as few of us today have seen, all that was implied both antecently and subsequently by the prayer "Restore unto me the joy of my salvation."

(b) *Direct attack of Satan.* The Puritans recognised the power and ubiquity of the forces of darkness. They recognised that Satan did indeed walk to and fro throughout the earth, that he was present at the most sacred moments, as when Joshua, the High Priest, stood before the Lord and yet had an adversary to resist him. Once again the basic doctrine of the Puritans affects their understanding of all other themes. They understood the full implications of the Fall and the depravity of human nature which has resulted therefrom. Satan, they said, has different modes of attack upon the child of God. First, they said, he can attack our reason. "On which," says Sibbes, "he worketh effectively because of his great ability to forge and invent false reasonings and arguments to overthrow our faith! Who, when young, outwitted our first parents when their reason was not depraved, but now *he* is grown 'that old serpent' and we are become 'children apt to be tossed to and fro.' Satan hath had time enough to improve his knowledge in! A student he is of five thousand years' standing that hath lost no time, but, as he is said to accuse day and night, so he is able to study both day and night: and he hath made it his chief, if not his whole, study to enable himself to tempt and plead against us. It is his trade. Therefore, as men are called lawyers or divines from their callings so he, the Tempter and the Accuser, from his employment. And by this, his long experience and observation he hath his set and composed machinations, his method of temptations which are studied and artificially moulded and ordered. Even such systems and methods as tutors and professors of arts and sciences have and do read over again and again to their auditors. The Apostle calls them darts, and he hath a whole shop and armoury of them ready made and forged, which are called the depths of Satan. Which depths, if in any point, are most to be found in this: for he is more especially versed in this great question and dispute—'whether a man be a child of God or no,' more than in any other. All other controversies he has had to deal with, but in particular ages as occasionally they were started, but this hath been the standing controversy of all ages since God hath had any children on earth. With every one of whom more or less he hath at one time or another had solemn disputes about it so as he knows all the advantages, windings, and turnings in this debate; all the objections and answers and discussions in it. Not only this, but he knows the several frames and temper of spirit of men as well as of their temptations. He knows all the several ranks and classes of men in the state of grace and according to their ranks with what sort of temptations to encounter them, for even as the gifts and operations of the Spirit are many and varied so also are men's temptations. Further, he is able undiscernably to communicate all his false reasonings, tho' never so spiritual, which he doth forge and invent and that in such a manner as to deceive us by them and to make them take with us."

Another mode of attack is an assault upon our conscience.

Wonderful indeed is the Puritan understanding of this subtle and all important point. Any child of God who is spiritually alert understands only too well his own repeated failures. Because of these failures, there is a right sense of shame. The child of God has but to see in the word any sin delineated to realise its lurking presence in his own heart. This induces a sense of shame and Satan is quick to seize upon this and to use it for his own ends. There is a profound difference between the presence of sinful tendencies in a Christian's heart and the predominance and power of those tendencies. Should those tendencies result in sinful action—should they gain an uppermost place in the Christian's heart and thinking, then the Holy Spirit Himself will be quick to convict and induce a right sense of shame; but Satan will come to a Christian when those evil tendencies are still only lurking, subdued, in his mind, and Satan will accuse the Christian because of them and produce within him a sense of guilt which God does not want him to have. In this way he loses the sense of God's favour and presence and Satan's purpose is achieved. Here again we should notice the masterly way in which the Puritans were able to distinguish between the true convicting work of the Spirit and the spurious convicting of Satan. They saw that the more truly humble a man is, the more sensitive he is concerning the corruptions of his own heart, the more able Satan is to attack him along this line. And the Puritans knew when to administer comfort in such cases.

Thus Satan is a most powerful foe, ever seeking to darken the soul of the child of God; and the child of God is helpless against him in his own strength. "None can take Satan off from a man but God. He must rebuke him: none else can. A poor soul fights with Satan in this darkness like unto a man that is assaulted by one that carries a dark lantern, who can see the assaulted and how to buffet him and follows him wherever he goes; whereas the poor man cannot see him or who it is that strikes him nor he aware how to ward the blow. Therefore the Apostle when buffeted by Satan knew not what to do but only to have recourse to God by prayer, for he could no more avoid or run away from these suggestions than from himself, nor could all the saints on earth any other way have freed him. None till God should cause him to depart."

(c) *The work of the Holy Spirit.* The Puritans taught that at times God Himself brings about this experience of desertion. They quoted and expounded Isaiah 50:10–11 in this connection and taught that "it is no new thing for the children and heirs of light sometimes to walk in darkness and for a time not to have any glimpse or gleam of light." At such a time the Christian may express himself in the words of Psalm 88, but he is also to stay himself upon God and await the gracious return of the Lord's known presence.

(d) *Its purpose.* The purposes which God may have in mind in permitting these experiences may be summarised as follows:

a) *To show God's power.*
   We need to be reminded that however long we have walked with God yet we are still kept only by His grace.
b) *To cause a man to long for heaven.*
   In a time of desertion the Christian's desire for the unbroken fellowship of heaven itself may well be strengthened and increased.

If the desertion be such that the Christian falls into sin, its purpose may be

c) *Chastisement.*
   The child of God is brought to deeper penitence and greater loathing of sin.
d) *To reveal the Christian to himself.*
   He begins to see what a sinner he really is, and the depths to which he can sink.
e) *To prevent worse sin.*
   The Christian may be so humbled by his fall into lesser sin that he avoids a greater sin into which he would otherwise have fallen.

If the desertion be such that the Christian loses the sense of God's favour, its purpose may be

f) *To let him taste the fellowship of Christ's sufferings.*
   The Lord drank the cup when His Father forsook Him. "And that cup hath gone round among God's people ever since."

g) *To cause him to feel the loss of the damned, and hence give him a real compassion for souls.*

h) *To prove to the Christian the reality of his love to God.*

In some cases a man may feel himself utterly lost—and at that point cry out from his heart, "If it please the Lord to damn me, let me be damned—only let the Lord do that which pleases Him."

This is agony at the time, but afterwards the Christian realises that such a prayer, putting God's good pleasure before his own eternal salvation, could come only from a renewed heart. And here is comfort and assurance indeed.

These gleanings from the Puritans are offered in all humility in the hope that we ourselves may better understand the varied experiences which are ours as God's children and Satan's enemies and that as we are called to be under-shepherds in Christ's flock, so we may be able to comfort others with the comfort wherewith we ourselves are comforted of God, to whose blessed name be glory. Amen.

Works:

Bolton: Directions for Right Comforting.
Baxter: Right method for a Settled Peace of Conscience.
T. Goodwin: A Child of Light walking in Darkness.
Symonds: A Deserted Soul's Cause and Cure.
Perkins: Works, vol. 1.
Owen: Exposition of Psalm 130.
Sibbes: The Bruised Reed, and the Saint's Conflict.
Greenham: Grave Counsels.
Gurnall: Christian in Complete Armour.
Matthew Henry: Commentaries.

4

THE LAW AND THE COVENANTS —
A STUDY IN JOHN BALL

E. F. Kevan

Ball was born in October 1585 at Gassington in Oxfordshire, and educated in Oxford. In 1610 he became minister of the church at Whitmore, Staffordshire, where he died in 1640. He has been called "one of the fathers of Presbyterianism in England." His greatest work, published posthumously in 1645, was "A Treatise of the Covenant of Grace"; according to Thomas Blake, "his purpose was to speak on this subject of the Covenant, all that he had to say in all the whole body of divinity." Such a method of arranging all theology under a system of covenants was an anticipation of Cocceius (1603–69) and the Dutch Federal school of Reformed theologians. Bali's book would probably have been enlarged had he lived; as it is, it is an elaborate and immensely learned volume. This paper summarizes the central aspects of his teaching.

I. The Covenants

"Covenant" in English represents the Hebrew "berith," rendered in the Septuagint and New Testament by *diatheke* (a testamentary disposition)—although, as Ball points out, "berith" never meant that in common Old Testament usage. Sometimes these biblical terms stand for an absolute, unconditional promise, sometimes for a promise with a stipulation attached.

Ball reviews the various stages in God's revelation of His covenants, as Scripture records them. Historically, seven stages may be distinguished: (1) the covenant made with Adam in innocence; (2) the covenant of promise made with Adam upon his fall; (3) the covenant of grace made with Abraham; (4) the covenant of grace under Moses; (5) the covenant made with David; (6) the covenant made with Israel after the Babylonian captivity; (7) the covenant revealed in Christ. Theologically, there is only one major distinction between the covenants: that of *works and grace*.

(A) The Covenant of Works

This was made with Adam in innocence. By it God "promises all good things, specially eternal happiness, to man *on just and favourable conditions,* and man promises to walk before God *in free and willing* obedience." "The form of this covenant stood in the special promise of good which man might expect *justly to receive as a reward for his work.*" It was imposed on man by God, and was in one sense a covenant of grace. "God enters into Covenant with man not as his equal but as his Sovereign, and man is bound to accept the conditions offered by his Creator. There is no equality of power and authority between God and the creature of such a kind that the creature may make a bargain with the Most High. The covenant is of God, and as such *is an expression of His free grace and love:* for although . . . the good is promised in justice for man's works, yet it is of grace that God is pleased to bind Himself to man . . . and it is far beyond anything that man deserves. Thus, though the reward is given in justice, it is also given in grace."

(B) The Covenant of Grace

All subsequent stages in God's dealings with man by covenant are parts of the covenant of grace. It was first announced in the Protevangelium, Genesis 3:15. "The Covenant of Grace entered immediately after the fall, and so may be called a Covenant of reconciliation . . . At the very instant when God was passing judgement on the several delinquents in the fall and pronouncing sentence against the tempter, He brought in the One Who would execute the sentence. In this execution there was unfolded the Covenant of Grace for the salvation of man whom the tempter had destroyed.

"The author of this Covenant was God, considered as a merciful and loving Father in Jesus Christ . . . The cause that moved the Lord to make this Covenant was *not any worth* or merit in man . . . neither can the cause be found in *the misery* into which man had brought himself . . . The only cause that moved God to make this Covenant was *His love, favour and mercy.*

"*This Covenant was made with Christ,* in and through whom man is reconciled to God: for since God and man were separated by sin; no Covenant could be made between them, no reconciliation could be expected, and no pardon could be obtained, but by means of a Mediator."

This covenant promises pardon and eternal happiness to sinful man "if he will return from his sin, receive by true faith the mercy held out to him, and walk before God in sincere and willing obedience." Plainly, "*man cannot be under the Covenant of Works and the Covenant of Grace at one and the same time* . . . He who is under grace cannot at the same time be under the law; and he who trusts for salvation from free and sovereign mercy cannot expect it from justice as the deserved wages of his good works."

"In its manner of administration this comprehensive Covenant of Grace *reveals great diversity,* for it has pleased God to *dispense it in different ways* but so far as its substance is concerned it is one, final, unchangeable and everlasting." The epochs of its administration divide broadly into two: those in which it was the *Covenant of Promise* (from Adam to Christ) and that in which it was fully promulgated as the *New Covenant,* following on the historical coming of the promised Mediator. The Covenant of Promise "appears in the following stages of development. The first stage is from (1) *Adam unto Abraham:* the second is from (2) *Abraham until the Covenant made with Israel* on the Mount, and the third is from (3) *Moses to Christ.* This last stage must be *sub-divided:* for the Covenant which God promised to make with Israel and Judah *after* their deliverance from the North Country was to exceed the *former* Covenant which He had made with their fathers when He brought them out of Egypt."

The Sinai covenant marked an advance in the revelation of the covenant of grace. It was "a clearer expression of this free gracious Covenant, extended as it now was to a people who had grown to a large number and who were about to be united in the forms of national life. The Covenant of Grace running down in Abraham's seed was every day being despised, as in the Ishmaelites, Edomites, Syrians and others. God therefore was pleased to bind the seed of Abraham together more strongly in a state Covenant, that things might grow better and not worse." Scripture calls the Mosaic dispensation the "old" covenant "not because it was first . . . but because it was to become old, to give place to the more excellent Covenant following, and finally to be abolished."

Ball argues strongly that the Old Covenant was a form of the covenant of grace. "That the Old Covenant was a Covenant of Grace may be demonstrated by that spiritual union which was brought about by God a little before the promulgation of the Law. It is described in the following words: 'Ye have seen what I did unto the Egyptians, and how I bare you on eagles' wings, and brought you unto myself. Now therefore, if you will obey my voice indeed, and keep my covenant, then ye shall be a peculiar treasure unto me above all people . . . ye shall be unto me a kingdom of priests, and an holy nation' (Exodus 19:4–6) . . . In the New Testament believers are called 'a peculiar people' and 'a people for peculiar possession.' This was the privilege of the Israelite which he obtained by this Covenant, and it is often mentioned to the praise of God's free grace and love towards them. 'The Lord hath chosen Jacob unto himself, and Israel for his peculiar treasure.' *This privilege,* however, *they could never have obtained by the Covenant of Works* . . . These are privileges granted in the grace of the Lord Jesus Christ, in whom believers are adopted, and made kings and priests to God . . . When the Lord gave His Law He began by a reminder of the evangelical promises He had given them and *the recent deliverance from Egypt* which had served as a type of His saving grace. It can hardly be questioned whether that Covenant in which man is bound to take God to be his Father, King and Saviour is the Covenant of Grace." Again: "It was of grace that God promised to be the God of Israel; and therefore the Lord, when He keeps the Covenant with Israel, *is said to keep the mercy* which He swore to their fathers and when He establishes them for a people to Himself, He is said to perform the oath which He swore to their fathers, to Abraham, to Isaac and to Jacob."

Ball points out that all the godly men of Israel understood their covenantal relation to God in this light. "The godly kings and people of Israel, repenting of their transgressions committed against God, many times renewed their Covenant, binding themselves to the Lord to be His people, to walk in God's law . . . But Jehoshaphat, Josiah, Nehemiah and other godly governors; who were well acquainted with their infirmities . . . would never promise punctual and exact obedience with the hope of deserving eternal life by that means . . . nor would they flatter themselves as though they could stand before the tribunal of God's justice in their own righteousness, when there was ample proof that no flesh could be justified in His sight. Without question they understood that God of His free grace had promised to be their God, and that of His undeserved and rich mercy He would accept their willing and sincere obedience, even though weak and imperfect in degree. All this, in effect, means that the Covenant which God made with them, and which they renewed, was a Covenant of Grace and is the same for substance as that which is made with the faithful in Christ in the time of the Gospel."

Therefore the Abrahamic and the Mosaic covenants are for substance identical: for "the promise is the same and the things required are the same. In the former God promises to be God sufficient to Abraham and to bless him with all necessary good for this life and the life to come: in the latter He promises freely and of His own grace and favour to be their God and make them a kingdom of priests and a holy nation to Himself. In the former He requires of Abraham that he shall walk before Him in integrity: in the latter He covenants that they shall obey His voice and keep His commandments. What is it to walk before God, but to keep His law?"

And the New Testament tells us that the law was always intended to subserve the gospel. " 'Christ is the end of the law for righteousness,' and 'the law was our schoolmaster to bring us unto Christ.' But if it did not point out Christ to men, or presuppose Him as One Who was promised, it could not bring them to Him; He is not the end of the Law if the Law did not direct to Him and require faith in Him."

Of the covenant made with Israel at the time of the return from exile, Ball says: "When we think of the new blessings that were added by the Lord at this time, (this) Covenant . . . may be called new but so far as the author, matter, form, end, effects and means of administration, teaching and application are concerned, it was one with the former"—and with it to be contrasted with the New Covenant in Christ which superceded it.

The New Covenant, promulgated upon Christ's coming, is one with its predecessor in *substance.* "They both flow from the free grace and mercy of God directed towards sinners in Jesus Christ. They are both the same in substance, the requirement of the obedience of faith and the promise of life everlasting. They both have the same object, Jesus Christ, Who, being promised to the fathers in prophetic Scriptures, God has in due time made known under the Gospel. They both have the same general end, namely, the praise of the glorious grace of God in Jesus Christ. Both Covenants are made with . . . sinners . . . who no longer rely on their own law-keeping, but put their trust in Him Who justifies the ungodly. In both, it is the same Spirit who seals the truth of the Covenant to all who are under Covenant." But the New surpasses the Old *in its administration,* in the following respects in it, (1) God's love is more fully manifested; (2) Christ is more openly revealed; (3) the promises are more spiritual; (4) Moses gives place to Christ as Mediator; (5) the blood is more efficacious; (6) the Law is written in the heart; (7) all nations are included in its scope; (8) the gospel is more powerful to secure its ends than ever the Law was; (9) the covenant people enjoy a maturity of relation to God. Grace was the same thing for believers before Christ as after, but its measure was not so rich.

The *external* administration of the covenant must at every stage be distinguished from the *internal,* which is not wholly coterminous with it. *"Externally,* this Covenant is made with every member of the Church, with parents and their children together . . . so many as hear and accept the promises of salvation and dedicate their children to God according to His direction. For what are the sacraments but seals of the covenant? *Savingly and effectually,* however, this Covenant is made only with those who partake of the benefits promised. According as the Covenant is made either outwardly or inwardly, so some are the people of God outwardly and others are the people of God inwardly and in truth . . ." The covenant is made, "not only *internally* with the heirs of promise" (i.e., by spiritual regeneration in effectual calling), but also *externally,* with all those who profess to receive the promises and dedicate themselves, or are dedicated by their parents, in the outward ceremony of dedication which God has prescribed. "If this Covenant had not been externally administered no unregenerate man could ever have been in the Church or have shared in the ordinances of religion. But by virtue of this Covenant, Cain as well as Abel offered sacrifice to God as a member of the Church." Similarly, Paul distinguishes Abraham's seed into the merely natural and that which was spiritual also (Romans 9:7–8). "All who descended from Abraham and all who were born in his house and bought with his money were counted for his seed," and circumcised accordingly; "thus Ishmael, Esau and others were circumcised, counted Abraham's seed and under Covenant, until they fell away and put themselves out of covenant . . . The whole nation of Israel . . . was accounted the seed of Abraham until the time of reformation, though many among them were wicked . . . In respect of the external administration of the

Covenant they were counted the seed (John 8:37–40): but they did not walk in the steps of the faith of Abraham, and therefore in deed and truth they were not the seed . . . Further . . . the Covenant reaches to all infants born of the seed under the Covenant . . . Your children 'are holy,' says the Apostle (1 Corinthians 7:14), they are holy by Covenant, even though by nature they are sinful . . ."

II. The Law

The covenant of works was based on law; its very title is based on the Scripture phrase "law of works." *"We do not find the word Covenant* used for the relation between God and man in the time of man's innocence . . . The phrases Covenant of Works and Covenant of Grace are not found in Scripture in so many words. The nearest we come to this distinction is where the law of works is described as opposed to the law of faith (Romans 3:27)"— which phrases, Ball thinks, are virtually equivalent to covenant of works and covenant of grace.

The Mosaic Law was never propounded to man as a covenant of works. *"It cannot be proved that God ever made a Covenant of Works with man in his fallen state* . . . " "The . . . Covenant of Works . . . does not allow for repentance of past sin. The Covenant made with the Israelites; however . . . contains the possibility of renewal after transgression and allows for repentance, Deuteronomy 4:30–31. If the Covenant may be renewed after transgression it is clearly of grace." The Mosaic enactment was the covenant of grace *"propounded in a way suitable to the time and purpose for* which it was made. It was given . . . first, that it might serve to reveal sin and drive the Israelites to flee to the mercy of God revealed in Jesus; and second, that it might be a rule of life to a people in Covenant . . ." This is the position taken by the Westminster Confession.

Ball understands the opposition between "law" and "grace" in the New Testament (Paul particularly) as follows: "Paul understood the force and meaning of the Law to consist in faith but because the Jews in their addiction to the letter of the Law gave no heed to the force and life of it, he proves that the Law when separated from faith comes to be the cause, not of life, but of death. What he does is to show that such a view and use of the Law not only lacks Christ, Who is the soul of the Law, but is even opposed to Him." Such "opposition" as existed between law and grace arose from a misuse of the law by the Jews. "The Gospel before Christ's time was in the Law as the corn is set in the ear"; but "if we think of the Law or Old Testament in the way that the Jews thought of it in the apostles' day, that is, altogether severed from the New, we find not only that they are two, but that they are two *opposites or contraries.*" The designed contrast between the Old and New was not, however, this; it was rather that which is expounded in Hebrews 8:7–10. Ball comments on this passage as follows: "What law was it which the Lord here promised to write in the hearts of His people? Was it not the law given before by Moses? . . . The words of the prophet about the writing of God's Law in the heart of man can imply nothing but this, that *the Law which previously and by the ministry of Moses had been delivered only in ink and paper should by the power of the Holy Ghost through the faith of Christ be written in the affections of the heart:* . . . God in Christ would not only administer outwardly the letter of the Law, whether in writing or preaching, but would by the regeneration of the Spirit give grace inwardly so as to accomplish obedience to it . . . *The Law is not opposed to the Law: but the writing to the writing.* Writing in tables of stone belonged to Moses, or to the Old Testament; writing in the heart to Christ, or the New Covenant." The contrast between Old and New is one not of content, but of administration.

Ball continues expounding this theme as follows: "The Law is a killing letter, says the apostle . . . but the same Law . . . is (elsewhere) styled a *lively* word, or lively oracles, that is, such as give life. The words of Paul therefore are . . . to be understood of the Law . . . *only as it was separated from Christ and the Gospel.* They are spoken in respect of men who rested in the Law and sought to be justified by it: whereas Christ was the end of the Law, which fact the Jews failed to perceive and thus perverted the true sense and scope of the Law . . . The Law considered *without Christ* wounds, kills and revives sin by means of men's corruption, but the Law considered *in Christ* and as it points to Him kills corruption and converts the soul."

In the epistle to the Galatians the apostle opposes the covenant of grace to the law in many things. For instance, he says that "the Law curses . . . and that it was four hundred and thirty years after the Covenant . . . and so forth. *But it is to remembered that in those passages the apostle is disputing against the Jews* who trusted in the works of the Law . . . who combined the law with Christ in the matter of justification, as if justification was partly by the works of the Law, an opinion which the apostle everywhere condemns as contrary to the intent and purpose of the Law. *The contrariety, then, of the Law to the Covenant of Grace is not in themselves, but in the ignorance, pride and hardness of heart of those who did not understand or who perverted the right end of the Law, as if it were given for justification* . . . according to the true meaning of the Law . . . the Law did not nullify the promise in any way, but rather established it." The law separated from grace is opposed to grace, but the law recognised as subservient to grace is itself grace.

The law, as well as pointing to Christ, has its use for the believer as a rule of life, and he continues under it in this sense, though he is no longer under it as a covenant of works. The stipulation in the covenant of grace is that men "(a) *must believe* in Him Who justifies the ungodly and (b) *must walk* before Him in all well-pleasing"; i.e. must take the law as his rule of life. Believing and obeying are organically connected. "Seeing also that it is the property of faith to work by love and to be fruitful in all good works, it is clear that if faith is commanded; *obedience is required* . . . not as the cause of life, but as the way to life and the fruit of faith . . . To whom God gives the power to believe in Him, to them He gives the power to obey and do all His commandments . . . To what end, we may ask, is remission of sins promised? Is it that man . . . might continue in sin? No, but that he should serve God in holiness and righteousness." This stipulation was made when the Covenant was revealed to Abraham (Genesis 17:1), and is repeated in the Mosaic covenant. Expounding the nature of the latter, Ball draws the following important distinction. "It is true that the promises rest on a condition of obedience; but conditions are of two sorts, antecedent or consequent. (a) It is an *antecedent* condition when the condition is the cause of the thing promised or given . . . (b) It is a *consequent* condition when the condition is annexed to the promise as a qualification of the subject. It was therefore in this latter sense that obedience to the commandments was a condition of the promise. *It was not a cause why the thing promised was granted, but a qualification in the subject who was capable of* receiving it . . . In this Covenant . . . *perfect obedience is commanded"*—but *"sincere obedience is approved,* even though it is imperfect." The standard of God's law is never altered or lowered, and all shortcomings are sin; but in the covenant of grace, where works are required, not as a ground of reward but as an evidence of faith, God graciously acknowledges and accepts that which is imperfect, provided it springs from faith and love.

"Sincere," "evangelical" obedience, though it is only an imperfect obedience, is graciously accepted from those who are in covenant with God. When Old Testament saints "bound themselves by oath to walk in all the Statutes . . . of the Lord they understood this. 'I have sworn, and I will perform it, that I will keep thy righteous judgments' (Psalm 119:106). Did the psalmist think himself able to fulfil the Law in every point? How will that stand with his prayer, 'Enter not into judgment with Thy servant: for in thy sight shall no man living be justified' (Psalm 143:2)? No, but he knew that the sincere and willing obedience which he promised and would perform would be received by the Divine compassion." Ball then cites Psalm 26:1; Isaiah 38:3; 2 Kings 23:25; 1 Kings 15:5; 23:43; 15:14; 2 Chronicles 15:12, and comments, "From these passages *we cannot prove* either that these servants of God fulfilled the Law of God perfectly, or that it is possible for men in this life to do so. *Nor can we prove* that the Law is given with such moderation, that the imperfections which attached to those . . . servants of God were not sins. *What we may quite soundly infer* . . . however, is that the Law as it was given to Israel makes allowance for sincere and earnest obedience, even though it is imperfect . . ." "This requirement of obedience (by the Law) must not be so understood as if it meant that if a man in his weakness offended in any one jot or tittle he would be regarded as a covenant breaker . . ."—for the law in the covenant of grace "calls for perfection but accepts sincerity." In their context as part of the covenant of grace, the words 'Do this and live' (Leviticus 18:5; Deuteronomy 4:1; 5:33; 8:1; 16:20; 30:16, 19; Nehemiah 9:29; Proverbs 4:4; 7:2; Ezekiel 20:11, 13, 21; 33:16, 19; Luke 10:28; Romans 10:5; Galatians 3:12) must not be interpreted as if they promise life on a condition of perfect obedience. They must be expounded evangelically . . . *describing the kind of person who possesses life eternal, not the cause why life . . . is conferred."* Law is not the way *to* life as wages, but it is the way *of* life as a gift. What the law requires is the very thing in which "life" consists. Life is not obtained by law-keeping, but is experienced in law-keeping. The "doing" envisaged by Scripture in these texts is that referred to in Exodus 19:5; Psalm 112:1; 116:3; 119:1–2; James 1:25. "All these passages are to be understood of sincere and upright walking: *they show who are justified and to whom the promises of life belong, but not why they are justified.* In like manner the apostle's words "The doers of the law shall be justified" (Romans 2:13) may be expounded evangelically . . . *of those who, being such as are already justified* by grace by faith and not for their works, *soundly obey the law.* These works are opposed to faith in the matter of justification, not that faith can be without them, but because they cannot be *causes together with faith* in justification."

The good works of "evangelical obedience" flow from faith, and the faith which justifies is that which also brings forth works. Hence Ball argues: *"a disposition to good works* is necessary to justification, being the qualification of an active and living faith. Good works of all sorts are necessary to the believer's continuance in the state of justification. . . ." And Ball goes on to lay down an important distinction concerning conditions in the covenant. "If when we speak of the conditions of the Covenant . . . we understand anything that is required on the sinner's part, as preceding, accompanying or subsequent to justification, then repentance, faith and obedience are all conditions: but if by conditions we understand what is required on man's part, as the instrumental cause of the good promised, then faith in the promise of free mercy is the only condition."

The doctrine which Ball elaborates is summed up in the Westminster Confession, 19: "Although true believers be not under the Law as a Covenant of Works, to be thereby justified or condemned; yet it is of great use to them . . . in that, as a rule of life, informing them of the will of God and their duty, it directs and binds them to walk accordingly . . . So as a man's doing good and refraining from evil, because the Law encourageth to the one, and deterreth from the other, is no evidence of his being under the Law and not under grace. Neither are the aforementioned uses of the Law contrary to the grace of the Gospel, but do sweetly comply with it."

5

Abridged from

MRS. HUTCHINSON AND
HER TEACHING

E. Braund

In 1817 a volume was published containing two works written nearly 150 years earlier by Mrs. Lucy Hutchinson, who has become widely known through the Memoirs of her husband, Colonel John Hutchinson, the Parliamentary Governor of Nottingham Castle during the Civil Wars. Though written by Mrs. Hutchinson after her husband's death, the Memoirs did not appear in print until 1806, but their immediate success then was undoubtedly the chief reason for the editor, himself a descendant of the Hutchinson family, subsequently publishing her remaining works which will be considered here after a brief sketch of the life of this remarkable Puritan woman.

Lucy Hutchinson, or Lucy Apsley as she was till she married, was born during the reign of James I, in 1620. Her birthplace and childhood home was the Tower of London, where her father, Sir Allen Apsley, was Lieutenant of the Tower until his death five years after Charles I came to the throne. Instructed by her mother, a godly Puritan woman of noble family, Lucy came to a knowledge of the truth as a young girl though, on looking back from old age, she could lament her continued preoccupation after that with a too-intensive study of classical writers which she was, however, later to put to good use.

Lucy's intellectual studies did not prevent her falling in love with John Hutchinson, the eldest son of Sir Thomas Hutchinson who sat in Parliament for Nottinghamshire. They were married in 1638, and the Memoirs which Mrs. Hutchinson later wrote provide a chronicle of the events of their life together, besides revealing her as a woman who, while drawing a tender portrait of a husband to whom she was devoted, could at the same time write detailed military history and set it clearly against the wider background of contemporary events and of the history of the Gospel in Britain.

On Civil War breaking out, John Hutchinson declared for Parliament, and not many months later was appointed Governor of Nottingham Castle and Town, which he held for Parliament throughout the first Civil War. Mrs. Hutchinson shared his hazards, living with him at the Castle which was often attacked, and on at least one occasion herself acting as surgeon to the wounded while also caring for the sick among the prisoners. Nor was her oral courage less evident than her physical bravery, and amidst the jealousies and feuds which were continually breaking out among Parliamentary supporters, she and her husband steadfastly pursued what they believed the Lord had called them to do. They also obeyed their conscience in matters of faith, although this led to them being spoken against by Presbyterians and supporting Separatists.

In 1646 Colonel Hutchinson was returned to Parliament in place of his father who had died. He favoured the Independents, and his wife took a keen interest with him in events as they moved to their climax. When, finally, the King was brought to trial, Colonel Hutchinson was one of the judges who signed the death warrant. During the Commonwealth he was a member of the first Councils of State, but after the expulsion of the Long Parliament by Cromwell he and his wife retired to the country and he took no further part in public life, since they both strongly disagreed with the power seized by the Army, and what they regarded as Cromwell's overwhelming personal ambition.

In the chaotic times following Cromwell's death, however, Colonel Hutchinson returned to Parliament, though shortly after the Restoration he was expelled as having been a regicide. Owing to his wife's strenuous efforts to save him, he was granted a pardon and allowed to retire to the country again, but in 1663 was arrested on a vague, and almost certainly false, charge of being implicated in a plot and was committed to the Tower of London. Though never brought to trial, after a few months the Colonel was transferred to Sandown Castle, a melancholy decaying place on the Kent coast. Having pleaded in vain to be imprisoned with him there, Mrs. Hutchinson took lodgings in Deal from where she walked over every day to care for her husband. After a while, however, she had to go home for a few weeks, and while she was away the Colonel caught a chill which proved fatal. Mrs. Hutchinson never saw her husband again, but he left her a message:

> "Let her," he said, "as she is above other women, show herself in this occasion, a good Christian, and above the pitch of ordinary women."

With her husband's death, Mrs. Hutchinson's life retreats into the shadows, but it was undoubtedly during the Restoration period, when she was faced with many financial and family problems, that she wrote her two books called "On the Principles of the Christian Religion" and "Of Theology," which are to be considered here.

The first of these was written specially for her daughter, and for a most practical purpose. Seeing her subject to many worldly temptations and living in an age of error and confusion, Mrs. Hutchinson believed the most important thing of all was that she should be well grounded in fundamental truths of the Christian faith for, as she writes, "Let but the judgment be fixed in the foundation truths, and the practice will not be so mutable and various as we see it in many professors." She maintained, too, that women should take particular care lest they be led away into errors.

Mrs. Hutchinson wrote her book, rather than simply recommending others to her daughter, because she wanted it to stand as a personal witness of all she regarded as of vital importance if her daughter was to lay a foundation of "sound knowledge for the building of a holy practice." Since the book, therefore, sprang from immediate and personal concern to promote her daughter's growth in the Christian life, it may be interesting to notice the way in which Mrs. Hutchinson felt she could best do this. At once we see she does not merely try to explain away her daughter's difficulties. Neither does she put her feelings in the first place, nor make happiness the primary reason for Christian living. Instead, her great concern is to present objectively those doctrines and principles she considers to be vital "foundation truths," giving positive expositions (of what I believe to be orthodox Puritan teaching) at the same time as issuing exhortations and warnings. By so doing, however, she in no way divorces the objective from the subjective, nor decries experience. Rather she believes spiritual meditation on objective truths to be a great means of leading to deeper experience of those truths and of promoting Christian living.

Mrs. Hutchinson's expositions bear the impress of her own spiritual meditation. Her judgment, too, is to be seen in her selection and presentation of those doctrines she considers vital for her daughter to be instructed in, and in this connection it is striking to observe how large a part of the book is devoted to truths concerning God Himself, His being, the Trinity, His attributes, His eternal and immutable decree, predestination, and His works n creation and providence. As regards the doctrine of election, Mrs. Hutchinson holds it to be "a great fundamental in our faith," and declares it should keep us humble before God; it should stir up our thankfulness to Him it should stay our souls in temptation, and exhort us to sanctity of life.

While ever seeking to direct her daughter's gaze upward to dwell on the majesty of God and the glory of Christ, Mrs. Hutchinson is equally concerned that she shall always do this through Scripture, the authority of which is unequivocally stated; and the book contains a solemn warning that "Christ is, in the Gospel, held forth to men to be received as their life and salvation, and they that seek a Christ anywhere but where God exhibits Him, that is, His own authorised Word, may find Christ of their own inventions, but shall never find the Christ of God, the alone Saviour of men."

Mrs. Hutchinson examines at length the person and work of the Lord Jesus Christ, and the work of the Holy Spirit in our salvation and sanctification. Only in the light of these truths does she expound what are called "privileges to believers purchased by Christ," such as peace and joy and liberty—and her very expression declares the way in which these are viewed.

The book includes a number of warnings, and among these are admonitions against people who would reject the Old Testament as of no use to believers, or who would preach that anyone once justified can fall into an unjustified state. In the controversy over the order of justification and sanctification, we are told neither can be without the other though "justification is perfect and complete, being by faith received and given us in Christ; but sanctification, being derived from Christ to us, and wrought in our souls, is perfected in the body by degrees, and admits of growth and remissions and intentions." Mrs. Hutchinson disputes with ministers who deny the preparatory work of convincing men they are sinners and who preach only the love of Christ, the grounds of her objection being that Scripture shows "that Christ and His apostles used the other method." Consideration of the biblical meaning of faith also leads to a further warning that "he that receives Christ by a true saving faith, receives whole Christ in all His offices, and as well submit to Him as a King, as embraces Him as a Saviour. . . ."

Love is the last vital truth which the book presents, and it is declared that none truly love God but those who love God only; and constantly; and for Himself more than for His blessings. He that loves God loves all things that are His, all those that love Him, and all His ordinances and His word. But although this consideration of "love" concludes the "foundation truths" of the book, Mrs. Hutchinson goes on at once to enumerate what she regards as the most essential principles for Christian living since, as she reminds her daughter, "to know all the truths and mysteries of Godliness, without living in and according to that knowledge, will be less excusable than ignorance."

These principles are not concerned with externals, but with the believer's attitude of heart and mind to God; and we may perhaps see here a connection between the emphasis in the first part of the book on the doctrines of God, and the primary importance attached to the soul's inward worship of Him as the basis of all Christian living in the second. The great principles laid down are that true inward worship of God, without which everything else is vain, must include a cleaving to Him, by which is meant in faith resting upon Him and all His promises, and longing and striving after communion with Him; and secondly, that there must be adoration of God, in which there are two essentials: self-abasement or self-denial; and exaltation of God.

It is shown that Scripture clearly teaches self-denial to be requisite to all true worship, and Mrs. Hutchinson maintains that the great way to stir ourselves up to this is to meditate upon what Christ has done for us. By exaltation or adoration of God is meant having high and reverent thoughts of Him which make us approach Him with a deep sense of His majesty and our own vileness. It is maintained, too, that where there is a true fear of God, which to a child of God does not mean slavish terror, there will be constant prayer and seeking after Him, and there follows an exhortation not to be content with vague wishes after Him. There can be no true adoration of God without inward obedience, exercised in the understanding and will, and also submission to God in all circumstances; while the last essential to all worship is said to be thankfulness, and Mrs. Hutchinson does not hesitate to assert that, of all sins, unthankfulness is the greatest.

It is obvious throughout the book that Mrs. Hutchinson herself delighted to meditate on the great objective truths of her faith and, thinking of them as she wrote, was constantly moved to praise. But as in her later life she thus came to dwell more and more upon these truths, she saw with increasing clarity the false webs of philosophy in which, when younger, she had been so nearly enmeshed; and I believe this to have been the chief reason for her embarking on her other book which is called "Of Theology." In it she surveys the position of man in sin and, making extensive use of her own knowledge of classical writers, attempts to expose the ultimate barrenness of philosophy and the impossibility of man attaining to a true knowledge of God by any effort of his own or by human reasoning. It is important to all Mrs. Hutchinson's thought, however, that she never means to decry man's faculty of reason as such, but only as it is set up in opposition to God or exalted above Him.

In spite of the involved form in which the book is written, with a mesh of close reasoning which often takes on a philosophical manner, its underlying argument proceeds logically from stage to stage as Mrs. Hutchinson develops her theme.

The book's first major argument is that by its very nature theology, by which is meant the study and knowledge of God and His revealed truths, cannot be reduced to purely human systems of intellectual study. Argument is drawn from the 1 Corinthians 2 from which it is concluded that "theology is a mysterious and divine wisdom which is neither circumscribed by those bounds, nor taught by those rudiments that all other arts and sciences admit"; also that "whoever would receive or understand the wisdom in the hidden mystery, it is necessary he should be instructed . . . by the Holy Ghost."

From this there follows an enquiry into the nature of the "divine wisdom," or theology, which includes both the knowledge God gives of Himself, and the way in which men are enabled to receive this knowledge. As regards the doctrine of God—that is, the knowledge He gives of Himself—the basic propositions laid down are that God alone knows Himself perfectly, and our immediate mirror is not God Himself but His word or gospel "in which with open face, by Christ, we behold the Glory of God." Theology, therefore, is divine truth itself, as it is revealed by God.

Further, all knowledge of God comes only by His own revelation, and here Mrs. Hutchinson adds the rider that all the word of God is committed to writing.

Proceeding to the way in which man in his first creation and entire nature was enabled to have this knowledge of God and to enjoy communion with Him, which is termed natural theology as distinct from the successive revealed word of God, the book teaches that man in his first creation had a two-fold dependence upon God. First, he was dependent upon Him as his Creator. Secondly, man as a rational being and distinct from all other creatures, also had a moral dependence upon God with moral obedience required of him, and was endued with that innate wisdom or light or law—the terms are varied—which enabled him to know what God required and to obey Him. Adam's theology is thus concluded to have been that "being constituted in a state of moral dependence upon God, and subjected to the Government of his Creator, and thereby capable of eternal blessedness in the enjoyment of his maker, he had an implanted law of those operations which were requisite to the attainment of that end, created together with him, and was moreover endued with wisdom enabling him to render the prescribed obedience according to the will and mind of God shining in the law."

This principle of a two-fold law of nature and moral law implanted within man, provides the basis for the rest of the book in which it is argued that though, by the Fall and sin, these laws within Adam were utterly corrupted and his communion with God broken, nevertheless relics of that first theology do in fact still remain in all men, though "corrupt and groaning." It is contended that all men have a sense of God, that He is to be worshipped and that He is judge of good and evil (Romans 1:19 is quoted in particular), and that they also have within them a law giving them a moral consciousness: and these are maintained to be the corrupt traces of Adam's true theology before the Fall. Conscience is cited as proving the existence of these principles within men, while universal experience is also held to confirm it—and the power of conscience.

The argument then proceeds from the internal sense of God

within men to the ways in which He reveals Himself eternally to all men through His works of creation and providence, and in a long digression the question is taken up as to whether this knowledge of God can bring men to salvation. Mrs. Hutchinson sees the whole controversy as hinging round two basic issues regarding God's will in giving the revelation of Himself in His works of creation and providence, and whether the means of these revelations are sufficient to save anyone. As regards the latter, the book's main conclusions are that though the works of God in creation and providence may bring men to knowledge of Him as their Creator and that He is to be worshipped and obeyed, this can only lead them back to a sense of law and to a covenant of works which men in sin cannot fulfil, and, while they show the goodness and patience of God towards mankind, this is not saving grace, and they reveal no placability towards men in sin. Moreover, and this is the truth everywhere emphasized, the works of creation and providence do not reveal the gospel of Christ, and therefore cannot of themselves bring men to salvation, nor can the blindness and prejudice of men's minds be removed except by the work of the Holy Spirit within them. The works of God do, however, render all men inexcusable before God since, "in the state wherein they might have known God, they have been wickedly ignorant of Him, notwithstanding His revelation of Himself in His Works." But in her arguments concerning the will of God in giving these revelations of Himself, Mrs. Hutchinson would seem to tend towards reducing His intentions to a form of rational argument, and to making His absolute sovereignty into an excuse for a lack of missionary enterprise.

Having in these ways established that neither the external nor the internal knowledge of God given to all men can save them apart from Christ, the rest of the book works out Mrs. Hutchinson's view of how men's efforts to arrive at a true knowledge of God apart from Christ have, in fact, not only failed but led them further from the truth. She argues that philosophy had its roots in those implanted laws within fallen men which are themselves the lingering traces of Adam's true theology, and that the first philosophers were those who, urged on by the sense of God within them and the revelation of Himself in creation, tried to feel after Him and by the exercise of their minds to arrive at Him. The study of ethics is said to have sprung from man's moral consciousness, while that of metaphysics was derived from man's sense of God. But though the philosophers, and particularly the Greeks, scaled great heights, they could not live up to their thoughts, nor could they arrive at true knowledge of God since their very minds, twisted by sin, led them away into endless contentions and speculations.

But there were other ways, too, in which relics of truth retained by men were corrupted. Mrs. Hutchinson claims that many early traditions had in them "particles of divine truth," but that instead of men benefitting from these to improve their knowledge, they further corrupted them. She accuses the Greek poets in particular of mingling traditions with their own fables, and vestiges of truth concerning God with the worship of false gods, until it was impossible for men with blinded minds to pick out one from another, and they were led into all sorts of pernicious errors and abominations, and to worship a multitude of gods.

Those concerned with law and government are also said to have been guilty of further corrupting the Gentiles' false religions by incorporating fables about gods and idolatrous worship into their laws for political ends. The wisest philosophers rejected this "political theology," but for all their efforts could not disentangle truth from false, and as superstitions and idolatries increased, many of the philosophers came to pour contempt on the whole multitude of gods. By these means, therefore, Mrs. Hutchinson maintains that all men's efforts to arrive at true knowledge of God not only proved hopeless, but led them to catastrophe. But, she declares at last, "God, from the foundation of the world, determined that, in His appointed time, a light should break forth to the Gentiles that sat in darkness. . . ."

In order to emphasise the power of the false religions and superstitions and philosophies which the light of the Gospel was to pierce, Mrs. Hutchinson takes the fifteen points by which Cardinal Bellarmine had asserted the true church might be discerned and shows that, in the sense they are used by the Roman Church, they might equally well be applied to the old gentile religions. While doing this with the explicit purpose of showing how strong was the hold of gentile religion to be overcome by the gospel, she is at the same time, however, surely implicitly contending that natural philosophy and religious superstition are to be found developing within the Roman Church, as they did among the Gentiles, and that both spring from the same root: namely, those corrupt relics of truth retained by man in sin which cannot bring him to true knowledge of God and salvation.

The main propositions around which Mrs. Hutchinson builds her book, therefore, are the two-fold law of nature and moral law which she claims as man's first theology before the Fall; the fact that relics of this, though corrupted by the Fall and unable to bring men to a true and saving knowledge of God, can still be traced in men by their sense of God and moral consciousness; and lastly, the contention that these principles within men were the main spring of gentile philosophy and religion. In this book her arguments concerning God's absolute sovereign will would seem to become too rational. But though we see here the weakness of her judgment with regard to this doctrine, we see its strength in her other book where it is shown to be a great cause of promoting holy living. Undoubtedly, too, it was Mrs. Hutchinson's deep sense of the majesty and holiness of God that led her in life to walk in that fear of the Lord of which she has left us her own description:

"This reverential fear begets a holy care and watch in the soul, suspecting and crying out to God to keep His citadel there . . . 'Tis a holy frame of spirit that keeps us always in a reverent awe and dread of the great majesty of God, and in an humble posture of soul before Him, yet cuts not off, but aggravates our delight in Him, our joy and our singing before Him. . . ."

6

RICHARD GREENHAM AND THE
TRIALS OF A CHRISTIAN

O. R. Johnston

I. Introduction

Greenham was the first of the great English Puritan pastors;
he pioneered the paths in pastoral dealing which the later, and in
some ways greater, Puritans followed. His twenty years of selfless
labour at Dry Drayton, a little village a few miles from Cambridge, to which he went in 1570, inspired many young men to
give their lives in similar ministries throughout England. Henry
Holland, his friend and admirer, spent four years collecting
tracts, letters, and written notes in order to give to the world a
lasting memorial of his apostolic labours and ripe Christian wisdom—the large volume of Greenham's collected works.

Greenham's conception of the Christian life, as this volume
reveals it, is briefly as follows. He sees the Christian as a pilgrim,

making his way through manifold difficulties along the road that leads to the heavenly city. His path lies through the vale of tears which is this mortal life. Great dangers beset him, and the way becomes harder rather than easier as he goes on. The main part of the duty of a true pastor is accordingly to show the Christian his difficulties and perils in their true—that is their scriptural—light, and him the way through and out of them.

For the purposes of this paper, we classify the trials and difficulties with which Greenham deals thus: (i) distressing states of mind and heart; (ii) temptations from the world, the flesh and the devil; (iii) afflictions, i.e. the assaults which are made upon our body, goods, or position in this life.

II. Distressing States of Mind and Heart

All Christians, says Greenham, periodically find themselves in such states; their inception is not marked and often we can trace no direct cause of them; but all know what it is to find themselves in them. We briefly review some of them.

(1) *Wandering thoughts.* Greenham was once asked "why a man after sundry and laborious reading . . . being desirous by meditation to apply the things read unto himself, was so much interrupted, and violently, unwillingly and suddenly drawn into other conceits." He replied, "It was *either* want of preparing and sanctifying our hearts by prayer before we set on so holy an exercise and therefore the Lord correcteth the pride of our wits and presumption of our hearts in being bold to work upon holy matters in our own strength; *or else* that we, resting upon a general purpose of thinking some good thing . . . did not fasten our mind constantly and continually upon some particular object, but ranging up and down . . . did not wholly and seriously set on the thing propounded to ourselves"—in fact, either lack of humility or lack of concentration.

(2) *Bouts of dread.* Sometimes for no apparent reason unaccountable terror invades the soul, "when we are alone, or . . . in

the night, being sent of God to humble us; the physician will say it is a melancholic passion, but I say it is the power of God's presence preparing us to prayer, or some such like service of God; which, when we feel, if we fall down before the Lord in prayer, we may find an unspeakable joy following it. . . ." Even if the physician is partly right, Greenham is not wholly wrong when he insists that a spiritual lesson must be learned from the onset of this state of mind; it must not be entertained or dwelt on, but prayed over and used as a lesson in humility.

(3) *Sinful desires and delusions.* These sometimes invade Christian souls; "sinking down so deeply in them that though they weep, pray and meditate . . . though they feel them with irksomeness and loathsomeness, as we feel sickness in our bodies—yet those motions will continually be in them without diminishing . . . We are not to martyr ourselves with disquietness of mind, because we are so pestered and thronged with wicked motions and assaults . . . For the godly shall not be so freed from sin, but that they shall be assaulted with evil motions, suspicions, delusions, vain fantasies and imaginations; the body of sin shall never be from us so long as we live. For the scum thereof is almost continually boiling and walloping in us, foaming out such filthy froth and stinking savour into our minds, that it is not only detestable to the mind regenerate . . . but it would make abashed the very natural man to look into so loathsome a sty of sin, and sinkhole of iniquity." Despite this, we need not despair: "if we feel this in ourselves, that we would fain love the Lord and be better, and being wearied and tired with our sins; long gladly to enjoy the peace of righteousness, and desire to please God in a simple obedience of faith—then let us comfort ourselves. . . ." We must confess the sin and seek repentance, but we may know as we do so that we are children of God.

(4) *Doubts.* When moods of doubt come upon the soul, "think with thyself that it is the mercy of God by them to cause thee better to discern of those temptations in others . . . how they make their first entry into a man's heart, how they gather strength, how

they agree with our corrupt nature, in what degrees they come to some growth, how the Spirit of God doth resist them, what be the means best to prevail against them. And thus if thou make profit by them, thou shalt so wonderfully search and descry . . . temptations in others, by an holy experience which God hath taught thee in self, that . . . thou shalt lay forth men's secret corruptions, as if thou wert in their bosoms; thou shalt be able also by the seed of sorrow in thyself to beget an unspeakable joy in others, who in time may be tempted as thou now art." It is in the school of spiritual doubts and conflicts that pastors are trained.

(5) *Deadness of spirit.* Feelings normally accompany faith, but not always. Spiritual insensibility is akin to bodily sickness: "as by some extreme sickness, life may be in one, yet it cannot be felt of the sick body, so in some great temptation, the Holy Ghost may be in us, and yet we not feel nor find his presence." In this state, the Christian must not "tarry to play till he find feeling but offer himself up into the hand of Jesus Christ"; and must take care not to be drawn into carnal joys ("taking his mind off it") lest he exile the working of God's Spirit. To one who complained that he was "comfortless for want of feeling," Greenham replied, "Oh brother, we hold Christ by faith, and not by feeling." Feeling "is but an effect and fruit of faith"; and faith may flourish most when feelings are least. "Although a man do not feel his faith sometimes under the cross, as indeed it falleth out often in the best children of God, yet when it shall please the Lord to send feeling, and deliverance, that man shall see that his faith was great . . . stronger, when he had not the feeling of God's favour, than it had been at some times, when he had great feelings."

(6) *Loss of assurance.* This point follows on from the last. Greenham speaks to it in his "Letter Consolatory for an Afflicted Mind." "There is sometime as it were an eclipse of our faith . . . but let us assure ourselves, that as the sun and moon do not perish in their eclipses, nor loose their light for ever so in this eclipse which happeneth to our faith, and sense of God's goodness the same . . . shall in good time be restored . . . unto our further and

more assured comfort. This have you seen in many of the dear children of God . . . You have felt it in yourself that there has been an interchangeable course of sorrow and comfort, of faith and fear, and that the one hath continually secceeded the other, that the same hand that humbled you, did raise you up again. . . ."

(7) *Hardness of heart.* In his "Letter against Hardness of Heart" Greenham differentiated between two sorts of hardness: that which is unrecognised for what it is (either a deliberate resistance to the Spirit and means of grace, or a careless continuance in sin without remorse), and that which is recognised (which leads some to desire a cure, and others despairingly and hopelessly to refuse all means of help). Greenham describes detailed remedies for cases of hardness of the second type, showing himself a master of spiritual therapeutics.

III. Temptations

(a) *The Christian in temptation: general remarks.* God never allows a Christian to be tempted in a way or to a degree which he cannot resist. 1 Corinthians 10:13 is one of Greenham's favourite texts. As we proceed in the Christian life, temptations increase. Sometimes we find ourselves "weaker in less assaults, having afore been stronger in greater temptations"; this may be partly because God was particularly good to us when first we came to Him, and partly because since conversion we have to some extent relapsed into carnal self-confidence, and, thinking ourselves strong, have become weak. Temptation reveals one's real character—"every man is that indeed that he is in temptation." The very facts of temptation, and resistance to temptation, are distinctive marks of regenerate men, and from our experience of them we may derive assurance. "By this, that Satan so busily and fiercely assaileth us, it doth appear that as once he lost his possession, and was cast out . . . by Christ, so now he findeth no peaceable entrance . . . and therefore there yet remaineth . . . the secret seed of faith still sustained and nourished by the Spirit of God in us, when we would

think it were utterly extinguished . . . Neither is there any more
sure testimony, either of our present deliverance begun, or of our
full and perfect victory in time to come, than this, that by the
word of God we do (though but weakly) resist the temptations of
the enemy, and continue in the battle against him, mourning indeed and travailing under the burden of affliction, but yet standing upright before the enemy so that he cannot . . . overthrow
and destroy us."

(b) *Satan's part in temptation.* "Satan hath so absolute power,
but a power by permission to try us: against which we must arm
ourselves by faith, which will assure us that either the Lord miti-
gate our temptation . . . or else, if he enlarge the trial he will increase our strength . . . We must also pray that the Lord give not
out that measure of leave to the devil which we give out to sin
. . . but that he would rather make Satan a surgeon to show us our
sins than a sergeant to confound us for them." Satan tries "to persuade many that the weakness of their body, and feebleness of
their brain proceedeth of their temptations, when indeed it
cometh of their own unstayed minds, wandering too much after
the motions of the devil, in that they not resting on the word, nor
depending on Christ, nor contenting themselves to be tried; nor
comforting themselves by meditation, attend too much and confer too often with the devil's illusions and temptations and they
complain of the effects and not of the causes of the temptations
being more grieved for their present sufferings, than for their
sins past. The root of this worldly shame is pride. . . ."

(c) *The relation of temptation to our own sinful state.* "When a
great temptation hangeth long upon us, it were good to seek for
some special sin in us, because we shall find that for some privy
pride or unthankfulness, or such like, a temptation remaineth
long with us. There is a train of corruption in us, and God often
punisheth one sin with another, which, if we espy not, but look
only to the grosser sins, we shall hardly be brought to humble our
souls . . . or to profit by the admonition of others." Temptation
thus often serves the useful purpose of bringing sin into the open

so that we see it clearly in all its foulness and can deal with it: "out-ward temptations do not hurt till our inward corruption doth yield: but rather they are as Surgeons to draw out our festered corruptions."

(d) *Particular temptations.* We mention three of the many with which Greenham deals. (i) This is how he comforted a man who thought he had *sinned against the Holy Ghost.* "Satan's temptations follow our affections. If we lightly account of sin he blears our eyes with God's mercies; if we begin to make a conscience of sin, he loadeth us with the judgments of God, being as ready now to aggravate this sin more than it is in itself . . . as before he would extenuate it to make it seem less than it was . . . You have sinned a great sin before the Lord in that you make a mock of the word which you know, yet if you turn to the Lord in fear and serve Him, your sin is remissible, howsoever Satan chargeth your con-science." (ii) *Riches* may be a temptation. "If we have wealth and riches, the Lord trieth us if we will be more thankful." Riches, though morally neutral in themselves, become a snare to those who have them. "Riches dim our eyes as a cloud, that we cannot see far with them . . . Poverty hath slain a thousand, but riches have slain ten thousand. They are very uncertain, they promise that which they cannot perform, neither can they afford a con-tented mind." (iii) *Godliness* itself becomes an occasion of temp-tation: "the more godly a man is, and the more graces and bless-ings of God are upon him, the more need he hath to pray, because Satan is busiest against him, and because he is readiest to be puffed up with a conceited holiness."

In all temptation, our first recourse must be to prayer. "Say 'Lord, thou makest me to possess the sins of my youth . . . how-beit, O Lord, grant I may by wisdom herein, make this temptation an holy instruction . . . oh turn this to thy glory and my salvation' . . . or if this do not prevail, give yourself with all humbleness to read the word of God, especially his promises, and be still at-tending on the means, waiting when the Lord shall enlarge your heart. Or if this do not help, go to some faithful brother, confess yourself to him . . . and be not ashamed to give God the glory by shaming yourself, and opening your corruption to him, that so he may pray for you . . . (James 5). Thus having prayed by yourself, and with another, and used the means of reading for your recovery . . . go to your calling, knowing that your prayers and the word of God, being as seed, must have some time between the sowing of thorn and the reaping of the increase and fruit of them. Above all, reason not with your temptation, dispute not with the devil, as though you could prevail of yourself. And as I would not that you should dispute with your temptation, so I would not you should despise it and make no account of it"—for the one course is spiritually as dangerous as the other.

IV. Afflictions

(a) *General positive principles.* The Christian is called to suffer, and his course will normally be hard. This principle does not of course hold good for all Christians at all times, but is a reliable rough guide to the experiences of a lifetime. "Although the godly shall escape hell in the world to come, yet they shall be punished in this world." However, this prospect must not daunt saints, for "it is a most certain thing in God's children, that the more their afflictions grow the more their faith groweth." Christians must grasp the fact that all things come to them from God, and for their good. Whatsoever is upon you is from the Lord, and whatsoever is from the Lord, to you it is in mercy, and whatsoever comes in mercy ought not to be grievous to you. What loss is it, when the losing of earthly things is the gaining of spiritual things? . . . All shall be for your good, if you make your use of all." Afflictions are sent for our profit, and we must learn to profit by them.

(b) *The connection between afflictions and sins.* Afflictions may be sent to make us appreciate fully the greatness of God's mercy when He bestows good gifts, without them we should be in danger of under-valuing this mercy. From this point of view, affliction need not have any direct connection with our sins. "Job served

God in truth and yet was punished, and so Lazarus; but this was not so much for their own sin as for the trial of their faith, and that after them the church might receive great comfort by their examples. For as it hurts not the gold to be put into the fire, both because it is thereby tried, and also made more pure—so it is not evil for the children of God to have their faith tried; if it be a strong faith it will bear the fire; if it be weak it will shine yet brighter." Yet affliction is sometimes sent as a warning. "The Lord often . . . by outward crosses draweth us from the state of security and untowardness to good works . . . Neither can we truly repent, until by some cross we know this world to be a place of sorrow, and not of mirth and delight . . . We must be as birds on a bough, to remove at God's pleasure, and that without resistance when the Lord shall visit us. And because we are too much given to think that we have the things in our own right, which we hold of the free goodness of God, we are taught in affliction how heinous unthankfulness it were to bind the Lord continually to entertain us in this life at so full charge and cost. . . ." One cardinal sin at least needs affliction as its cure—fleshly security, and the slothfulness in good works to which it leads. Affliction serves to terminate this condition by humbling us. "It is the wisdom of God joined with mercy for the preserving of his children in humility and thankfulness (if they forget to spy out and be humbled for their inward corruptions), either to let them fall into some sin, to punish their pride . . . or else (which is his more merciful chastisement) to break them with some cross, until their hearts be bruised." Affliction, acting as it does to call attention to our sins, may thus reinforce the message of the law, and prepare us for faith. Affliction is either of the body or of the mind, of these the Lord sometime to humble us doth send the one, sometime the other, sometimes both, and all to humble us . . . when as he seeth by reason of the corruption of our nature, that the preaching of the law is not sufficient to humble us, and strike that terror into our hearts which might make us duly prepared to receive . . . the sweet and comfortable promises made us in Christ . . . Now if affliction be such a notable thing, and the Lord worketh even eternal life thereby often times to those whom he hath elected

and called to be his, how lovingly ought they to embrace it to
whom the Lord doth so fatherly offer it? How patiently and
cheerfully ought they to bear it, inasmuch as they thereby may
assure themselves that Cod hath severed them from the world,
and from those on whom he meaneth to show no mercy in the
day of his wrath? And as for those whom the Lord as yet hath
laid no scourge upon them, let them not long for it, but let
them lay the law of God and the threatnings thereof unto their
hearts to humble them thereby. It is better to be humbled
thereby than by affliction, and yet better by affliction than not
at all. . . ."

(c) *Particular afflictions.* We mention five out of many which
Greenham treats. (i) *Persecution,* the Christian's common lot,
serves to distinguish the children of God: "so long as God's children and worldlings walk as it were together, it is hard to distinguish (them) . . . but when they are severed by persecution, it will
surely be seen who be the children of God, and who be the heirs
of the world." (ii) *Scorn and reproach* was Greenham's own lot: "he
said, although he was subject to many and grievous reproaches,
yet two things did ever comfort him; this one, that his heart was
well, did not evil affected to many men; secondly, that going
alone, he could humble himself and pray to God that the authors
of such reproaches might be pardoned." He shows with pene-
trating insight how the regenerate should face reproach. "It is
our corruption that we are more grieved when we suffer as well-
doers, than when we suffer for evil-doing. For this is the logic of
the world: 'I am grieved that I am thus dealt with because I never
deserved it; had I done anything worthy of punishment it would
not have grieved me, though I had been punished.' Thou speak-
est like a foolish man . . . Whether is it better to suffer, when thy
conscience is free and suffereth not, or when with thy outward affliction thou art afflicted also of thine own heart? And is it not a
glorious thing to suffer for well doing wherein thy cause of grief
is the less . . . ? For if the cause of affliction rather than affliction
itself should grieve thee, then affliction without cause of affliction—being for God, his cause—should rather comfort thee."

(iii) *Being abandoned by one's friends* should prompt us to self-examination: maybe we have been unkind to our friends, or sought the favour of man more than of God, or perhaps fleshly love or hypocrisy is being corrected, or God may be trying our faith to see whether we love Him for His own sake—for "the Lord oft sequestreth our friends far from us to knit and glue us nearer to himself." In any case, one must not suppose one's trouble to be unique and become immersed in self-pity. (iv) *Personal loss* of other kinds (children, or goods) should prompt us to self-examination in a similar way; our main concern should constantly be to find out and learn the lesson which affliction has been sent to teach us. (v) *Continuing poverty while others grow rich* ought not to rob the Christian of his contentment and glad acquiescence in his lot. "If the Lord show lesser mercies to us than to others, we have no cause to complain because He is no debtor so we must not envy them that have greater gifts, for if we have any it is more than (our) due or than we have deserved, and this will teach us to be contented with that which we have had. Let us then look on what we have and give God thanks for it, and know that if we should have more, He would give more, yea if we consider that they that have much must make the greater account, and that we are unfit to do so, will thank God that we have no more than we have."

(d) *Two dangers* beset the afflicted Christian. The first is *self-pity.* "Let us now learn to hold all the passions of impatience in bondage, both by comparing our evils with the wonderful mercies of God, and our small suffering with the intolerable conflicts of our forefathers. For there is no greater cause of our despairing under the cross than when Satan persuadeth us that never any were handled so roughly . . . Wherefore, lest our infirmities should over-master us . . . let us call to mind the Saints of God . . . to the end that by them we may learn that, according as God dealeth forth the gifts of the Spirit, thereafter doth he send greater afflictions, both to make them the more esteemed, and also to cause a more plentiful fruit of their faith." The second danger is *spiritual recklessness.* Greenham outlines it in the following words—"when our afflictions do not drive us to God, nor cause us more humbly to hear and seek His work, but rather to stop our ears, and to run from it, and to seek unlawful means, let us then mourn secretly and heartily unto God for the direction of God's Spirit, for that case is dangerous."

V. Conclusion

We have tried to let Greenham speak for himself on the trials of the Christian life. But, of course, trials are not the whole of the Christian life; there is abundant joy and comfort for the believer, more than many Christians ever know, and Greenham has much to say on this side of the matter too. His account of the Christian life, like that of all the greatest Puritans, is admirably balanced. However, in this paper we have confined our attention of necessity to one aspect of the picture only. We close with some comments on the teaching we have reviewed.

(i) It is *admirably realistic.* The state of the church in Greenham's day was unsettled, and so were the minds of many of its members. One result of the conflict of convictions within Christendom was to throw men's consciences into turmoil. There was no settled pattern of middle-class life with its comfortable middle-class morality. Men needed rooting and establishing on sure foundations; they needed to learn the truly Christian attitude towards the changing circumstances, the strains and stresses of life. This Greenham set himself to teach, and with great success, as we have seen.

(ii) It is *strongly doctrinal.* Greenham bases his instruction on a thorough grasp of the doctrines of the universal sinfulness of man, of the efficacy of the cross of Christ for the putting away of the sins of the elect, of regeneration by the Holy Spirit, and the certainty of a glorious heavenly inheritance. Whether we label this teaching Calvinistic, Puritan, or simply scriptural, we cannot but admire the deeply experimental grasp of these doctrines which provided Greenham with his starting-point.

(iii) It is *sane and profound.* Evangelical Christians today will adjudge it helpful at the deepest level. Greenham's advice is practical, Christ-centred, humbling, and heart-warming. His informal pastoral classes would lose none of their usefulness were he alive to hold them in our time. Such pastoral wisdom as his is one of our greatest needs.

(iv) It *glorifies God.* There is a singular lack of self-advertisement in Greenham's writing. He is content to honour the word of God and to glorify the Saviour. It is precisely for this reason that his teaching did good in his own time, and can still do good to God's children today.

Part 2

Servants of
the Word

୵

1957

1

THE PURITANS AND
THE LORD'S DAY

J. I. Packer

I

If we are to profit from studying Puritan teaching on this or any subject, our approach to it must be right. For it is all too easy for admirers of the Puritans to study their work in a way which the Puritans themselves would be the first to condemn. Thus, we can have a wrong attitude to the men; we can revere them as infallible authorities. But they would scarify us for such a gross lapse into what they would regard as Papalism and idolatry. They would remind us that they were no more than servants and expositors of God's written word, and they would charge us never to regard their writings as more than helps and guides to understanding that word. They would further assure us that, since all men, even Puritans, can err, we must always test their teaching with the utmost rigour by that very word which they sought to expound. Or,

87

again, we can make a wrong application of their teaching. We can parrot their language and ape their manners, and imagine that thereby we place ourselves in the true Puritan tradition. But the Puritans would impress on us that that is precisely what we fail to do if we act so. They sought to apply the eternal truths of Scripture to the particular circumstances of their own day—moral, social, political, ecclesiastical, and so forth. If we would stand in the true Puritan tradition, we must seek to apply those same truths to the altered circumstances of our own day. Human nature does not change, but times do; therefore, though the application of divine truth to human life will always be the same in principle, the details of it must vary from one age to another. To content ourselves with aping the Puritans would amount to beating a mental retreat out of the twentieth century, where God has set us to live, into the seventeenth, where He has not. This is as unspiritual as it is unrealistic. The Holy Spirit is pre-eminently a realist, and He has been given to teach Christians how to live to God in the situation in which they are, not that in which some other saints once were. We quench the Spirit by allowing ourselves to live in the past. And such an attitude of mind is theologically culpable. It shows that we have shirked an essential stage in our thinking about God's truth—that of working out its application to ourselves. Application may never be taken over second-hand and ready-made, each man in each generation must exercise his conscience to discern for himself how truth applies, and what it demands, in the particular situation in which he finds himself. The application may be similar in detail from one generation to another, but we must not assume in advance that it will be so. And therefore our aim in studying the Puritans must be to learn, by watching them apply the word to themselves in their day, how we must apply it to ourselves in ours.

This point is crucial for us who believe that modern evangelicalism stands in need of correction and enrichment of a kind which the older evangelical tradition can supply. It seems that modern evangelicalism is guilty of just this error of living in the past—in this case, in the recent, late-nineteenth-century past. We are too often content today to try and get along by re-hashing the thin doctrinal gruel and the sometimes questionable ideas about its ethical, ecclesiastical, and evangelistic application which were characteristic of that decadent period in evangelical history. But the answer to this situation is emphatically not that we should retreat still further, and start living, not now in the nineteenth, but in the seventeenth century. Such a cure would in many ways be worse than the disease. We certainly need to go back behind the nineteenth century and re-open the richer mines of older evangelical teaching, but then we must endeavour to advance beyond the nineteenth-century mentality into a genuine appreciation of our twentieth-century situation, so that we may make a genuinely contemporary application of the everlasting gospel.

And this principle is as relevant when we study the subject of the Lord's Day as it is anywhere. For here, surely, is a subject on which fresh thinking about the contemporary application of biblical principles is long overdue. Our thoughts and speech about it often betray a degree of negative legalism as it is. If we rigidly imposed on ourselves the application of the fourth commandment which the Puritans worked out in terms of their own age, we would merely increase and perpetuate that legalism. Yet, if we resist the temptation to take over this application ready-made, and set ourselves to re-apply God's law realistically to our own present-day situation, we shall find in the Puritan expositions an incomparably rich and suggestive presentation of the positive principles that must guide our judgment in this matter.

II

First, however, we must fill in the historical background of our study. The Puritans created the English Christian Sunday— that is, the conception and observance of the first day of the week as one on which both business and organised recreations should be in abeyance, and the whole time left free for worship, fellowship, and "good works." This ideal was never generally accepted by Continental Protestants: as Baxter observed, "England hath been the happiest in this piece of reformation" (Works, 1838 ed., 3:906). The history of the Puritan achievement spans a century. At the end of the sixteenth century, it was the Englishman's custom after church was over to pass the rest of Sunday in "frequenting of bawdy stage plays . . . may-games, church-ales, feasts and wakes; in piping, dancing, dicing, carding, bowling, tennis-playing, in bear-baiting, cock-fighting, hawking, hunting and such like, in keeping of fairs and markets on the Sabbath . . . ; in football playing, and such other devilish pastimes" (P. Stubbes, *Anatomie of Abuses*, 1583). Serious Christians ("Puritans" in the popular sense) grew increasingly concerned about this. The "Puritan" point of view on the subject received its first full statement in print in Dr. Nicholas Bolind's *True Doctrine of the Sabbath* (1595), though the first exposition of it to be written seems to have been Richard Greenham's *Treatise of the Sabbath,* which was privately circulated for some years prior to this. James I's *Declaration of Sports* (1618) laid it down that, apart from bull- and bear-baiting and bowls, all the popular games of the day might be played on Sundays after church. In fact, James hereby "simply reiterated what had been the law of the State and of the Church since the early days of the Reformation" (W. B. Whitaker, *Sunday in Tudor and Stuart Times*, p. 95), but his Declaration brought consternation to the rapidly growing body of Puritan clergy and laity. In 1633 Charles I republished it, and ordered the bishops to see that all clergy read it from their pulpits; some refused to do so, and lost their livings as a result. What things in the country were like at this time appears from these words of Baxter.

"In my youth . . . one of my father's own tenants was the town piper, and the place of the dancing assembly was not a hundred yards from our door, and we could not on the Lord's day either read a chapter, or pray, or sing a Psalm, or catechize or instruct a servant, but with the noise of the pipe and tabor and the shoutings in the street continually in our ears; and . . . we were the common scorn of all the rabble in the streets and called Puritans, Precisians, Hypocrites, because we rather chose to read the Scriptures than do as they did . . . And when the people by the book (i.e., the declaration, 1633) were allowed to play and dance out of public service time, they could so hardly break off their sports that many a time the reader was fain to stay till the pipe and players would give over, and sometimes the morris dancers would come into the church in all their linen and scarves and antic dresses, with morris bells jingling at their legs, and as soon as common prayer was read did haste out presently to their play again. Was this a heavenly conversation?" (3:904).

But Puritan teaching had its effect. As a result of Baxter's work at Kidderminster, what had previously been a brawling, drunken, irreligious community was so changed that "on the Lord's day there was no disorder to be seen in our streets; but you might hear a hundred families singing psalms and repeating sermons as you passed through the streets" *(Autobiography,* Everyman ed., p. 79). A similar reformation took place in many other places where Puritans ministered. The Long Parliament and its successors, prompted by Puritan convictions, passed a series of ordinances forbidding games, trading, and travel on Sunday. Finally, in 1677, when the Puritans were out of power and in disgrace, a violently anti-Puritan Parliament passed the Sunday Observance Act, which repeated, and confirmed, Commonwealth legislation on this subject. It prescribed that all should spend Sunday, not in trading, travelling, "worldly labour, business, or work of their ordinary callings," but in "exercising themselves . . . in the duties of piety and true religion, publicly and privately." The significance of this piece of legislation is clear. England had come generally to accept the Puritan ideal for Sunday. Royalist and republican, conformist and nonconformist alike were agreed on it. The Puritan teaching had created a national conscience on the subject; and this despite the fact that the Caroline divines had consistently opposed the Puritan view.

III

Against this background of history we now turn to the Puritan teaching itself.

(i) The Meaning of the Fourth Commandment
(Exodus 20:8–11)

Here the Puritans advanced on the Reformers. These latter had followed Augustine, Aquinas, and Mediaeval teaching generally in denying that the Lord's Day was in any sense a Sabbath. They held that the Sabbath, which the fourth commandment prescribes, was a Jewish typical ceremony, foreshadowing the "rest" of a grace-faith relationship with Christ. So Calvin explains it: "the analogy between the external sign and the thing signified is most apt, inasmuch as our sanctification consists in the mortification of our own will . . . We must desist from all the acts of our own mind that, God working in us, we may rest in him, as the apostle teaches (Hebrews 3:13; 4:3, 9)" (Institutes 2.8.29). But now that Christ has come, the type is cancelled, and it would be as wrong to perpetuate it as to continue offering Levitical sacrifices. Calvin appeals here to Colossians 2:16, which he interprets as referring to the weekly day of rest. He allows that, over and above its typical significance, the fourth commandment also reaches the principle that there must be public and private worship, and a day of rest for servants and employees, so that its full Christian interpretation is threefold: "first, that throughout our whole lives we may aim at a constant rest from our own works, in order that the Lord may work in us by His Spirit; second, that each man should diligently exercise himself in devout meditation on the works of God, and . . . that all should observe the lawful order appointed by the Church for hearing the word, administering the sacraments, and public prayer; thirdly, that we should avoid oppressing those subject to us" (2.8.34). But he speaks as if he regards this as being all that the commandment now prescribes, and finds nothing in it, in its Christian sense, to prohibit work or play on the Lord's Day out of church time. All the Reformers spoke in the same way. Yet the extraordinary thing is that their statements in other contexts show that "the Reformers, as a body, did hold the divine authority and binding obligation of the fourth command, as requiring one day in seven to be employed in the worship and service of God, admitting only of works of necessity and mercy to the poor and afflicted" (P. Fairbairn, *Typol-*

ogy of Scripture, 2:142; see App. A, pp. 514ff. for the evidence). Why they never saw the inconsistency between asserting this in general terms and yet denying that the Lord's Day has this *character* is a standing puzzle.

The Puritans, however, corrected the inconsistency. They insisted, with virtual unanimity, that, while the Reformers were right to see a merely typical and temporary significance in certain of the detailed prescriptions of the Jewish Sabbath, yet the principle of one day's rest for public and private worship of God at the end of each six days' work was a law of creation, made for man as such, and therefore binding upon man as long as he lives in this world. They pointed out that, standing as it does with nine undoubtedly moral and permanently binding laws in the Decalogue, it could hardly be of a merely typical and temporary nature itself. In fact, they saw it as integral to the first table of the law, which deals systematically with worship: "the first command fixes the object, the second the means, the third the manner, and the fourth the time" (Jonathan Edwards, Sermon 2 on *"The Perpetuity and Change of the Sabbath,"* a fine statement of the Puritan position, Works, 1840 ed., 2:95). They noted that the fourth commandment begins, "Remember . . ." thus looking back to a pre-Mosaic institution. They observed that Genesis 2:1ff. represents the seventh-day rest as God's own rest after creation, and that the sanction attached to the fourth commandment in Exodus 20:8ff. looks back to this, depicting the day as a weekly memorial of creation "to be observed to the glory of the Creator, as an engagement upon ourselves to serve him, and an encouragement to us to trust in Him who made heaven and earth. By the sanctification of the Sabbath, the Jews declared that they worshipped the God who made the earth . . ." (Matthew Henry on Exodus 20:11). The Puritans further pointed out that the commandment declares God to have sanctified the seventh day (i.e. appropriated it to Himself) and blessed it (i.e. "put blessings into it, which He has encouraged us to expect from Him in the religious observance of that day" (Henry on Exodus 20:11); and that Christ, though he reinterpreted the Sabbath law, did not cancel it, but rather established it, by keeping it Himself and showing that he expected

His disciples to continue keeping it (cf. Matthew 24:20). All this, they argued, showed that the seventh-day rest was more than a Jewish type; it was memorial of creation, perpetually obligatory for all men. So that when we find the New Testament telling us that Christians met for worship on the first day of the week (Acts 20:7), and kept that day as "the Lord's day" (Revelation 1:10), this can only mean one thing: that by apostolic precept, and probably in fact by dominical injunction during the forty days before the ascension, this had been made the day on which men were henceforth to keep the Sabbath of rest which the fourth commandment prescribes. The Puritans observed that this change from the seventh day of the week, the day which marked the end of the old creation, to the first, the day of Christ's resurrection, which marked the start of the new, was not precluded by the words of the fourth commandment, which "merely determined, that we should rest and keep as a Sabbath every seventh day . . . but . . . in no way determine where those six days shall begin . . . There is no direction in the fourth commandment how to reckon the time . . ." (Edwards, p. 96). Therefore nothing hinders the supposition, which the New Testament seems to require, that the apostles actually made this change. In that case, it becomes clear that the condemnation (in Colossians 2:16) of Jewish Sabbatarianism has nothing to do with the keeping of the Lord's Day at all. Such, in outline, were the considerations on which the Puritans based their doctrine of the Lord's Day, which is well summed up in the Westminster Confession, 21.7–8.

(ii) The Character of the Fourth Commandment

"The Sabbath," wrote Matthew Henry, "is a sacred and divine institution, but we must receive and embrace it as a privilege and a benefit, not as a task and a drudger. First, God never designed it to be an imposition upon us, and therefore we must not make it so to ourselves . . . Secondly, God did design it to be an advantage to us, and so we must make and improve it . . . He had some regard to our bodies in the institution, that they might rest . . . He had much more regard for our souls. The Sabbath was made a day of rest, only in order to its being a day of holy work, a day of communion with God, a day of praise and thanksgiving, and the rest from worldly business is therefore necessary, that we may closely apply ourselves to this work, and spend the whole time in it, in public and private . . . See here what a good master we serve all whose institutions are for our own benefit . . ." (On Mark 2:27).

This quotation fairly sums up the Puritan approach to the Lord's Day. Here we would merely underline three of Henry's points, and add a fourth by way of corollary.

(a) *Sabbath-keeping means action, not inaction.* The Lord's Day is not a day for idleness. "Idleness is a sin every day: but much more on the Lord's Day" (J. Dod, On the Commandments, p. 143). We do not keep the Sabbath holy by lounging around doing nothing. We are to rest from the business of our earthly calling in order to prosecute the business of our heavenly calling. If we do not spend the day doing the latter, we fail to keep it holy.

(b) *Sabbath-keeping is not a tedious burden, but a joyful privilege.* The Sabbath is not a fast, but a feast, a day for rejoicing, in the works of a gracious God, and joy must be its temper throughout (cf. Isaiah 58:18). "Joy suits no person so much as a saint, and it becomes no season as well as a Sabbath" (G. Swinnock, The Christian Man's Calling, 1:239). "It is the duty and glory of a Christian to rejoice in the Lord every day, but especially on the Lord's day . . . To fast on the Lord's Day, saith Ignatius, is to kill Christ; but to rejoice in the Lord this day, and to rejoice in all the duties of the day . . . this is to crown Christ, this is to lift up Christ" (T. Brooks, Works 6:299). Joy must be the keynote of public worship; Baxter in particular deplores drab, mournful services. There must be no gloom on the Lord's Day. And those who say that they cannot find joy in the spiritual exercises of a Christian Sunday thereby show that there is something very wrong with them.

(c) *Sabbath-keeping is not a useless labour, but a means of grace.* "God hath made it our duty, by his institution, to set apart this day for a special seeking of his grace and blessing. From which we may argue, that he will be especially ready to confer his grace on those who thus seek it . . . The Sabbath day is an accepted time, a day of salvation, a time wherein God especially loves to be sought, and loves to be found . . ." (Edwards, p. 102).

(d) *Sabbath-breaking brings chastisement;* as does the abuse of any God-given privilege and means of grace. Spiritual decline and material loss accrue to both individuals and communities for this sin. The good gifts of God may not be despised with impunity. Thomas Fuller thought that the Civil War, Brooks that the fire of London, came as judgments on the nation for Sabbath-breaking.

The admirably positive and evangelical character of this approach to the Lord's Day could scarcely be bettered.

(iii) Practical Principles for Keeping the Lord's Day Holy

The Puritans were methodical men, and nothing if not thorough; and we find them giving detailed attention to this aspect of our subject. Four principles in particular fall to be considered here.

(a) *Preparation must be made for the Lord's Day.* First, the Puritans tell us, we must realise the importance of the Lord's Day, and learn to value it rightly. It is a great day for the church and for the individual, a "market-day for the soul," a day for entering the very "suburbs of heaven" in corporate praises and prayers. We must never, therefore, let our Sundays become mere routine engagements; in that attitude of mind, we shall trifle them away by a humdrum formality. Every Sunday is meant to be a great day, and we should approach it expectantly, in full awareness of this. Therefore we must plan our week, so that we may make the most of our Sabbaths. Haphazard improvidence will preclude our profiting here, just as it will in any other enterprise. "That policie and discretion which we see in natural men about the market of their bodies, we must learn about the market of our souls: they will be providing, and thinking before, what they must buy . . . and sell there . . . so, if ever we will make good markets for our souls, we must (all the week before) be preparing our hearts . . . that we may then be burdened with no sin nor worldly care . . . we must . . . , stop out all distractions and encumbrances, and raise up our hearts against deadness and dullness . . . if ever we will comfortably and profitably spend the Lord's day in the Lord's work" (Dod, p. 138f.). Preparing the heart is the most important matter of all, for the Lord's day is pre-eminently a day for "heartwork" (Baxter, 1:470). From this point of view, the battle for our Sundays in usually won or lost on the foregoing Saturday night, when time should be set aside for self-examination, confession, and prayer for the coming day. Richard Baxter's Young People's Fellowship used to spend three hours each Saturday evening preparing together for the Sabbath in this way. "If thou wouldst thus leave thy heart with God on the Saturday night," Swinnock assures us, "thou shouldest find it with him in the Lord's-day morning" (1:230). The last rule for preparation comes from the supremely practical mind of Richard Baxter. "Go seasonably to bed, that you may not be sleepy on the Lord's Day" (1:472).

(b) *Public worship must be central on the Lord's Day.* The day must be built round public worship, morning and afternoon or evening ("the publike exercises are twice at the least to be used every Sabbath" [Greenham, *Works,* 1611 ed., p. 208]). Private devotions must take second place to this, if one or the other for any reason has to go. But we must get up on Sunday mornings in time to prepare our hearts afresh to praise and pray and hear God's word preached "for if we come rudely into the Lord's House from brawling or chiding at home or so soon as he is out of his bed . . . the Word shall be but a tediousness and serve to the further hardening of his heart" (Dod, p. 145). Puritan services might last anything up to three hours, but the Puritans had little sympathy with those who complained at their length. Baxter's comment is simply that those who found a church service tedious, and yet could spend a far longer time in a public house, or at a public entertainment, without boredom, must have very bad hearts; though he then takes occasion to speak a word in season to preachers and suggest to them "an honester way to cure peoples weariness. Preach with such life and awakening seriousness . . . and with such easy method and with such variety of wholesome matter that the people may never be weary of you. Pour out the rehearsal of the love and benefits of God, open so to them the privileges of faith, the joys of hope, that they may never be angry. How oft have I heard the people say of such as these, I could hear him all day and never be weary! They are troubled with the shortness of such sermons, and wish they had been longer . . ." (3:905).

(c) *The family must function as a religious unit on the Lord's Day.* (See the Westminster Larger Catechism, p. 118). The head of the house must conduct family prayers twice, take the family to church, and examine and catechise the children and servants afterwards to make sure that they had thoroughly absorbed the sermon. The principle here is that the man of the house has an inalienable responsibility to care for the souls of the household, and that it is on the Lord's Day supremely that he must exercise it. The Puritan pastor, unlike his modern counterpart, did not scheme to reach the men through the women and children, but *vice versa.* Was he not perhaps wiser, and more scriptural too?

(d) *The pitfalls of legalism and pharisaism must be avoided in regard to the Lord's Day.* These wrong attitudes threaten here, as in all other spiritual concerns. Legalism, the habit of mind which stresses what one must *not* do on the Lord's Day and stops there, and pharisaism, the habit of mind which is all too ready to censure others for real or fancied lapses in this matter, are both a violation of the spirit of the gospel. Baxter, as we should perhaps expect, has most to say about them, and he counters both with a constructive evangelical principle of judgment: "I will first look at a man's positive duties on the Lord's Days how he heareth and readeth and prayeth and spendeth his time, and how he instructeth and helpeth his family, and if he be diligent in seeking God, and ply his heavenly business, I shall be very backward to judge him for a word or action about worldly things that falls in on the by . . ." (3:908). Here, surely, is Christian wisdom.

IV

The above passages speak for themselves, and need no further comment. We close with a testimony and an admonition. The testimony is that of Lord Chief Justice Sir Matthew Hale.

"I have found by a strict and diligent observation that a due observance of the duties of the Lord's Day hath ever had joined to it a blessing upon the rest of my time, and the week that hath been so begun hath been blessed and prosperous to me, and on the other side, when I have been negligent of the duties of the day, the rest of the week has been unsuccessful and unhappy in my own secular employments. This I write, not lightly or inconsiderately, but upon long and sound observation and experience."

The admonition is from Thomas Brooks.

"For a close, remember this, that there are no Christians in all the world comparable for the power of godliness and heights of grace, holiness, and communion with God, to those who are more strict, serious, studious and conscientious in sanctifying the Lord's Day . . . The true reason why the power of godliness is fallen to so low an ebb, both in this and in other countries also, is because the Sabbath is no more strictly and conscientiously observed . . . And O that all these short hints might be so blessed from heaven as to work us all to a more strict seriousness and conscientious sanctifying of the Lord's Day . . ."(6:305f.)

2

THE SAVOY CONFERENCE, 1661

G. Thomas

I. Introduction

The Savoy Conferences called by the King, met for the first time on April 15, 1661 "in the Master's lodging" in the Savoy. It was a conference between bishops and Episcopalian divines on the one hand and persons of Presbyterian views on the other, who were to undertake a revision of the Prayer Book "for the giving satisfaction to tender consciences and the restoring and continuance of peace and unity in the churches under our protection and government." But right from the outset the Anglican bishops made it perfectly clear that they did not intend to co-operate, and after four months, during which the Presbyterian delegates were bullied and shouted down, the Conference ended amid mutual recriminations. Nothing was accomplished. Had the Conference been a secular affair between politicians and business men, it would have been deplorable. Between two different parties in the church of Christ such an incident becomes inexcusable.

Now we may well ask why this was. The King had returned amid universal rejoicings. So far as the Anglicans were concerned (and the King for that matter), they were lucky to be back after twenty years in which, largely as a result of Archbishop Land's policies, the Church of England had been in the wilderness. And surely, since they were not yet certain of the extent of the reaction in their favour, they would have been wise to have proceeded cautiously.

It was not to be. A little group of High Churchmen right at the centre of the Laudian tradition rendered this impossible. During the years of exile, both at home and abroad, this little group had worked and plotted with untiring perseverance and ruthless determination. Their achievement was that they became identified in people's minds with the authentic voice of Anglicanism and with the Royalist cause. When the Restoration came they were ready. Their goal was to recapture the establishment without any conditions or concessions, and in the event they were brilliantly successful. Within a year of the King's return they occupied every position they had sought to win.

But if that is true, they were considerably assisted by the gross mistake of the Presbyterians in England in inviting the King to resume the throne unfettered by any conditions regarding the ecclesiastical settlement. The Presbyterians had a strong bargaining position with the King; was it not a Presbyterian Parliament that invited him to return? Yet Monk insisted on inviting him back unconditionally, and Presbyterian ministers waited on him at the exile's court, not as equal parties negotiating a settlement, but as suppliants. All that had been won at the cost of bloodshed and misery was abandoned. It was a colossal mistake.

There is still a third thread running through this narrative and that relates to the difficulties in which moderate men and parties found themselves. In the case of denominations the two extremes, having no basis for agreement with one another, were the Independents and the extreme Presbyterians on the one hand, and the Laudians on the other. But there were also moderate Presbyterians holding the intermediate position and regarded by the extreme Presbyterians as traitors, while—and this is vital to an understanding of the matter—the Anglicans loathed the Presbyterians with a hatred which seems at times, as we read their letters, almost hysterical. It was likewise a difficult time for such moderate men as Baxter and Manton among the Presbyterians and bishops like Reynolds, who were actually on the same side at Savoy, but who, as the full tide of Laudianism swept in, were forced to take sides.

The tragedy was that at the Restoration the Presbyterians treated with the Anglicans for comprehension within the National Church, and the watchword was comprehension, not tolerance. Baxter and his friends considered they had a case for such comprehension. After all the two essential characteristics of the Church of England are that it is governed by bishops and has a Prayer Book, and the moderate Presbyterians believed in both, subject to modifications. They desired that bishops should be of the old, primitive mould, ruling with the consent of presbyters, and that the Prayer Book should be revised so as to be more scriptural. These views they put forward in a series of discussions with the bishops at the Restoration. But they met the High Church Laudian school at the height of its power, and it is difficult to resist the feeling that revenge played no small part in the behaviour of the latter. The Savoy Conference was bound to fail.

II. The Resurgence of the Laudians During the Interregnum

The following reasons are suggested for the fact that fifteen years after Archbishop Laud's execution, his party was dictating the course of the Reformation settlement.

Firstly, there was Cromwell's tolerant religious policy. It is an interesting historical fact that persecuted people begin their agitation for freedom, not when the persecution is at its height but when it begins to abate. So it was here. Cromwell's policy aimed at securing the widest possible toleration within the national church consisting with the safety and security of the state. Reor-

ganising his church on the plan which John Owen had presented
to Parliament in 1654, Cromwell appointed commissioners to examine all candidates for livings as to their being fit and able persons to preach the gospel. But the church was comprehensive, including Presbyterians, Independents, and Baptists among those
holding livings, while although the Liturgy had been prohibited
in 1645, many Anglicans remained in their livings and sometimes
used portions of it from memory. Outside the national church
liberty was offered, under Cromwell, to "all such as do profess
faith to God and Jesus Christ," only Popery and Anglicanism being excepted as idolatrous and politically dangerous. But, in fact,
Sir Charles Firth says that "congregations of Royalists continued
to meet in London throughout the Protectorate, and the Government winked at their use of Anglican services and ceremonies." This toleration, while relieving the pressure on Anglicans, confronted them with a problem as to their own policy and,
since Cromwell's liberality did not stir them up to united hatred,
they split into three groups.

First, there were those who, though preferring the old ways,
loyally supported the Cromwellian establishment. Second, there
were those who, while conforming outwardly, put up as much
passive resistance as possible. Third, there were the Laudians
who, having no dispensation from their bishops to refrain from
using the Prayer Book, would have nothing to do with the new order at all, and it is they who, assuming leadership of the scattered
Church of England, became identified in people's minds with the
Royalist and Anglican causes. Ably led by Henry Hammond and
Gilbert Sheldon, their work within the sphere of Cromwellian tolerance is the second reason for the Laudian revival.

The third reason lies in the fact that they were indefatigable
in propagating their cause, producing a remarkable number of
theological writings asserting the High Church position, and suc-
cessfully spreading their doctrine among the landed gentry.

But perhaps the most important factor in the resurgence of
Laudianism is that the Laudians in exile captured the hearts of
the King and of his chief adviser, Edward Hyde, later Earl of
Clarendon. Not only were the King's ecclesiastical advisers all

men of the Laudian stamp, but his political advisers were High Churchmen of similar views. Most significant of all they abhorred the Presbyterians against whom they made it their business to secure the King, though at the same time keeping him from the advances of the Roman Catholics who were offering their support.

Then Cromwell died and Independency as a political force died also. Monk marched on the capital and recalled the Convention Parliament. Negotiations opened with the King, who issued the worthless Declaration of Breda. What followed was vague and academic, and when in 1660 the King returned to the acclamation of the multitude, he was unhampered by any conditions.

III. The Recapture of the Establishment Immediately Prior to Savoy

Dr. R. S. Bosher *(The Making of the Restoration Settlement,* 1951) points out that two courses were open to Hyde. One, which was strictly legal, was to argue that all that had happened during the Commonwealth and Protectorate was illegal, and that since the Church of England had previously been established by law as the national church, it had only to resume the privileges which had never been legally taken from it.

The other possibility was to acknowledge that the last twenty years could not so easily be forgotten, and that it was right to negotiate with the Presbyterians regarding the church settlement. In view of Charles' promises at Breda, one might assume that he had adopted this view and abandoned the first.

In point of fact, Hyde did not dare act on the first view, and Baxter gives the reason perfectly, saying, "When they came in, it was necessary that they should proceed safely and feel whether the ground was solid under them before they proceeded to their structure . . . Therefore, it was necessary that moderate things should be proposed and promised." The first thing they did was to attempt to win over those of the old Presbyterians, both laymen and ministers, who were held in high esteem in the state. Among others, Baxter was offered and refused the See of Hereford, while such men as he, Calamy, and Manton were appointed chaplains to the King. Moreover, the King not only made a proclamation against the expulsion of present incumbents, but opened negotiations with the Presbyterian leaders for a comprehensive church settlement. After consulting with their friends, Baxter and the other leaders proposed a modified form of Episcopacy and a more scriptural Prayer Book.

But all this time the King had been filling the church with Laudians, and suddenly the Presbyterians in Parliament awoke to the danger, with the result that the Anglicans suffered a major defeat in the passing of the Bill for Settling Ministers. This caused the King and Hyde to take fright. Parliament was adjourned for two months, and in order to keep the Presbyterians quiet the King issued his famous Declaration to compose religions differences— though at the same time appointing now Laudian bishops.

Although the Puritans and Anglicans were largely agreed on the terms of the Declaration, the former were by now becoming suspicious and endeavoured to give it legal force by transforming it into a Bill. This forced the Anglicans into the open and in the ensuing Commons debate they opposed it tooth and nail, defeating the Presbyterians. After this, the attack on the Puritans proceeded apace and to plead the Declaration was useless. But then, on March 19, 1661, a popular outburst against bishops at the Guildhall in London and the election of four Presbyterians to office caused the government to take fright again. Six days later the King issued his warrant summoning representatives of the Anglican and Presbyterian parties to meet at the Savoy. But by the time they did meet, it had become clear that the Guildhall election had only been an isolated political freak. The Anglicans accordingly went into the Conference in a spirit of uncompromising truculence which foredoomed it to failure.

IV. The Conference Itself

The King's warrant appointed twelve bishops and twelve Presbyterians, with nine other divines on each side as assistants, to supply the place of any that were unavoidably absent. Among the Episcopal divines we note the names of Gilbert Sheldon, Bishop of London, George Morley, Bishop of Worcester, and John Cosin, Bishop of Durham, while among the nine coadjutors were Dr. Earle, Dr. Barwick (the King's Messenger when in exile) and Dr. Peter Gunning. It was a Laudian array. The Presbyterian divines included Edward Reynolds, Bishop of Norwich, Calamy, Manton, and Baxter; and among the coadjutors, were Dr. Jacombe and Dr. Bates. The terms of reference were precisely stated.

1. "They were to advise upon and review the Book of Common Prayer.
2. They were to compare the Prayer Book with the most ancient Liturgies used in the church in the primitive and present times.
3. They were to take into grave and serious consideration the various forms and rubrics in the Book, and the objections and exceptions raised against it, and they were to advise and consult upon the same.
4. They were to make such reasonable and necessary alterations, corrections and amendments as should be agreed to be necessary or expedient for the satisfaction of tender consciences and restoring and continuing the peace and unity of the church, with the proviso that they were to avoid all unnecessary abbreviations or alterations."

As soon as the Conference had met, Sheldon insisted that nothing could be done until the Presbyterians brought in their exceptions to the Prayer Book and their suggested additions and alterations in writing. He used the flagrantly untrue argument that the Presbyterians had sought the Conference, while in fact the King had offered it. Much put out by this maneuver, the Presbyterians urged the King's Commission requiring them all "to meet together, advise and consult." But Sheldon was immovable, and Baxter persuaded his brethren to consent, feeling it would be wise for them to agree beforehand on their exceptions lest they should disagree among themselves in the course of the talks. He also thought that unless they put their cause into writing they might be misunderstood by the people, posterity, or foreigners. Events proved him to be right.

In dividing their work, the Presbyterian brethren undertook to formulate exceptions to the Book of Common Prayer, while Baxter went off on his own to draw up the Additions or New Forms. He completed the work in a fortnight and admits he did not have the time to give the matter the accuracy he desired. We cannot here consider Baxter's exceptions, but he regarded "the faults of the Common Prayer to be chiefly disorder and defectiveness, and so that it was a true worship, though imperfect."

When Baxter returned to his brethren he found them just beginning on their work of exceptions, and his attitude to this is vital in view of subsequent charges against him of combativeness. He says of one brother's enumerations of corruptions in the Liturgy: "it was refused because we would be as little querulous as possible, lest it should hinder our direct accommodation and what passages soever seemed to make the Common Prayer Book odious, or saver of spleen and passion, they did reject, whoever offered them."

We shall consider the brethren's exceptions, then the debates which ensued, and finally some Anglican excuses for the failure of the Conference.

1. *Exceptions.* The brethren's exceptions fall into two parts, general and particular. We can only very briefly touch on the general exceptions.

They pointed out that it was a hundred years since the Liturgy had first been completed, and there was reason to amend it now so as to satisfy scrupulous consciences. They proposed the following:

(i) The prayers and the Liturgy must contain nothing doubtful that would lead to separation.
(ii) The first Liturgy having been drawn up to embrace as many Papists as possible, it should now be composed as

to gain upon the judgments and affections of the truly Protestant.

(iii) Repetitions and responses between desk and people, and responsive reading of Hymns and Psalms should be omitted.

(iv) The Litany should be made into one solemn prayer.

(v) There should be deleted from the Liturgy all observation of Lent and Saints' Days.

(vi) Nothing in the liturgy should exclude the gift of extempore prayer in Public Worship; since this was a special qualification for the work of the ministry bestowed by Christ for the edification of His church.

(vii) Even little blemishes—these were men of principle worshipping the God of Order—should be rectified. The Prayer Book should contain new translations of the Bible.

(viii) As the Scriptures alone contained everything necessary to make a man wise unto salvation, the Apocrypha should not be read at services.

(ix) No phrase should be used in any of the offices which presumed all present to be regenerated or converted, or in an advanced state of grace.

(x) The term "Minister" and not "Priest" should be used.

(xi) They objected to short prayers and proposed one long methodical prayer in place of the separate Collects.

(xii) They regarded the Liturgy as defective in forms of praise and thanksgiving.

(xiii) They criticised the Catechism for its omissions. On this Baxter wrote, "In the Catechism there are omitted some of the Essential Attributes of God without which He cannot be rightly known. There is also omitted the Doctrines of the Law made to Adam, and of Man's Fall and the Doctrine of our Misery is insufficiently touched. The Person, Office and Properties of the Redeemer are so insufficiently opened as that we should think the essentials of Christianity are omitted, were it not that they are generally expressed in the Creed itself, which is more full than the explication of it. There is no mention of the Holy Scriptures in it, and the Doctrine of the Covenant of Grace is very defectively expressed, and so is the Doctrine of Sanctification and other parts of the Work of the Holy Ghost, and the whole Doctrine of God's Judgment and Execution, and that of Man's duty and even the nature and use of the Sacraments, in which it is fullest: as will appear with a true comparing it with what we offer."

(xiv) The Surplice, the Cross in Baptism, and kneeling at the Lord's Supper were brought forward as the usual instances of ceremonies judged unwarrantable by learned and pious men, and exposing many orthodox, peaceable, and pious ministers to the displeasure of their superiors. The brethren argued that by the imposition of such ceremonies people had been forced to forsake the churches or to worship otherwise than their consciences dictated, while ministers had been compelled to leave their livings. Was all this worth the cost of such impositions? It was a moving and irresistible plea.

The particular exceptions included the following:

(i) With regard to the Communion Service the brethren considered that intending communicants should give their names to the curate on the day before, and not on the night before or on the Sunday morning, and that the minister should have power to admit or expel communicants. They also emphasised the manual elements, i.e. breaking of bread, and that the minister should, when distributing the wine and bread, use the Saviour's words and not repeat them to each communicant

(ii) They specially objected to the Baptismal office, and refused to agree that Christ would accept any child presented in Baptism by the church. They desired that it should be unlawful for ministers to baptise children whose parents were atheists, infidels, heretics, unbaptised, or notorious sinners. They did not like sponsors, but declared that the parents were the right persons to dedicate a child to God.

(iii) With regard to Confirmation, they argued that it was not sufficient qualification for children to recite from memory the Creed, the Lord's Prayer, and the Ten Commandments, and to answer the questions of the Catechism. They also objected to the imposition of hands by the bishop, as seeming to put a higher value on Confirmation than upon the Sacraments.

(iv) In the Marriage Service they considered the ring indifferent, and had certain observations on the order for the Visitation of the Sick. With regard to the order for the Burial of the Dead, they desired the insertion of a rubric declaring that the prayers and exhortations were not for the benefit of the dead but of the living.

2. *The debates.* To read in Baxter's Reliquiae what happened when the Presbyterians presented their exceptions is a sorry story. They met the Laudian bishops at the height of their aggressiveness, and Baxter says, "they would not by any importunity be interested at all to debate as in the King's Commission, nor give any of their opinions about those papers."

Baxter mentions two incidents typical of the bishops' attitude. Dr. Sterne, Bishop of Carlisle, attacked him for using the term "in the nation" rather than "in the Kingdom," and Bishop Cosin complained that Baxter threatened the bishops with numbers when he begged them to have compassion for the consciences of so many of his brethren! When the bishops talked of the antiquity of Liturgies, Baxter asked them to name any Prince who had ever imposed one form of prayer or Liturgy for uniformity on all the churches in his dominions, and proved to them from the instances of Basil and the church of New Caesarea and others that every bishop chose what forms he pleased for his own church—which they could not deny.

Baxter says he perceived less compassion in these men, and less regard to the scruples and tenderness of godly people afraid of sinning, than he would have thought possible among Protestants. For their part the bishops became increasingly angry, particularly with the fact that though always courteous Baxter treated them with a disconcerting frankness of utterance. They accused him of representing them as persecutors, though in point of fact he was only telling them what he, and they, knew they intended to do. The Conference ended with nothing achieved.

3. The Anglicans endeavoured to place the blame for the failure of the Conference on the shoulders of Richard Baxter. Dr. Ferne in particular criticised him for his part in the debates, conducted in syllogistic form, as to whether kneeling at the Communion was sinful and scoffed at his "strange syllogisms." He also declared that at the Conference Baxter seemed "to show more boldness and ignorance than reason, for the most part," while Dr. Sanderson said that he had never met "a man of more pertinacious confidence and less ability in all his conversation."

We must examine these charges. Allowing for all Baxter's love of dispute, the evidence seems to show the Laudian party were the combative party at the Conference. Moreover, ignorance is a strange charge to level against the author of the "Reformed Pastor" and "The Saints' Everlasting Rest," while, if it were true, why had he but recently been offered the See of Hereford? It is noteworthy that the bishops did not seem fully to answer Baxter's "strange syllogisms." No; what the bishops did not like—and Dr. Ferne's own language betrays this—was that Baxter could not be bullied and that he treated them as equals. We have seen at the beginning of this section how anxious he was, when the exceptions were being prepared, to avoid points of dispute; but he refused, for the sake of his own and that of his brethren, to come as a suppliant.

V. The Results of the Savoy Conference

Although Savoy achieved nothing, the astonishing thing is that in 1661 the Prayer Book was revised and that the Book which was issued in 1662, when the Laudian Party was in full control, is the Book which is with us today. Why were the cherished desires of the High Church Party rejected, and why did the Book contain some of the minor proposals put forward by the Puritans? The answer is that it was watched by the laity of Parliament who, though anti-Puritan, were equally anti-Papist and had no sympathy with Laudianism. We can say, in the final assessment, that the Book preserved the balance so dear to Anglican hearts of not erring too much either on the side of Rome or of Geneva. But the evangelical will say that in 1661 a great opportunity was lost to comprehend moderate Presbyterians within the Established Church.

With regard to these Presbyterians, they soon came under the full blast of the Clarendon Code. But in the wise providence of God it has been, especially since the final ban was lifted in the last century, the tension between Churchman and Dissenter, each representing a vital and integral part of the nation's life, which has contributed so largely to the greatness of England. Who knoweth the mind of the Lord or who shall be His Counsellor? "For of Him, and through Him and to Him are all things: to Whom be Glory for ever. Amen."

Discussion after the paper centred on these three questions.

1. How far is comprehension a justifiable ideal in a gospel church?
2. How are evangelicals to bear their witness and seek to exert influence in the affairs of larger ecclesiastical organisations, not consistently evangelical?—by staying in to fight, or by going out? What principles could justify either course?
3. How are we to avoid the danger of the ecclesiastical mentality, which habitually opts for comprehension at the cost of compromise in preference to clear-cut formulations of truth and applications of principle, just because the latter, by their very definiteness, create a risk of division? It was pointed out that this is an acute problem in all the churches today.

3

THOMAS SHEPARD'S "PARABLE OF THE TEN VIRGINS"

O. R. Johnston

I. Introduction

Thomas Shepard was a dissenting minister born in 1605; he fled to New England for reasons of conscience after narrowly escaping arrest in 1635, and he died at Boston, New England, after an exemplary pastorate, in 1649. "The Parable of the Ten Virgins" was first published in 1659. It is a collection of his sermon notes, a little expanded, for weekly lectures on Matthew 25 delivered between June 1636 and May 1640. Formally the work is not easy to follow, though the matter itself is pure gold. Most of the reader's difficulties spring from the fact that the work is simply an expansion of the preacher's notes, e.g. uneven style, lack of balance in various sections, some sections verbatim, others condensed. There are texts without references, but above all, an amazing (even for a Puritan!) proliferation of divisions and sub-divisions.

As each new verse or portion of a verse comes under consideration, there are one or more *Doctrines* (or *obs*[ervations]), i.e. formal propositions of a general scriptural truth carefully and con-
cisely expressed. Then follow multitudes of sub-divisions. There
are many omissions and incorrect numerations among these.
There would be much work for a modern editor here—the reader
of any early version would be wiser not to try to grasp the structure of the work on any scale greater than that of the paragraphs
of the page he is reading. These remarks are valid even for the
1855 edition (King, Aberdeen and Nelson, London) used in the
preparation of this paper and to which all page numbers refer.

The style is elliptical and even cryptic, conjunctions and ad-
verbs are often omitted and thus the tone of voice and the connection of the thought is not always as clear as it might have been.
The language is homely, and often vividly illustrative, e.g. a comment on the self-righteous who will not apply to the Great Physician: "Kitchen physic is not far to fetch" (40); a remark on those
who "never yet loved the Lord Jesus unless it be from the teeth
outwards" (44); or on the sinful extreme of "swallowing down all
the flies that be in the cup" by thinking too charitably of all that
profess faith. The man under temptation is described as being
like a "poor laden horse when spur-galled and the load heavy"
who will "lie down in the highway till rest and provender be given
him" (591). Or this longer illustration, reflecting Shepard's own
journey to the New World, perhaps: "Men that live on land and
love the smoke of their own chimneys, never look out to other
coasts and countries or to a strange land, but seamen that are
bound for a voyage and have a pilot with them that has seen the
coast they look for; so men that live in this world and are well
here look not after Christ and his coming, but they have a pilot,
the Spirit to show them this day, this coast" (140).

The content of the work is not purely exegesis—the length
makes this obvious—nor is it even solely theological in the narrow sense. In each new section when a new verse or part of a verse
or *Doctrine* comes under consideration, we progress from exegesis to theology and thence to practical divinity, the application of
the truth to Christian experience. It is this which forms the vast

bulk of the work, which makes it a characteristic Puritan master-piece and forms the work's great and lasting claim to the title of an evangelical masterpiece.

II. Exegetical Principles

It would be as well first to see the broad lines on which Shepard expounds the parable. "It is clear that by the kingdom of heaven here is meant the external kingdom of Christ in this world, that is, the visible church . . . in which kingdom some are wise, some foolish, all profess Christ, look for the coming of Christ, for salvation from Christ" (20). Though the ideal is a completely pure church "all church members are and must be visible saints . . . virgins espoused to Christ, escaping the pollutions of idolatry and the world" (29), yet "there is and will be a mixture of close hypocrites with the wise hearted virgins in the purest churches" (178), and the subject of the parable and of Shepard's exposition is therefore the characteristics and detection of the Gospel hypocrite. The time spoken of he takes to be particularly the days immediately preceding the second advent of the Lord Jesus Christ, yet the truths in the parable are capable of a more general application to the church throughout the gospel age (27–29). The fact that *five* were wise and *five* foolish simply suggests, says Shepard, that "a great part were sincere and a great part false," for we must not "rack and torment parables" but "chiefly look unto the scope" (i.e. aim, intention) of them (178). It is worth noting in passing that Shepard does give sober and yet detailed teaching of the events preceding the Second Coming of Christ in judgment in the course of his exposition (482ff.).

III. Theological System

Throughout his work, though in no way a slave of a man-made system, Shepard shows a firm grasp of the biblical theology, the doctrines of grace sometimes labelled "Calvinism." As with all the other great Puritans, this is the source of the strength, the warmth, and the depth of Shepard's preaching. In this work we find the great scriptural truths evident in their practical application.

1. *Election.* In explaining how hypocrites in virgin churches reveal themselves, at least before the Lord, in a neglect or an ineffectual use of the means of grace, he writes, "This neglect is one of the great means by which God executes His eternal rejection of men, and hence here they ever do fail. . . and hence, as all the elect are to be certainly carried through all means to their end, and this is proper to them, so hence the best hypocrite, being never appointed certainly to come to this end, ever fails in the use of means, there he is and shall be forsaken of God and forsake God" (231). Ultimately all depends upon God and His electing decree.

2. *The plan of salvation.* In explaining the duty of constant readiness to meet Christ, Shepard ends the consideration of one verse thus: "Look over all the Lord's love, turn over all the leaves of it. The Lord has called me. Why? Because Christ has redeemed. And why that? Because the Father has chosen. And why me? To glorify His grace. And why me rather than another? No reason, but He would. This, I doubt not, will be the work of heaven, I am glorified because called, because redeemed, because elected" (108).

3. *Perseverance.* In explaining how the graces of the Spirit are constant and eternal in the souls of the faithful, Shepard says, "See how far they fall short of saving grace who serve the Lord by fits and starts and whose hearts follow after the Lord and make much of the Lord only in good moods . . . That is *not* the Spirit of grace which accompanies salvation which is alive today but dead tomorrow" (344).

4. *Justification and sanctification are inseparable,* for the man who, for Christ's sake, is accounted righteous is being made righteous by the sovereign work of the Holy Spirit. "The Lord doth not only out of the riches of His grace accept us in Christ, but out of

the same love sends down the Spirit of grace . . . the Lord works thereby such a change as is not to be found in the most refined hypocrites breathing" (203). Or, as is pointed out in another connection, "Hence see the deceit of that sinful opinion, that (maintains that) true sanctification is to see that I have no sanctification; and cleanness of heart to see nothing but uncleanness . . . poverty of spirit is a grace peculiar to them that shall have the kingdom of heaven, but to see no grace is common to those that shall be shut out of the kingdom" (437–38).

5. *Hell.* The punishment of the unsaved is a dread reality. "The loss of God is the greatest loss, for it is the utmost and the last plague upon the damned in hell" (36)—such words recur as a solemn warning on many occasions. We may not be happy about the idea that the souls of the damned are in "Satan's custody" or "in the hands of devils" (549–50) but in reaction to such mediaeval inventions let us not discard the thoroughly scriptural warning of the danger of eternal torment, which (though a motive of fear) is used on more than one occasion by Shepard. "God hath sanctified affliction, death, and the fear of them for this end: to awaken the secure sinner . . . it is not hypocrisy to be awakened partly by fear to the apprehension of these things . . . the awakening of conscience is that whereby the Lord prepares for grace" (414). The same reasons would clearly be given by Shepard if accused of moving men by the fear of hell.

IV. Christian Experience

Christian experience is analysed and depicted by a master hand in "The Parable of the Ten Virgins."

1. *Its beginnings.* The gospel ordinarily first comes to the soul through the word preached by a minister, for there "the Spirit of Grace is most abundantly dispensed" (471). The offer of Christ's love comes to all men and to every individual man, it is a real, earnest, and completely free offer of mercy (567–70), and there

are no possible objections which are valid on behalf of those who reject it (570–72). To close with Christ a man must, of course, know something of Him. As a couple see and know something of each other before they are espoused, so there must first be "an act of understanding" (117), and a man must come to know Christ, not by report, from His works, by bare letter (i.e. a mere theoretical knowledge), but in the glory of His person, covenant, and grace. Then comes faith which "pitches on and closeth with the person of Christ Himself, for Himself," not with some right-eousness He may give, or with the promises alone, or for peace, consolation, or joy, but with Christ Himself (117–131). And such a committal immediately involves separation, for "whoever looks for everlasting communion with the Bridegroom of the church, Jesus Christ, must be virgins divorced from all others, and es-poused only to Jesus Christ" (30).

2. *Its continuance.* In one sense, much of the book deals with the continuing of the Christian in the way of grace, but there are three useful and characteristically Puritan emphases which recur in Shepard's work. Firstly, the Christian is not to expect an easy way; indeed, things will in all probability go hard for him, but he is to remember that all God's dealings with him have one ulti-mate purpose—to advance the glory of His grace. "Do you not observe it? Sometimes you shall find the Lord so strangely carry-ing matters as if he did not love nor care for His people, against the hair and grain of their desires, and when all comes to wind-ing up, it is to advance grace. All a man's good days and bad days, all God's frowns and smiles, all the Lord's food and physic, all God cares for, works for, plots for it is to do His people no more hurts than this—to advance His grace in them and by them, all His hewings and hammerings of you, nay, His knocking you to pieces and new melting and casting of you, it is that you may be vessels of His glorious grace, that you may be able to live in the air of God's grace; to suck in and breathe out grace, and let all the power of hell seek to blur it, yet grace shall conquer" (102). Secondly, Christians must expect to be kept hungry and empty, and cut short of many spiritual blessings which they might rea-

sonably claim. This is the Lord's will. They do not get peace and rest in this world "that they might lay up their peace and find all in Himself," they are not allowed to seek and find too much good in themselves and from themselves "that they might look for help and righteousness in another." All blessedness, all supply of our many wants, we are to obtain in Christ, and in particular the free grace and love of the Father, eternal life, conquest, and victory over all our enemies and the immutable certainty of standing and persevering in the state of grace (113–15).

3. *There is the important duty of exhorting one another.* "We shall find that, as it is in a town where men are all asleep, one bell-man, one waking Christian will keep life and spirit and the power of godliness in many, and when he sleeps, all are fast. Nothing in the World brings security sooner upon men than sleepy company . . . O let every man get up and fall to this work of mutually exhorting! go visit one another, go and speak often to one another" (360). This, Shepard goes on to say, is part of our warfare—indeed, if we neglect it, the backsliders' sins will be ours. We must know our brethren, enquire about them; if we cannot help more positively, then we must "relate our own condition" and even "speak often of the sins of others" and perhaps enter into a solemn engagement to exhort one another; in particular we should "provoke one another to frequency in ordinances," e.g. prayer meetings, fasts, etc.

4. *Its dangers.* There are many dangers, and the book abounds in practical warnings and advice. Slackness may follow a good beginning: "Many Christians at their beginnings grow and thrive and abound in the fruits of righteousness—but afterward (are) so poor and ragged. O the two or three first years, how frequently in prayer, meditation! O what sorrow and peace! but after this, now they can find little good they can get, little growth they make, unless it be downward; little life they have, and what ado to keep it, or to get a good spiritual meals meat! This is the reason of it: when they first began, then the enemy was out and they were up and . . . conquered and had the spoils, but since they have grown secure and loved to sleep" (375). Besides sleepiness

there is the poison of love for the worldly which may be found even in God's dearest saints, "in their hungry lustings and dropsy desires after the sweet things of this world for there may be "inordinate lustings after lawful things in themselves" (159). On page 538 Shepard mentions seven choking sins, but, as we might expect from his subject matter, it is spiritual slumber which most engages his attention; it is analysed in all its varied initial stages, of which eight degrees are specified (368–70). As a result of a Christian's becoming slack or stumbling, he may become impoverished and useless; he may draw upon himself the chastisement of his heavenly Father in various corrective providences, sickness, loss of dear ones (521) and other calamities, and finally he may even become unready to meet Christ, as is movingly described in the following passage: "Hence see the reason why some godly people die so uncomfortably and with such distress of spirit— they have not lived in an expectation of Christ, and hence they cry out themselves; they thank (their ministers) for their love but God has otherwise thought of them . . . and what is the reason of it? What need I speak? (They) themselves will tell you, and have done it 'O I have lived thus and thus before you, but my heart in secret has gone after the world . . . I have neglected the Lord secretly. I have seldom thought of or prepared for death, and I had thought to have been better but the Lord has met with me . . .' As it has been with some, so take warning lest it be so with you; you may be saved alive, yet to suffer wreck upon the shore is uncomfortable" (77).

V. The Gospel Hypocrite

If this parable proves one thing for Thomas Shepard, it is the reality and importance of one problem—the existence of the gospel hypocrite. This follows from his exegesis of the parable, but he is never tired of underlining and analysing it. It is his main theme: there are those in the church who are not of it, members of the church visible who belong not to the church invisible, those who seem to have been weaned from the world but who are yet not joined to Christ. We may only touch on a very few of the aspects under which this theme is examined in the course of the work.

1. *The gospel hypocrite and common grace.* God works all good that exists or comes into existence; there are many who have a kind of faith that is not saving faith, but who are yet assiduous in Christian duties. Their power to live thus comes from God, but it is his work in common grace, not the work of his saving grace, special grace. "Unto some men especially . . . the Lord gives a power to act and live and move and to do many spiritual duties; or good duties from themselves . . . Now how comes this about? Why, the Lord gives that power to act . . . Hence all terrors and comforts and duties of conscience are from God, so the historical faith of the Gospel, which many have . . . and joy from this, and reformation of life upon this, none of these are natural to the soil of a man's soul, but all are planted there by God" (53).

2. *The knowledge of Christ which does not save* is a subject into which Shepard enquires in detail, for "foolish virgins may have some light in their lamps, some sight and knowledge of Jesus Christ." He then goes on to show what this knowledge may consist of (297–99)—knowledge born of "common fame and human private instruction . . . as (for example) that Christ is the Saviour of the world, is come, is dead, is risen, is at God's right hand, that in Him God's justice and mercy is reconciled, that there is mercy with Him for the greatest of sinners, etc." Such non-saving knowledge, again is all that can be ascribed to those who have seen Christ in the flesh with their own eyes, eaten and drunk with Him, moreover, seeing Him in His wonderful works and glorious kingdom and government, noting the deliverance of His people, etc., this will not save; the same may be said of a man who has a clear apprehension of the letter and teaching of Scripture about Christ. Neither will a man be saved by raptures, ecstasy and visions whose subject is Christ.

3. *The work of the Spirit of God in hypocrites.* The great and often striking enlightenment that some men experience who are yet

proved not to be true believers is to be attributed directly to the Holy Spirit. "The Spirit of God comes upon many hypocrites in abundant and plentiful measure of awakening grace . . . as upon Balaam . . . the grace and Spirit of God come suddenly and plentifully upon many a man, which gives them a time of flourishing; it comes not from imitation or education or moral persuasion only, but physically from the Spirit of God . . . (but) it is only awakening grace, for renewing grace savingly to change their nature is not given . . . and though it doth come upon them thus, yet it doth never rest within so as to dwell there, to take up an eternal mansion for Himself . . . hence it doth decay by little and little as a man that dwells not, but sojourneth for a little time in a house" (428), and the passage continues with the examples of King Saul and the branch that is withered in John 15. In the following section, Shepard goes on to show how grace decays in such persons.

   4. *Varieties of hypocrisy are most searchingly delineated* on many occasions, as for instance when Shepard is dealing with the inward principle from which men act. The great question is whether "all my sorrows, prayers, reformation, profession is but a paint, an appearance, a fashion, a church-craft" (270). Thus, a man is a hypocrite, a foolish virgin in the sense of the parable, *first,* "when a man's principle is nothing but the power of created nature expressing itself and setting the best face forward, in the gilded rottenness of some moral performances, wherein a man saith that he does what he can." *Second,* "when a man's principle is the power of holy example, whereby many a one is drawn to do more than he otherwise would . . . it sometimes falls out that the Lord sets before men's eyes some pattern Christians; hereupon they think thus: here are two contrary ways, they cannot both lead to heaven, their way is better than mine and doubtless leads to life, mine doth not, therefore let me live like them." *Third,* "those whose principle is nothing but external applause and praise of men, and this will carry a man beyond all the best examples, nay, sometimes to be singular and a man alone; a Pharisee's trumpet shall be heard to the town's end, while simplicity walks through the town unseen." *Fourth,* there are "those whose principle is

nothing else but their own gain of outward blessings"; and *fifth,* "those whose principle is nothing else but the strength of natural conscience, which will set men a-doing, when they have neither praise from men, not gain from Christ from their labour." *Sixth,* in this section we have "those whose principle is the fear of death and hell, raised not so much by the power of conscience as by the power of the Word." In the whole of this section (271–75), Shepard's acute mind works faithfully on the data of Scripture, and the headings above do scant justice to the searching exegesis (and indeed, the remarkable psychological insight) of the New England divine.

5. *The experience of the gospel hypocrite* is compared with that of the truly regenerate in the following moving passage, which finds many echoes in other parts of the work. "Hypocrites have awakening grace, and are much troubled; they have enlightening grace and know more than many Christians: they have affecting grace, and are wonderfully taken with the glad tidings of the Gospel, but satisfying grace, or that grace that brings them to full rest, and satisfying sweetness in God, not only to their consciences but to their hearts . . . this they never came to . . . this is the last end and fruit of the redemption of Christ so to satiate as not to desire other things, and there to stay, though the heart doth oft not feel the same sweetness" (452).

We are not surprised to find that on more than one occasion Shepard imagines a conversation between himself and a hypocrite, and in each case the objections are solemnly and scripturally answered, the objectors experience is dissected and then contrasted with the experience of a real saint, and an exhortation to true repentance and faith in Christ follows (e.g. 190–91).

VI. Conclusion

Thomas Shepard's "Parable of the Ten Virgins," some of the main themes of which we have examined above, is certainly a lengthy and involved work. We might almost say that it demands a special technique of the reader who would read it to his profit. But despite what has been said about the presentation of the material, and the occasional scholastic hair-splitting which not every reader will find justified, the work can only be classed as a masterpiece of the thorough, sound, and practical Reformed Christianity which we associate with the names of the very greatest Puritans. The exegesis is meticulous, sane, and balanced. The doctrine has breadth, depth, and height; it is massive and intensely moving, as is the word from which it is dug. Shepard's aim is to make every man examine himself in the light of Scripture, and the tone is experimental and urgent throughout. In its healthy solemnity and the amazing depth of its biblical psychology, it puts twentieth-century evangelical Christianity to shame. Yet this is our inheritance. This man preached our gospel. The issues at stake in the gospel made him preach arid write as he did. "O! the heavy wrath of God on a world of poor, blind ignorant men that have no hope, no hope of Christ, no hope of glory unless a flattering dead hope. What a sad thing it is to think of a number of men that are buried in the world, and never to awaken till they see Christ in the clouds of heaven coming to be revenged on them. O! methinks I see them down before the judgment Seat and crying out 'O! that we had known of this day! O! Alas that I had hope! but not such an hope, but am now deceived.' O! It is otherwise with saints; they shall find that they hoped for, and infinitely more . . . behold the Lord cometh that shall deliver and redeem them! O! see their blessedness and let it draw you to make up a match with Christ, that never did it yet. He has been wooing of you, longing for you . . . Give thyself this day to Him and take Him only, when nothing thou hast can be so pleasing to Him. And now you may look and believe what one day you shall feel to your everlasting comfort" (146).

Discussion centred upon the pastoral problems presented by the existence of "gospel hypocrites," who profess the truth, exhibit the appearance of good works (they do what Christians are expected to do), and have some kind of love, joy, and peace (they like Christians and Christian society, and feel happy), yet are not genuinely regenerate. It was agreed that there is no "standard experience" of conversion whereby true converts may infallibly be distinguished from others: for there is no aspect of Christian experience, taken in isolation, which cannot be counterfeited in the experience of a hypocrite. The chairman summed up as follows:

(i) We must recognise how real, constant, and universal is the danger of self-deception as to one's spiritual state. Shepard's warnings speak to every Christian's condition. Self-examination is every Christian's need and duty.

(ii) The gospel hypocrite's fault is that God's will and glory and his own relationship to God, never become his chief concern. In times of revival, religion is "in the air," and such times produce a crop of "temporary believers," swept along by the movement, though never heartily committed to God. Any vigorous religious movement may produce hypocrites in this way: indeed, the ordinary life of the churches does so constantly. But the problem is to discern the hypocrite, and to enable him to discern himself and to see his lack, of which he himself is unaware.

(iii) The safe rule for discerning such cases is to take and apply all the scriptural tests of true faith (for which see 1 John, etc.) together. None alone can yield a sure diagnosis. This is the real point of Shepard's constant insistence that this feeling, that experience, that attitude of mind, is by itself no infallible sign of grace—though the point that all the tests must be applied together is partly obscured by the minuteness and detail of his analysis of each one separately. The truth is that regeneration affects the whole man, but the hypocrite's temporary faith does not; hence he is lacking somewhere, though not everywhere. A synoptic view of him in the light of *all* the tests will most quickly show us the truth about his condition.

(iv) We must preserve the balance of scriptural truth in teaching this subject. Too much emphasis on self-scrutiny reflects a morbid depression in ourselves (as it did in Shepard, who was notoriously a melancholic) and induces a similar depression in those we instruct. Morbid introspection is sin, and has nothing to do with scriptural self-examination.

4

JOHN BUNYAN AND
HIS EXPERIENCE

Owen C. Watkins

(Note: Numbers in parentheses refer to paragraphs of *Grace Abounding*).

Dr. Robert Harris, who succeeded John Dod at Hanwell, used to say that a preacher had three books to study, the Bible, himself, and the people. It is the purpose of this paper to say something of how Bunyan studied himself and interpreted what he found to the people.

In *The Pilgrim's Progress* one of the things that helps to retain our interest to the end is the great variety of adventures that befalls Christian; he meets many kinds of people and travels through many kinds of country. Yet all this variety is actually *variation* between times of affliction and times of comfort. This is Bunyan's message about his experience of the Christian life: that God reveals Himself to His people as much in times of tempta-

tion as in times of peace, and that both will lead them nearer to
the glory which is unchanging.

Bunyan relates his experience in *Grace Abounding*, written
during his first imprisonment, "for the support of the weak and
tempted people of God." He describes it as "something of a relation of the work of God upon my own soul, even from the very
first until now, wherein you may perceive my castings down, and
raisings up; for he woundeth, and his hands make whole." There
was no single or dramatic moment at which he became conscious
of his rebirth, but from the time when "the thoughts of religion
were very grievous" (10) there were four incidents which all had
a lasting effect: (1) The reading of two books of practical divinity
which his first wife had inherited from her father (15); this broke
down his prejudice against religious observance. (2) A sermon
on Sabbath breaking convicted him of sin (20–22). (3) A rebuke
from a woman as ungodly as himself put him to secret shame for
his swearing (26–28). (4) The overhearing of a conversation
about the work of grace on the soul opened his mind to perceive
the glory of the kingdom of heaven (37–38).

Bunyan was now in the position of Christian on the first
page of *The Pilgrim's Progress*. "And now, methought I began to
look into the Bible with new eyes, and read as I never did before
. . . . indeed, I was never then out of the Bible, either by reading
or meditation, still crying out to God, that I might know the
truth, and the way to heaven and glory" (46). And there are
many remarkable correspondences throughout Bunyan's own
story with the adventures of his pilgrim. The wicket gate, which
Christian must pass through, is foreshadowed in the autobiography in what Bunyan calls a dream or vision; here he became
aware of the happiness of professing Christians as being like the
warmth and comfort of people on the sunny side of a high
mountain, while he shivered in the cold and clouds outside a
great wall which surrounded them; and in this wall there was a
narrow gap through which he struggled to pass (53–54). This is
a typical example of how Bunyan's imagination gave concrete
form to scriptural imagery, and so why he was able to write the
greatest allegory in the language: his mind instinctively per-

ceived spiritual reality after this manner, as his remarks in paragraph 55 indicate.

Christian's first difficulty on his journey is the Slough of Despond; and Bunyan himself had quickly been assaulted by doubts as to whether he was one of the elect, or whether the day of grace for him was not already past: "I was often, when I have been walking, ready to sink where I went, with faintness in my mind" (62). By quoting Romans 9:16 to him Satan repeatedly tempted him to despair. "Therefore, this would still stick with me, How can you tell that you are elected? And what if you should not? How then? O Lord, thought I, what if I should not, indeed? It may be you are not, said the tempter; it may be so indeed, thought I. Why then, said Satan, you had as good leave off and strive no further, for if, indeed you should not be elected and chosen of God, there is no talk of your being saved; 'For it is neither of him that willeth, nor of him that runneth, but of God that sheweth mercy'" (59–60).

The instruction that Bunyan received through the fellowship of the Baptists in Bedford is represented in *The Pilgrim's Progress* by Interpreter's House and by the advice of Evangelist and Good Will; we may note particularly the emphasis on the need for guilt of conscience to be taken off only by the blood of Christ, otherwise "a man grew rather worse for the loss of his trouble of mind, than better" (86).

Bunyan's first experience of the love of Christ for his soul was the result of a sermon on Canticles 4:19, "Behold thou art fair, my love, behold thou art fair." These words ran through his thoughts and kindled his spirit; "yea I was now so taken with the love and mercy of God, that I remember I could not tell how to contain till I got home. I thought I could have spoken of his love, and of his mercy to me, even the very crows that sat upon the ploughed lands before me" (92). We think of Christian, who had a merry heart and gave three leaps for joy when the burden fell off his shoulders.

So despair and comfort alternated in Bunyan's experience; difficulties were overcome in order that other trials further along the road might in their turn be tackled and overcome. Christian has to endure the hardships of the Valley of Humiliation, of Vanity Fair and of Doubting Castle; and the first and last of these are the counterparts of two periods of equally ferocious temptations in Bunyan's life. Only a week or so after his great experience of forgiveness, what Bunyan calls "a very great storm" came upon him: "it came stealing upon me, now by one piece, then by another; first, all my comfort was taken from me, then darkness seized upon me, after which whole floods of blasphemies . . . were poured upon my spirit, to my great confusion and astonishment" (96). And his struggle in prayer (107) is like Christian's combat with Apollyon, who commanded the pilgrim to forsake his new Master. The subtlety of the tempter is conveyed very powerfully in *Grace Abounding.* Bunyan remembers that his periods of comfort and zeal for God, however overwhelming at the time, invariably fade away. "Well," he said, "I will watch, and take what heed I can. Though you do, said Satan, I shall be too hard for you, I will cool you insensibly by degrees, by little and little. What care I, saith he, though I be seven years in chilling your heart if I can do it at last? Continual rocking will lull a crying child asleep. I will ply it close, but I will have my end accomplished. Though you be burning hot at present, yet, if I can pull you from this fire, I shall have you cold before it be long" (110). The slow grip of despair induced by these words is that felt by Christian in the Valley of the Shadow of Death, and the reference to the crying child gives us a strange awareness of the malignity of the unseen powers of evil. Bunyan's deliverance, both now and later, came from constant meditation on the promises of the gospel and their conditions (111–16).

The second great period of trouble recorded in *Grace Abounding* was much more distressing. This was a temptation to sell and part with Christ, to exchange Him for the things of this life. He was haunted by this for a whole year together, but nothing could diminish its power, and finally, worn out with the struggle, he felt the thought pass through his heart, "Let him go if he will" and thought also that he felt his heart consent to it. At once he was plunged into the most fearful despair, and there seized upon his soul the words of Hebrews 12:16–17: "Or profane person, as Esau, who for one morsel of meat, sold his birthright; for ye know, how that afterward, when he would have inherited the blessing, he was rejected, though he sought it carefully with tears"

(141). "These words were to my soul like fetters of brass to my legs, in the continual sound of which I went for several months together" (144). Indeed, for over two years he had few moments of relief. But he was not passive; his intellectual activity was incessant; he continually searched the Scriptures for some guidance as to the true nature of his sin and its remedy. He tried to find parallels: David, Hezekiah, Solomon, and Peter were all guilty of terrible things, but his was most like that of Judas. He had insuperable difficulty in prayer; his desire to come before the mercy seat was constantly frustrated. He was mocked by Satan, who among other things told him at one time that since he had rejected the only mediator with the Father, he must pray for God the Father to be mediator between the sinner and His Son, and at another time that Christ indeed pitied him but had not died for that particular sin. Such thoughts were not the less grievous because he was fully aware that they were essentially ridiculous. But he was mocked most not by Satan, nor by the terrible warnings of Scripture, but by all the promises and most gracious words of the gospel. "Every time that I thought of the Lord Jesus, of his grace, love, goodness, kindness, gentleness, meekness, death, blood, promises, and blessed exhortations, it went to my soul like a sword; . . . Oh, thought I, what have I lost! What have I parted with! What have I disinherited my poor soul of!" (183). Thus the eternal constancy of God, which often comforts the believer, brings only terror when he despairs of salvation.

Bunyan's experience of this was not by any means unique, but among all the seventeenth-century accounts which have survived his is the one which speaks to us with most power, and which also shows us most clearly how the Christian should react to such an attack. Comparison with two other memoirs will help us here.

In a book called *Spiritual Experiences* published in 1653, there is an account by a young man, signing himself E.R., which includes an episode frequently found in Puritan autobiographies. The memory of some sin convinces the believer that he is a reprobate, and he refuses to listen to any word of comfort. We usually read of his being visited by his pastor who reasons with him for many days in a vain attempt to alleviate his despair. And so it is with E.R., for he says, "my parents did send for Mr. Knew-stubs, a Minister in Edmundsbury, and one Mr. Rogers another Minister of Dedham, who tooke a great deal of pains with me, and asked me whom I did believe in, and I told them that I did believe in God that he would damn me, and they asked me if God would damn me because I did believe in him; I answered no, but it was for that sin committed against God, and my innocent sister, and they asked me, whether I was not sorry for that act, and I told them yes, for I had cause to be sorry, for I must be damned for that sin" *(Spirituall Experiences,* 359). Later, when told that Christ would pardon a repentant sinner, "I told them no, that he would never open my heart but with terror, for I was born to be damned, and must be damned, and that Christ never died for such a sinner as I was" (ibid., 362). The preachers' formidable learning and biblical exposition are of no use, because the victim seems to have searched every possible Scripture for himself. Prayer, ingenuity, and earnest persuasion are likewise without effect, for they are matched by answers even more ingenious. Time and again we read how the Puritan physicians of the soul appeared to make no impression on this obstinate refusal to listen to reason: the victim abandoned himself to all his morbid fears, and seemed almost to take a perverse delight to resisting all attempts to help him and in his uniqueness as the one soul whom not even God Himself could save.

Such perversity is spoken of in Mrs. Hannah Allen's *Satan, his Methods and Malice Baffled* (1683). She made several attempts at suicide and quotes many remarks which show how she clung to her misery. On hearing a woman swear in the streets, she would say to her companion, "Ah, cousin, I have abhorred such company all my life, I hope they shall not be my companions to eternity" (13). When she would not get up in the mornings, and in other ways led her aunt to complain of weariness, she replied, "Ah, but what must I do, that must have no rest to all eternity" (27).

Now there is no trace of such wilfulness in Bunyan. He never surrendered; he was constantly seeking and was ready to grasp any vestige of hope. But even in his most miserable moments he wanted truth rather than comfort. His knowledge of his own heart and of the grace of God led him to shun a false peace obtained by closing his eyes to any of the facts as he saw them. Thus many Scriptures were brought home to his heart which seemed to lift his burden, but as he followed their implications ruthlessly to a conclusion, every way of escape was found to be a blind alley. This was indeed dreadful at the time, but looking back, he could say, "I never saw those heights and depths in grace, and love and mercy, as I saw after this temptation. Great sins do draw out great grace; and where guilt is most terrible and fierce there the mercy of God in Christ, when showed to the soul, appears most high and mighty" (252). Nevertheless the Christian is not to seek out temptations, and Bunyan explicity claimed that his trials were partly the result of having disregarded the Lord's command that we should pray to be kept from temptations to come. (See 237–39.) And so Mr. Greatheart points out to the pilgrims the bones of one Heedless, who was "foolishly venturous."

His incessant reasoning from the Scriptures eventually pointed the way back to peace of mind. He became convinced that his brief periods of comfort were indeed conveying true spiritual comfort from God, and after much questioning concluded that it was not possible for a soul that had sinned the unpardonable sin to receive such comfort. So he got courage to reconsider the texts which condemned him, and concluded that he had been wrongly informed about the nature of his sin. And the way in which the Scriptures worked on his soul is nowhere seen more clearly than in the climax of this period of testing, where the texts of condemnation and of promise struggled within him until "this about the sufficiency of grace prevailed with peace and joy." (See 204–15.) Bunyan experienced the Scriptures almost as physical presences. The Bible, he says, "was so fresh, . . . that I was as if it talked with me" (63). He constantly refers to it in physical terms: "The glory of these words was then so weighty upon me." "Then would the former sentence fall like a hot thunderbolt again upon my conscience." "This sentence stood like a millpost at my back." And in most references to his spiritual condition there is this almost physical sense of strain. "I should find my heart to shut itself up against the Lord, and . . . my unbelief to set, as it were, my shoulder to the door to keep him out." "I found myself as on a miry bog that shook if I did but stir." These images hardly seem to be images at all, but a direct description of the man's experience as it actually was. This surely is why he can bring home to the reader the truths of Scripture with all the full power of personal experience. And so we do not just understand his condition, but in some measure know and feel what he felt.

Of other autobiographies in the Puritan tradition, the one which recounts an experience most like Bunyan's is that of John Rogers, an Independent minister who later became a notorious Fifth Monarchy Man. Anyone who reads Rogers's story however, which is printed in his treatise on church government *Ohel or Bethshemesh, A Tabernacle for the Sun* (1654), can see at once why Bunyan is still widely read today when Rogers is not. It is ultimately a question of the nature of his experience, for after ending on a note of complete assurance, Rogers went on to embrace more and more extreme religious and political opinions, but we do not feel convinced by his story because he paints his past in such lurid colours, condemns all his past attitudes out of hand, and concludes that now at last he is entirely right. Bunyan, on the other hand, while no less conscious of the great gulf between despair and assurance, can still speak at the end of his story of "seven abominations" in his heart. One quotation from Rogers, followed by one from Bunyan's preface, must suffice to indicate the relevance of a man's style to the substance of what he is really trying to do when he writes.

Rogers: "The more I read the more I roared in the black gulf of despair . . . I have run into barns, stables, house of office, anywhere . . . on purpose to pray, sigh, weep, knocking my breast, curse that ever I was born; wishing I were a stone . . . . for fear of hell and the devils, whom I thought I saw every foot, in several ugly shapes and forms (according to my fancies) and sometimes with great rolling flaming eyes (like saucers) having sparkling firebrands in the one of their hands, and with the other reaching at me to tear me away to torments! O the leaps that I have made! the frights that I have had! the fears that I was in!" (*A Tabernacle for the Sun*, 426–27).

Bunyan: "I could also have stepped into a style much higher than this in which I have here discoursed, and could have adorned all things more than here I have seemed to do, but I dare not. God did not play in convincing of me, the devil did not play in tempting of me, neither did I play when I sunk as into a bottomless pit, when the pangs of hell caught hold upon me, wherefore I may not play in my relating of them, but be plain and simple and lay down the thing as it was."

The lesson for us is surely that in relating any experience of holy things it is frivolous to use heightened language or pious cliches, which may hinder the passage of the truth. We must try to "lay down the thing as it was." And we can certainly say that in Bunyan's case it was the directness and forcefulness with which he portrayed the heights and depths of his experience that enabled him to succeed in his aim to support "the weak and tempted people of God."

This paper has perhaps been more concerned with the depths than the heights. In conclusion, then, it may be profitable to recall another Puritan writer who can give us a tangible link between the heights of Bunyan and the hope of glory which sustained an earlier generation of Puritans. We are all familiar with that great passage at the end of the Second Part of *The Pilgrim's Progress* where the pilgrims are called one by one across the river. They all in turn receive their summons, make their bequests, and enter into their eternal inheritance. It is an idealised picture of the passing of faithful pilgrims, and it is true to the Puritan tradition, for fifty years before Bunyan wrote these words Edward Bagshaw had described the death of Robert Bolton, that son of thunder and consolation, in words hardly less noble than Bunyan's.

"About a week before he died, when his silver cord began to loosen, and his golden bowl to break: He called for his wife, and desired her to bear his dissolution, which was now at hand, with a Christian fortitude, a thing which he had prepared her for by the space of twenty years, telling her that his approaching death was decreed upon him from all eternity, and that the counsel of the LORD must stand, and bad her make no doubt but she should meet him again in heaven. And turning toward his children, told them, that they should not expect he should now say anything to them, neither would his ability of body and breath give him leave, he had told them enough in the time of his sickness and before, and hoped they would remember it, and verily believed *that none of them durst think to meet him at that great Tribunal in an unregenerate state* . . . The night before he died, when the doors without began to be shut, and the daughters of music to be brought low, and he lying very low with his head, expecting every moment when the wheel should be broken at the cistern, yet being told that some of his dear friends were then about him to take their last farewell, he caused himself to be lifted up, and then like old Jacob bowing himself on his bed's head, after a few gaspings for breath, he spake in this manner. *I am now drawing on apace to my dissolution* . . . . *Hold out faith and patience, your work will speedily be at an end:* And then shaking them all by the hands, prayed heartily, and particularly for them, and desired them *to make sure of heaven, and to bear in mind what he had formerly told them in his ministry, protesting to them, that the doctrine which he had preached to them for the space of twenty years was the truth of GOD, as he should answer for it at the Tribunal of CHRIST, before whom he should shortly appear.* This he spake when the very pangs of death were upon him. Whereupon a very dear friend of his taking him by the hand, and asking him if he felt not much pain, *Truly no* (said he) *the greatest I feel is your cold hand.* And then speaking to be laid down again, he spake no more until the next morning when he took his last leave of his wife and children, prayed for them and blessed them all, and that day in the afternoon about five of the clock, being Saturday the 17 day of December, Anno Dom. 1631 in the LXth year of his age, yielded up his spirit to GOD that gave it, and according to his own speech celebrated the ensuing Sabbath in the Kingdom of Heaven" (Edward Bagshaw, *The Life and Death of Mr. Bolton;* in Bolton's *Works,* 1641, 33–35).

The following points were considered in discussion:

1. How far is it right to present Christian truth in an imaginative form, as Bunyan does in *Pilgrim's Progress?* Imagination, it was observed, is a gift from God, and, as such, has its proper

use—in this case, to make truth vivid (for Bunyan's book is simply an extended illustration of Scripture principles). The danger here, however, is that imagination should cease to be a handmaid of truth, and its use a means to an end, and that it should be employed simply to entertain. This is always wrong in the sphere of revealed truth; we are not told to make the gospel entertaining. Again, if our attention is diverted from the truth being presented to the medium of its presentation, and our use of the resources of imagination becomes a self-conscious striving after effect, or aping of someone else, we fall into error, and indeed do harm by distracting our readers' or hearers' attention from our message to ourselves. Bunyan's own artless absorption in his message, and the consequent naturalness and integrity of all his imaginative writing, is a lesson to us all.

2. Why is Bunyan's intensity of experience rare today? Partly, no doubt, because men of Bunyan's psychological make-up are rare in any age; but is it not also because we preach a different doctrine today—a less exalted doctrine of human sin, and a more superficial doctrine of faith ("believism"). Shallow doctrine creates shallow spirituality.

5

THE PURITAN PRINCIPLE
OF WORSHIP

W. Young

Expressed more precisely, the subject of the present study might be formulated as "The regulative principle of Reformed worship in the Puritan writers, and its application to the element of sung praise in worship."

The importance of the regulative principle of worship for the origin and essential character of the Puritan movement appears from the following definition of Puritanism given by Prof. Horton Davies in his standard work on "The Worship of the English Puritans" (Chapter 1, p. 1). "Puritanism is most accurately defined as the outlook that characterised the radical Protestant party in Queen Elizabeth's day, who regarded the Reformation as incomplete and wished to model English church worship and government according to the Word of God."

The application of this principle may be said to enjoy a certain primacy with respect to worship rather than to church government; yet in the Reformed conception both are, in their essential structure and procedure, entirely prescribed in Holy Scripture according to the regulative principle as understood by Reformed theologians, and especially the Puritans. In actual historical fact, Puritanism began with the application of this principle to worship and later became increasingly concerned with its reference to church government and relations between church and state. While on the latter issues the Puritans divided into diverging camps, all were of one mind as to applying the regulative principle to the worship of the church, and an adequate understanding of it is necessary for a proper comprehension of the significance of the Puritan movement in the past, and of its relevance to our present problems.

The Puritan principle of worship was no invention of the Puritans, but was that formulated by Calvin and adopted by all the Reformed churches. It stands out in contrast to the Lutheran view which held that what is not forbidden in the word of God may be allowed in the worship of God, and regarded ceremonies in worship as to a large extent things indifferent (adiaphora), i.e. things neither commanded nor forbidden in the Scriptures. The thirty-fourth of the thirty-nine Articles of the Church of England follows the Lutheran line in its statement that "it is not necessary that traditions and ceremonies be in all places one, or utterly like; for at all times they have been divers and may be changed according to the diversity of countries, times and men's manners, as that nothing be ordained against God's Word."

As opposed to the Lutheran, the Reformed view has uniformly been that only that which is prescribed by the word of God may be introduced into the worship of God. Calvin formulated this regulative principle with clarity and applied it with great consistency in the Reformation at Geneva. It is implicit in his celebrated definition of pure and genuine religion as "confidence in God coupled with serious fear—fear, which both includes in itself willing reverence, and brings along with itself such legitimate worship as is prescribed by the law" (Institutes, 1.2.3). The corruption of pure religion by the introduction of forms of worship invented by man was for Calvin a mark of the vanity and blind-

ness of fallen human nature. In arguing against idolatry and image worship and in distinguishing true religion from superstition
he appealed uniformly to this regulative principle, while his discussions of ecclesiastical legislation show how pervasively this
principle had penetrated his outlook as the chief ground for rejecting the traditions of men.

Calvin found the regulative principle of worship established
by the second commandment of the decalogue, which he expounded thus: "As in the first commandment the Lord declares
that he is one, and that beside him no gods must be either worshipped or imagined, so he here more plainly declares what his
nature is, and by what kind of worship he is to be honoured, in
order that we may not presume to form any carnal idea of him.
The purport of the commandment, therefore, is that he will not
have his legitimate worship profaned by superstitious rites.
Therefore, in general, he calls us entirely away from the carnal
frivolous observances which our stupid minds are wont to devise
after forming some gross idea of the divine nature, while at the
same time he instructs us in the worship that is legitimate,
namely, spiritual worship of his own appointment" (Institutes,
2.8.17).

In Calvin's refutation of the claims of the Church of Rome,
the regulative principle of Reformed worship provided a charter
of Christian liberty. In his doctrine and practice, as in that of the
Puritans in the following century, it was a liberating power, cut-
ting off at the root the tyrannical impositions of men in the worship of God by asserting that the Christian is free from the commandments of men in this matter, for, it was insisted, God is the
only law-giver, and His will is the perfect rule of all righteousness
and holiness. Consequently, human ceremonies devised for the
worship of God and imposed upon the conscience as of necessary
obligation, are contrary to the word of the Lord. Though directing his arguments towards abuses prevalent in his own day, Calvin
recognised this regulative principle as applicable to all ages, and
wrote thus: "But if, without any regard to circumstances, you
would simply know the character belonging at all times to those
human traditions which ought to be repudiated by the church

and condemned by all the godly, the definition which we formerly gave is clear and certain—viz. that they include all the laws enacted by men, without authority from the word of God, for the purpose either of prescribing the mode of divine worship, or laying a religions obligation on the conscience, as enjoining things necessary to salvation" (4.10.16).

The witness of the Reformed creeds to the regulative principle of worship is along the lines laid down by Calvin; and among these the Westminster Confession of Faith and Catechisms contain the consensus of English Puritan and Scottish Presbyterian judgment in this respect. Whatever difference of opinion there was in the Assembly as to church government, there was agreement as to the regulation of worship, and the following statement of the position defined by the Westminster standards may be safely taken as expressing the unanimous Puritan conviction on this subject.

1. The regulative principle is a consequence of the sufficiency of Scripture. Nothing need, nor may, be added to the word of God as a rule of faith and practice. Therefore, only what is prescribed by God's written revelation may be admitted in His worship.

2. The mode of prescription need not be that of explicit command in a single text of Scripture. Approved example or demonstrably applicable principle warrants an element of worship as surely as does an express precept. For example, all would agree that Scripture principles warrant the admission of women to the Lord's table, although no express command or approved example can be adduced.

3. The regulative principle does not entail an impossible demand that an indefinite number of minute circumstances concerning the worship of God should be deduced from Scripture. Such details as the time and place of worship for a Christian congregation are not minutely prescribed.

4. Yet this does not mean that all circumstances are adiaphora. The circumstances not prescribed by the word of God are only such as are "common to human actions and societies"— and only some such.

5. The general rules of the word of God are to be observed in the ordering of these circumstances "by the light of nature and Christian prudence." An act of worship is never a thing indifferent (i.e. something neither commanded nor forbidden by God), though some civil actions and even some circumstances accompanying acts of worship may be thus classed among the adiaphora.

6. With respect to matters of faith and worship, human laws over and above the word of God, even though not directly contrary to it, have no binding force.

In his well-known "Medulla Theologica" (Eng. Trans., "The Marrow of Sacred Divinity," 1642), William Ames, professor at Franeker, discusses the principle of worship systematically, and the following is a brief summary of certain of his arguments and definitions. He states that instituted worship is the means ordained by the will of God to exercise and further natural worship. That only certain means are permitted is declared in the second commandment, which forbids all means of worship devised by men, under the title of "graven" and "images." Only God Himself can either understand what will be acceptable to Him or add that virtue to any worship whereby it may be made effectual and profitable for us. We make the Lord our God and give Him the honour due to Him, by (among other things) subjecting ourselves to His authority and ordinances in religious worship. All the means ordained by God for His worship, both general and special, should be observed by us: for God must be worshipped with His own worship, totally and solely, and nothing must be added, taken away, or changed (Deuteronomy 12:32). Opposed to this instituted worship, is "will-worship" devised by men, and its sin may be called under the general name of superstition. This is unlawful in that undue worship, in respect either of manner or measure, or of matter and substance, is offered to God. Religious teaching by images and all those ceremonies ordained by men for mystical or religious signification, are thus condemned.

Jeremiah Burroughs, in his treatise on Gospel-Worship (1648), proceeds from an account of the strange fire offered by Nadab and Abihu to formulate the regulative principle of worship: "That in God's worship there must be nothing tendered up to God but what he hath commanded, whatsoever we meddle with in the worship of God, it must be what we have a warrant for out of the Word of God" (p. 8). Moreover, Burroughs concludes, it is not enough that a thing is not forbidden in worship, but it must be commanded. He makes the standard Puritan distinction, however, between the elements and circumstances of worship, terming the latter "natural and civil helps" and declaring, "It's true that there are some things in the worship of God that are natural and civil helps and there we need not have any command: as for instance, when we come to worship God and the congregation meets, they must have a convenient place to keep the air and weather from them, now this is but a natural help, and so far as I use the place of worship as a natural help, I need have no command." But he goes on to say that if he would put anything in a place beyond what it has in its own nature, then he must have a command, and he sums up thus: "If any creature that you make any use of in a way of religion beyond that it hath in its own nature, if you have not some warrant from the Word of God . . . it is superstition."

The following brief quotation from further Puritan works show the emphasis placed on the regulative principle in worship:

The work *"English Puritanisme containeing the maine opinions of the rigidest sort of those that are called Puritanes in the Realme of England"* (1605) by W. Bradshaw, declares, *"In primis,* they hold and maintaine that the word of God contained in the writings of the Prophets and Apostles, is of absolute perfection, given by Christ the Head of the Churche, to bee unto the same, the sole Canon and rule of all matters of Religion, and the worship of God whatsoever. And that whatsoever done in the same service and worship cannot bee justified by the said word, is unlawfull. And therefore that it is a sinne to force any Christian to doe any act of religion or divine service, that cannot evidently bee warranted by the same."

W. Perkins in *"A Warning against the Idolatrie of the last times and an instruction touching Religious or Divine Worship"* (1608) writes, "The second way of erecting an Idoll is, when God is worshipped otherwise, and by other meanes, than he hath revealed in the Word. For when men set up a devised worship, they set up also a devised God . . . " and later he continues, "The 2nd point, is the role of worship: and that is, that nothing may goe under the name of the worship of God, which He hath not ordained in his owne word, and commanded to us as His owne worship. For we are forbidden under paine of the curse of God either to adde or to take away anything from the precepts of God in which He prescribes His owne worship. Again, the Lord forbids us in His worship to follow after our owne hearts and eyes, or to walk in the ordinance of our forefathers, but onely in His commandments. And He holds it a vaine thing, to teach His worship, and feare by the precepts of men . . . All voluntarie religion and will-service, is utterly condemned. "

Again, Perkins in *"A Golden Chain, or the Description of Theologie"* (1608) declares, "For God is not worshipped of us, but when it is His will to accept our worship: and it is not His will to accept our worship, but when it is according to His will."

When applied, the regulative principle provides objectivity in worship, by which is meant in this connection simply conformity to the law of God as opposed to subjectivity, or rather subjectivism, in worship. Subjectivity in a good sense—that is, heartfelt sincerity and reverence—is of the essence of true worship, but this, where it exists, will invariably tend to that worship which is agreeable to the will and word of God. Opposed to this is subjectivism in worship, where the forms followed arise, not from the revealed will of the Lord, but from the desires, inclinations, imaginations, and decisions of men: and to this the Reformers and Puritans applied the biblical term will-worship.

An increasing trend toward subjectivism in worship has marked the practice of professing Protestantism since the seventeenth century, and corresponds with a general trend in modern thought and life. The Puritan principle in the sixteenth and seventeenth centuries was insisted on in opposition to the tyrannical exercise of power on the part of an authoritarian church. In the twentieth century, while authoritarian churches still display their characteristic traits, the glaring evil especially in Protestant circles is unbridled license on the part of individuals and groups within the churches. The Puritan principle stands as a principle of order and of liberty, between the extremes of tyranny and anarchy in worship. It is not legalism, for it neither inculcates salvation by works nor admits of any impositions beyond the commandments of God. Legalism, whether in Judaism or Christianity, has involved essentially the rejection of sovereign Divine grace and of the sufficiency of God's word; and Puritanism, far from being legalism in this proper usage of the word, is the one system that has in its distinguishing principle opposed legalism most consistently. If Puritans have sometimes fallen into legalistic errors, this has been in spite of and not the natural result of their allegiance to the regulative principle of worship.

The Puritans were concerned with ceremonies and with the imposition of liturgies, but since the eighteenth century a major deviation from the regulative principle in the direction of unbridled subjectivism (which could also be illustrated in a multitude of other particulars), concerns the musical aspect of the service of worship. The flood of uninspired lyrics which has inundated a declining Protestant church has been matched by other musical accompaniments that have transformed churches into theatres and concert halls.

In the eigtheenth century, William Romaine protested against the crowding out of divinely authorised and inspired psalmody by the introduction into public worship of humanly composed ditties. He referred in particular to Isaac Watts's compositions, though acknowledging Watts himself never intended to thrust psalms from the worship of the church as some of his followers were to do. But Watts was, in fact, responsible for two innovations in the service of sung praise, both in the direction of subjectivism in worship. He prepared imitations of the psalms to supersede the metrical versions commonly used in the Puritan churches, while his more drastic innovation was the introduction of a collection of hymns of his own composition. In defending both these departures from standard Puritan practice, he attempted to produce scriptural warrant for the introduction of uninspired hymns from Revelation 5:9; 14:39; and 15:3. But his general arguments entail a modification of the regulative principle in worship by transferring the content of praise from prescribed matter to a thing indifferent, and in this, even more than in the innovations themselves with their far-reaching consequences, lies the deepest deviation of Watts from the Puritan position with respect to worship.

Coming now to a consideration of authentic Puritan teaching with respect to the content of sung praise, reference may be made first of all to the witness of the Puritans at the Westminster Assembly of Divines in their mention of singing of psalms as among the authorised elements of worship, and in their concern for a metrical psalter which would bear a faithful rendering of the text of the psalms.

John Cotton, teacher of the church at Boston in New England, in his *"Singing of Psalmes a Gospel-Ordinance"* (1647) first justifies vocal singing in the worship of God, giving three main proofs. The first is the commandment of the Lord by Paul, in Ephesians 5:19; Colossians 3:16; 1 Corinthians 4:15–16. From these Cotton deduces, "that singing of Psalmes in the New Testament is to be dispensed in Christian churches, not only with inward grace in the heart, making melody to the Lord, but also with outward audible lively voice." He argues also from 2 Kings 3:15 and 1 Samuel 10:5–6, while from Psalms 108:1 and 57:7–8 he finds that singing of psalms honours God with our glory, i.e. our tongue. To the objection that "these gracious effects and fruits of singing Psalmes to plead as much for singing and playing with instruments, as for singing with voyces," Cotton gives, along his replies, one main ground for the Puritans' objection to instrumental music in worship. "Singing with instruments was typicall, and so a ceremoniall worship, and therefore is ceased. But singing with heart and voyce is morall worship, such as is written in the hearts of all men by nature."

Second, Cotton proves vocal singing in the worship of God from the example of Christ Himself and of His saints and disciples in the New Testament, and his third proof is from the prophecies of the Old Testament foretelling with approval that such singing would be practised in the days of the New (Isaiah

52:8). He then proceeds to the heart of the matter, namely, the content of sung praise in worship—and states his view that not only the psalms of David, but any other spiritual songs recorded in Scripture may lawfully be sung in Christian churches; that any private Christian with a gift to compose a spiritual song may frame it and sing it privately; and that if upon any special occasion in the public thanksgiving of a church, a member with a spiritual gift composes a psalm, he may sing it before the church, though the reservation is added that such gifts are not ordinarily bestowed.

Proceeding to the issue as to whether, then, the scriptured psalms are appointed by God to be ordinarily sung in Christian churches or whether they should be laid aside and only spiritual songs composed by church members sung, he declares, "The former we hold to be the Truth, others the latter" (p. 16). In stating reasons for restricting the content of sung praise in worship to inspired songs, Cotton takes the texts Ephesians 5:19 and Colossians 3:16, and argues, "In both . . . places, as the Apostle exhorteth us to singing, so he instructeth us what the matter of our Song should be, to wit, Psalmes, Hymnes, and spirituall Songs. Now those three be the very titles of the songs of David, as they are delivered to us by the Holy Ghost himselfe . . . Now what reason can be given why the Apostle should direct us in our singing to the very titles of David's Psalmes, if it were not his meaning that we should sing them?"

Here we should observe that Cotton bases his argument on the regulative principle, taking his reasons for faith and practice "from the commandment or exhortation of the Apostle." Sung praise is to be restricted in its content to divinely inspired songs, not simply because they are inspired and therefore superior in quality to the best uninspired compositions, but basically because inspired psalms and songs are warranted by express command and approved example, while uninspired compositions lack such warrant. Cotton's interpretation of psalms, hymns, and spiritual songs as referring exclusively to the inspired compositions of Scripture is standard Puritan exegesis (and this is evident from, e.g. N. Byfield's Commentary on Colossians 3:16).

To arguments for supplanting psalmody by the hymns of uninspired writers, or at least for introducing such hymns, based on the references to singing a new song in Psalm 96:1; Revelation 5:9; and 15:3–4, Cotton replies that there is no estate or condition that can ever befall the church, but that there is a suitable Scripture-psalm provided, and that when these are chosen for each new occasion and sung by God's people with new hearts, they will ever be found new songs. Moreover, David's exhortation to sing a new song pertained to those under the Old Covenant as well as to us under the New, and yet they upon new occasions sang the old songs of David. In expounding the song of Moses and of the Lamb (Revelation 15) Cotton argues that Moses' song (Exodus 15) and the psalms of David may justly bear those titles. And with regard to the new song mentioned in Revelation 5:9–10, he says that this "may either be understood metonymically for a Doxology or Thanksgiving, which the Saints in the Church should give to Christ upon occasion of his revealing a cleare exposition of the Revelation; or else, if it be understood literally that they sang that very song, as it is it here penned by the Holy Ghost, then it appeareth that at such a time that song shall be translated into number and metre, fit to be sung, and shall be sung by the Church . . . And thus, this place onely sheweth, that it will be lawfull to sing other songs, beside that of David and Asaph; but yet such onely as are penned by an infallible Spirit, or else upon speciall occasion, by men of spiritual gifts which we deny not."

Thomas Manton, in his exposition of James 5:13 (1653) observes that singing of psalms is a duty of the gospel. Although he does not forbid the singing of other songs besides Scripture-psalms, he has no other grounds to give for this except the testimony of Tertullian's "Apology." Nevertheless, he proceeds to argue that scriptural psalms may be sung, and beyond this that they are fittest to be sung. Reason, he declares, proves they may be sung, for the word does not set a limit that would exclude them; and they are part of the word of God, "full of matter that tendeth to instruction, comfort and the praise of God which are the ends of singing; and therefore unless we will bring a disparagement upon the Scriptures, we cannot deny them a part in our Spiritual mirth. Besides, thus hath it been practised by Christ himself, by the apostles, the servants of the Lord in all ages . . ." In his further argument that Scripture-psalms not only may be sung, but are fittest to be used in the church, Manton gives as his judgment that "upon the whole matter I should pronounce that so much as an infallible gift doth excell a common gift, so much do scriptural Psalms excel those that are of a private composure."

To conclude, the importance of the regulative principle of Reformed worship is eloquently proclaimed by John Owen in his work on Communion with God where the third thing in which he states that the saints' chastity towards Christ consists is "in his institutions or matter and manner of his worship." He writes, "Christ marrying his Church to himself, taking it to that relation, still expresseth the main of their chaste and choice affections to him, to lie in their keeping his institutions and his worship according to his appointment . . . On this account those believers who really attend to communion with Jesus Christ, do labour to keep their hearts chaste to him in his ordinances, institutions and worship, and that two ways.

"1. They will receive nothing, practice nothing, own nothing in his worship but what is of his appointment. They know that from the foundation of the world, he never did allow nor ever will, that in anything the will of the creatures should be the measure of his honour, or the principle of his worship, either as to matter or to manner . . .

"2. They readily embrace, receive, and practise everything that the Lord Christ hath appointed. They inquire diligently into his mind and will, that they may know it. They go to him for directions, and beg of him to lead them in the way they have not known . . . This I say they are tender in. Whatever is of Christ, they willingly submit unto, and accept of, and give up themselves to the constant practice hereof. Whatever comes on any other account they refuse" (Owen, *Works,* ed. Gould, I. Isoff).

The following questions were raised in discussion after the paper:

1. If the regulative principle of worship as here expounded as valid in its application to hymns, would it not require us equally

to seek in Scripture authorized verbal forms of prayer for use in public worship? Is it a sufficient answer to say that the two cases are not parallel, since God has given us no authorized verbal forms of prayer (the Psalter being a public hymn book but not a public prayer book)? If this answer is not sufficient, is doubt thereby cast on the correctness of the proposed interpretation of the principle in regard to hymns?

2. Is the principle as stated a legalistic aberration, prompted partly by reaction against the licence of those who, like the Quakers, set the Spirit against and above the word, and going, not merely beyond Calvin (though it does: see Horton Davies, op. cit.), but beyond Scripture itself? Is it natural exegesis to equate the psalms mentioned in 1 Corinthians 14:26 with the contents of the Psalter exclusively? If not, does not that text (which contains no hint of censure) prove that under certain circumstances sung praise not contained in the Psalter may be admitted in public worship without dishonour to God? And if so, does not this cast doubt on the interpretation of the regulative principle which the paper expounds? Is it sufficient, in reply to this, to dismiss 1 Corinthians 14 as reflecting the extraordinary circumstances of the apostolic age to such a degree that it yields no guidance or relevant precedent in this mater for public worship in later days, now that the extraordinary gifts of the Spirit are withdrawn? If not, must we not conclude that there is a risk of quenching the Spirit by ruling out hymn singing in public worship—especially in view of the references to hymn-singing as the natural consequence of being filled with the Spirit and nourished by the word (Ephesians 5:18; Colossians 3:16)?

6

DAILY LIFE AMONG
THE PURITANS

E. Braund

"The nature of man is more apt to be guided by example than
by precept," wrote the elder Edmund Calamy in his preface to a
book containing a number of Puritan biographies. And undoubtedly one of the main reasons for such accounts being issued was that while honouring the memory of the people concerned, they should also provide examples for other Christians in
their daily living.

It is the purpose of this paper to try to show something of
what a number of these early biographies, together with autobiographical writings, reveal of the way their subjects were striving to
live, and through their example to see how men and women
among the Puritans in England were exhorted to conduct themselves day by day. First, however, it is necessary to define more
precisely both the sources from which information is drawn and
who among the Puritans are being considered. For this is by no

155

means an attempt to make a general survey of how all Puritans lived in this country during the sixteenth and seventeenth centuries, but has in view simply a number of accounts which are, I believe, representative of a distinctive body of Puritan biographies and autobiographical writings.

These works began to appear before the end of the sixteenth century, and continued to be issued in greater numbers during the following century. They include lives of the earlier Puritans, those who had sought for further reform within the established church of England, but most of those belonging to the later period and included here were Presbyterians. In using the term "the Puritans" in future, therefore, it is to such people that we are referring.

The biographies under consideration are by no means limited to ministers, and they afford an eloquent testimony to the fact that the Puritan movement touched all strata of society in this country. They were, however, written about people regarded by their contemporaries as outstanding Christians and, with the purpose of example in mind, authors tended to concentrate on the particular excellencies of their subjects' daily lives. On the other hand, the autobiographies and diaries of the people themselves provide searching records of their knowledge of their own hearts and of their failures, and it is from such X-rays of the soul, as well as from the accounts of others, that we shall try to glimpse men and women among the Puritans as they lived day by day, often in the midst of difficulty and suffering. In so doing we may perhaps also see the outworking of revival reaching through their individual lives into many varied spheres in this country, and being a means leading to profound changes in our national life.

Accounts of the Puritans at once reveal a basic pattern of daily living to have been followed by men and women irrespective of their place in society or their age. Their lives, too, in their varying circumstances, were dominated by the same fundamental characteristics. We see them above all as people consumed by the consciousness of being in the hand of Almighty God; and such knowledge, together with an awareness of the corruption of their own hearts, made them walk with sobriety. But they were also characterised by the totality with which they tried to live every part of their lives to the glory of God, and indeed a note of urgency runs through many accounts. Yet theirs was no mere activism, and in all that befell them they endeavoured not only to be resigned to God's will but to be thankful. Moreover, their lives were marked by the strict emphasis they placed on observing public and family worship, and on their own private duties day by day. But more than that, they exercised intense discipline with themselves, seeking to bring their every thought and action into accordance with God's word, and to this end some among them wrote down principles, drawn from the Scriptures, as daily rules by which to walk.

We shall follow the ways whereby the Puritans tried to regulate their daily lives to God's glory, by looking at their conduct at home in their households, and then by tracing their private duties throughout the day. First, however a brief mention of their various professions and interests—for unless called to the ministry, the Puritans did not neglect secular work, and a life of idleness was strongly deprecated. They also engaged in intellectual pursuits, music, and certain recreations. But they were careful not to let these activities interfere with Christian duties and sought to conduct their businesses in conformity with scriptural principles, their attitude towards their work being summed up by Lord Chief Justice Sir Matthew Hale, who reminded himself in his own daily resolutions that the chief end of his ordinary calling was to serve God in it.

Coming now to daily life in the Puritan home, the authority and serious responsibilities of the master of the house were stressed. But his wife was no mere cipher and shared with her husband in the material and spiritual care of those in their house, for all of whom they regarded themselves as accountable to God. In discharging these responsibilities and ordering their own lives day by day, great importance was attached to Sabbath observance, and biographies give a picture of the way that the Lord's Day was spent in many households.

Preparation for it took place regularly on Saturday evenings, when men and women examined themselves and their conduct

during the past week. Indeed, the whole of the day before taking
the Lord's Supper was often set apart for prayer, fasting, and self-
examination. On the morning of the Lord's Day many were up at
least as early as on weekdays for further preparation before going
to church, and the joy with which such people looked forward to
the day is noteworthy. Heads of families were not only strict in their
own attendance at public worship, but made it their duty to ensure
their household's presence too, and the following account describes a Cheshire squire, in the late sixteenth century, on his way
to church. Setting out on foot, we read that he called "all his family about him, leaving neither cook nor butler behind him, nor any
of his servants but two or three to make the doors and tend the
house. And taking then his tenants and neighbours, as they lay in
the way, along with him, he marched on with a joyful and cheerful
heart, as a leader of the Lord's host toward the house of God."

After public worship in the morning the exact procedure for
the rest of the day might vary between households, but in all the
whole day was observed as to the Lord and heads of families instructed their children and servants. It was their invariable custom
either to repeat the sermon from the notes they had taken, and
which they also used for private meditation, or to require each
member of the household to give an account of what he or she remembered. In this respect, the method of John Rowe, a Devon-
shire man, is typical. It is said of him that "as soon as dinner was
ended he would repeat the sermon to his family: after that was
done, the times of public worship in the afternoon drew on, then
he would hasten to the congregation. When public worship was
ended, he would first spend a considerable time in secret, then in
the repetition of the sermon that was preached in the afternoon
and calling his family to an account of the things they had learnt."
Psalms were often sung after supper, while in certain households
the mistresses examined and prayed with their maids before finally the Lord's Day ended with men and women resorting to further private prayer when they retired for the night.

From the Lord's Day we come to the ways the Puritans led
their ordinary day to day lives. There were, however, certain days
on which particular events took place. People are described as

travelling miles to attend weekly lectures, which were commonly preached on market days in the various centres. Days of thanksgiving and fast days were also held, when services went on "with great strictness and solemnity from eight in the morning till four in the evening." And at home, too, blessings were marked by days given up by the entire household to thanksgiving, while not only were family fast days observed, but men and women kept private fasts either at stated intervals or for some specific reason, as when a diarist records, "being under the rebukes of God's chastising providence, I set apart a day to humble my soul with fasting and prayer, that I might obtain from God a sanctified use of my afflictions."

But important as were these fast days and days of thanksgiving in the lives of the Puritans, they were additional to the ordinary daily routine of their homes which will be summarised here under three headings.

First: Family worship. This was regarded as a vital daily duty by people of all ranks in society and took place morning and evening, everyone in the house being required to attend. In the morning it was held before worldly business crowded in and, except in households of the Puritan nobility where there was a chaplain, the head of the family conducted it himself. After opening with prayer (and on account of the weakness of servants and children Paul Baines advised heads of households not to pray for more than a quarter of an hour at a time), there followed Bible readings often accompanied by brief comments on the passage which had been carefully prepared from sermon notes or books. The singing of a psalm was also frequently included in morning worship, and Philip Henry declared, "Those do well that pray morning and evening in their families, those do better that pray and read the Scriptures, but those do best that pray and read and sing the psalms."

When evening came the whole household, with any visitors present, assembled again. The form of worship was sometimes identical with that in the morning, but frequently more time was given in the evening to exposition of the Scriptures and possibly to questioning members of the household as to what had been read that night or during the preceding week.

Second: The conduct of Puritan households during the rest of the day, and the further care given by masters and mistresses to the religious instruction of their servants.

Although no longer specifically engaged in an act of worship, biographies reveal the Puritans endeavouring throughout the course of the day, by example and exhortation, to live and conduct their households as in the sight of God.

In their own personal lives the discipline to which reference has already been made is seen being worked out, and a young woman in her early twenties is described as ordering "her soul first, and then all other things were set in the exactest order . . . She had digested her hours into methods for affairs, repasts, reading of books." Idleness, vain conversations, and unnecessary visits were all avoided, and when in company with Christians, people took seriously their duty of edifying and exhorting one another. Meal-times also provided occasions for spiritual discourse and instruction in Puritan homes. But heads of families were at the same time mindful of setting an example by the very way they ate, and among a list of questions for daily self-examination, the following occur: "Did I eat, drink, for the glory of God? Did not I mock with God when I pretended to crave a blessing and return thanks?"

In some households the servants had a portion of Scripture or of a religious treatise read aloud to them after every meal, and during the rest of the day mistresses—including those among the aristocracy—took every opportunity of examining and talking with their maids on spiritual subjects, and possibly of reading books aloud to them. Added to this, once or twice a week the servants were catechised together in the evenings by the head of the house who regarded this as a necessary duty to be strictly carried out, while also on occasions taking them apart to question them separately about their souls.

In these ways, therefore, accounts of the Puritans show what they regarded as their responsibility in the spiritual care of their servants, and how in fact they tried to fulfil it. But no picture of daily life in their households would be complete with reference at least to our third heading, namely:

The importance attached by husbands to the spiritual care of their wives, and that of parents for the instruction of their children.
Most biographies dwell upon the wife's recognition of her husband's authority and her duty of submission to him, but at the same time the husband's responsibility for looking after her spiritually as well as materially is made clear.

With regard to their children, parents took secular education seriously but their first concern was to bring up children in a knowledge of the truth. In so doing, they recognised the importance of example as well as instruction, and while exercising firmness many fathers ruled their families with love. Of Samuel Fairclough it was said that "as a father he maintained his authority, and as a good father he did exercise great clemency," and Fairclough was not alone in this.

Parents began teaching their children from the word of God when they were still very young and were concerned to do so in such a way as, like Philip Henry, "to bring them to understand and love it." The children were also taught strictly to observe public and family worship, and were catechised regularly with the servants. As they grew up and left home, too, their parents sent them letters of spiritual advice, and among such we find a Puritan mother writing to her undergraduate son in terms which not only show her concern for him but also something of her own spiritual life, as she says, "In some proportion it is, with the soul, as with the body, there must be a good diet, we must feed upon the Word of God, which when we have done we must not let it lie idle, but we must be diligent in exercising of what we know, and the more we practise, the more we shall know. Dear Ned, let nothing hinder you from performing constant private duties of praying and reading. Experimentally, I may say that private prayer is one of the best means to keep the heart close with God . . . it is a sweet thing to open our hearts to God. . . ."

Thus, by example and instruction, the Puritans brought up

their children and conducted the life of their households. But within this ordered round, they performed their own private duties and tried to keep their hearts in a spiritual frame throughout the day. Avoiding too much sleep, the nobility as well as those in humbler positions rose early, often between four and five o'clock. On waking it was their deliberate endeavour to set their thoughts on God, and the following description is typical of the importance men and women placed on the ordering of waking thoughts. "When he first waked," we read, "his constant care was to set his heart in order, and to fit it for holiness all the day after, offering the first fruits of the day and of his thoughts unto God."

As soon as men and women were up, they usually spent a time of private prayer which, united with Bible study and meditation, might last anything up to four hours before family worship took place. After that, definite periods were set apart during the day when people stopped their ordinary activities to pray by themselves, some doing so as often as seven times each day. Nor were these brief telegraphic prayers, and a mother writing directions for her children warned them "to set out a due proportion of time for the duty of prayer: a slightly, huddled prayer is a blind sacrifice . . ." Finally, on retiring to bed at night there followed further prayer.

A period was also set aside each day for private Bible reading with prayer, while women as well as men consulted commentaries and spent time regularly in reading expository works. Books were found helpful, too, in the duty of meditation which many performed daily, testifying to the great blessing they derived from disciplined thinking on great scriptural truths, and in advising people as to their subjects for meditation, Baxter declared, "Great Truths will do great works upon the heart. Meditation on great and weighty truths make great and weighty Christians."

Those truths to which people very often appear to have directed their thoughts were of God Himself and the person and work of the Lord Jesus Christ. But death was also a subject on which the Puritans meditated much, some doing so daily, and we find the Countess of Warwick noting in her diary that such thoughts "had this effect upon me, to make me in an extraordinary awakened frame, in which the things of another life were much realised to me, and did make very deep impressions upon me. And my soul did follow hard after God, for grace to serve Him better than ever yet I had done."

Apart from these set periods of prayer, meditation, and Bible study, the Puritans tried at all times to keep a close watch on their own spirits and actions, and every evening would give themselves to self-examination which, again, was regarded as a vital duty. "Go down into the secrets of your hearts, try and fear, fear and try," wrote one young man, and men and women made no mistake in imagining self-examination to be an easy task, or in under-estimating the deceitfulness of their own hearts. To help them in this duty, many kept diaries in which they inexorably recorded all their daily failings alongside God's mercies to them. From these diaries we see that, ever fearful lest they should be deceived into resting upon a false assurance, they periodically tried themselves by the Scriptures with regard to the very foundations of their faith and evidences of their state. In their nightly self-examination, too, men and women not only recalled every action of the day but, reaching down further, searched into the motives from which actions had sprung and questioned their feelings as to what they rested on. "I am jealous of myself," sighed one, "lest the fear of the rod do trouble me more than my grief for sin." And Owen Stockton, probing his heart for its motives, confessed, "When I have been disquieted by the actings of my sin, that which hath recovered me to my former peace, hath not been (that I could find) God speaking peace through the Blood of Christ, but rather from the intermission of temptation and the cessation of those sins."

But while accounts of the Puritans reveal them constantly to have been examining and disciplining themselves and their households, they also show that they were intensely and actively concerned in their daily lives on behalf of fellow Christians and unbelievers. This is seen first in their prayer life, when they are described as wrestling with God for the souls of others and spending whole days in prayer for the nation and church. But their concern did not stop with fervent prayer, and extended to practical care for other Christians. In particular they helped and supported ministers, but they also gave money to causes aiding Christians in distress both at home and abroad, while day by day they tried to seek out and help individuals who were in trouble, or who were sick and aged.

The Puritans we are considering did not preach unless called to the ministry, but a number were instrumental in bringing faithful ministries to their own, and other, neighbourhoods. Moreover, they were importunate in private conversations with unbelievers, and it would seem that urgent concern sometimes led them to accost strangers on the roads or in the fields and to talk with them of eternal issues. Nor did they neglect the material needs of others, and although fellow Christians were the first objects of their charity, both men and women regarded it as part of their Christian duty to give alms to the poor and to relieve want and suffering where they could. Indeed, their active concern for social conditions and for the public good reached out to affect many and varied spheres of the nation's life.

In tracing the daily lives of the Puritans, as they emerge from their biographies, we have therefore seen that while they attached great importance to public and family worship, to the ordering and instruction of their households and to their own private duties, yet active care for others and acts of charity also played a vital part in their conception of Christian living. In closing, it remains only to mention their spiritual experience as it is revealed through their writings.

It must be said at once that many knew doubts and conflicts, and all were well aware of the plague of their own hearts. But while disclosing heart-searchings, diaries, and letters also reveal deep soul-joys and longings after Christ, and the following short extracts from among the writings of men and women who were neither ministers nor leaders, speak for themselves:

First, a young man in his early twenties, John Janeway, could exclaim, "Oh, let our souls be overcome with the thoughts of this love of Christ . . . When shall it have its proper effect upon us, to make us to desire more earnestly to be like our beloved! . . . If we have at any time experienced the more lively and full incomes of this Spirit of Christ, how did it set the heart on fire! . . . Did we never experience what this meaneth? Then let the remembrance of the sweetness of it, renew it in us."

Second, a Mrs. Clarke, writing after the death of her youngest child, testified, "Though I lay long under the burden of that loss, yet in this time did the Lord sweetly manifest His special love to my soul, assuring me that He was my gracious and reconciled Father in Christ, whereby my love to Him was much increased and even inflamed, so that by His grace it wraught in me more diligence and carefulness to maintain and preserve these evidences of His love."

Third, in recording the mercies of God on his fiftieth birthday, Sir Edward Harley, wrote, "How precious are all thy thoughts of love unto me, O God! How great is the sum of them! . . . Oh Lord, I am the clay, be Thou my potter. Fashion this house of clay to be Thy temple. Make me a vessel of praise and service to Thy Majesty. Be not ashamed to be my God."

While deriving their assurance and evidences for their state from the written word of God, there was another assurance which men and women are described as knowing, as in the case of a certain alderman of Exeter of whom it was said, "God gave to him the testimony and seal of His Spirit and so assured him of his eternal love in Christ, and of his adoption and eternal happiness of heaven." People having this assurance urged others to seek it by prayer, diligent use of the means of grace, and by self-examination, while so far from making those to whom it had been given careless in their duties. John Rowe echoed the experience of others also when he observed, "This testimony doth always when it comes, raise the soul to more desires after more intimate union and communion with God, works more self-abhorrency and more care to please God and fear to displease Him and (in a word) drives me nearer to God, whereas false-flashes leave the soul loose."

Finally, there are instances of men and women being given extraordinary spiritual experiences in such measure that they could scarcely contain themselves for the glory and joy that was theirs, but could declare with the Cheshire squire, John Bruen, "They were so wonderful and unspeakable that whether I was in the body or out of the body, with Paul I cannot tell." Not infrequently such experiences are recorded of people on their deathbeds, and it was said of Dr. Samuel Winter that the night before he died he was given such a glimpse of the glory of heaven that although previously he had thought he had studied and knew as much of it as any man, he then "saw that all the divines on earth were but children in the knowledge of the great mystery of heavenly glory which the Lord that night had given him a clearer sight of than ever formerly he had."

Such accounts make it clear that there were men and women among the Puritans who were given deep experimental knowledge of the love of God in Christ. We have already seen they were people who walked with a sense of the majesty of God and the corruption of their own hearts, and that such knowledge made them stir themselves up to thankfulness to God in all circumstances. It may be that, as we look at them living by rule and disciplining their days as intensely as they did, the questions will occur, Were there tendencies in their way of living which provokes reaction and an opposite emphasis? And can this be traced in the history of the mid-seventeenth century? But if there were any such tendencies and if there were those who, as biographers point out, were guilty of formalism, yet the desire of the class of Puritans whose daily living we have traced, may undoubtedly be summed up by Joseph Alleine when, in speaking of his own daily rules, he declared, "I cannot say I have already attained, but this is that my heart is set to learn, that in all that I do, whether sacred or civil actions, still I may be doing but one work, driving on one design, that God may be pleased by me and glorified in me."

The chairman, summing up, pointed out that there is no justification whatever for the difference that undoubtedly exists between Puritan daily life and that of Christians today. We desire to have the Christian life made easy, and to take it easily, but only spurious Christianity comes easily; true godliness demands self-discipline, self-examination, and a serious single-mindedness, and is unattainable without them. The paper summons us to question ourselves as to our practice and to learn afresh to walk in the old paths.

Part 3

A Goodly Heritage

༂

1958

INTRODUCTION

J. I. Packer

This booklet contains shortened versions of the six papers read at the 1958 Conference of the Puritan and Reformed Studies Group of the Tyndale Fellowship for biblical Research. By way of introduction to them, something may here be said about the convictions which have brought this Group, with its annual "Puritan Conference," into being. The Group exists because its organisers believe that historic Reformed theology in general, and the teaching of the great Puritans in particular, does justice to certain neglected biblical truths and emphases which the church today urgently needs to re-learn. This is not, of course, to imply that Puritan expositions of Scripture are infallible and final, or that the Puritans always succeeded in balancing truth in exactly the right proportions; nor is it suggested (forsooth!) that the way to solve the problems which face Christians of the twentieth century is to teach them to walk and talk as if they were living in the seventeenth. What is meant is simply that the Puritans were strongest just where Protestants today are weakest, and their writings can give us more real help than those of any other body of Christian teachers, past or present, since the days of the apostles. This is a large claim, but it is not made irresponsibly. A moment's thought about the facts of the case will show its justification.

169

Consider the characteristic features of Puritan Christianity. The great Puritans were men of outstanding intellectual power and spiritual insight, in whom the mental habits fostered by sober scholarship were linked with a flaming zeal for God and a minute acquaintance with the human heart. All their work betrays this unique fusion of gifts and graces. They had a radically God-centred outlook. Their appreciation of God's sovereign majesty was profound; their reverence in handling His word was deep and sustained. They were patient, thorough, and methodical to the last degree in searching the Scriptures; hence their grasp of the various threads and linkages in the web of revealed truth was firm and clear. They understood the ways of God with men, the glory of Christ the Mediator, and the work of the Spirit in the believer and in the church, more richly, fully, and accurately, perhaps, than any since their day. And their knowledge was no mere theoretical orthodoxy. They sought to "reduce to practice" (their own phrase) all that God taught them. They yoked their consciences to His word, disciplining themselves to bring all activities under the scrutiny of Scripture, and to demand a theological, as distinct from a merely pragmatic, justification for everything that they did. They applied their understanding of the mind of God to every branch of life, seeing the church, the family, the state, the arts and sciences, the world of commerce and industry, no less than the devotions of the individual, as so many spheres in which God must be served and glorified. They saw life whole, because they saw its Creator as Lord of it all, every moment, every circumstance, every department; and this gave them a theological world-view, a God-centred ideology, a social, cultural, and ecclesiastical programme, the implications of which have not even yet been fully explored.

Nor is this all. Knowing God, the Puritans also knew man. They saw him as in origin a noble being, made in God's image, destined to rule God's earth, but now tragically brutified, as well as brutalized, by sin. They viewed sin in the light of God's law, lordship, and holiness, and so saw it in its threefold character, as transgression and guilt, as rebellion and usurpation, and as uncleanness, corruption, and inability for good. Seeing these things, and knowing as they did the ways and means whereby the Spirit brings sinners to faith and new life in Christ, and leads saints, on the one hand, to grow up into their Saviour's image, and, on the other, to learn by experience their own utter nothingness and entire dependence on grace, the Puritans became superb pastors. The depth and unction of their "practical and experimental" expositions in the pulpit was no more outstanding than was their skill in the study in applying spiritual physic to sick souls. By the light of Scripture, they mapped the often bewildering terrain of the life of faith and communion with God as thoroughly and to as large a scale as any evangelical theologians have ever done (see *Pilgrim's Progress* for a pictorial gazetteer to the whole), and their acuteness and wisdom in diagnosing spiritual malaise and setting out the appropriate biblical remedies could scarcely be surpassed. The Puritans remain the classic pastors and teachers of Protestantism, just as Whitefield and his friends stand unchallenged as its classic evangelists.

Now, our present point is that on every one of the subjects mentioned, modern evangelicalism urgently needs to learn what the Puritans have to teach. Other Christians of other ages have left us equally classical statements of biblical teaching on other matters, no doubt, and all sufficiently important in their place; but it is here, in the realm in which the Puritans stand supreme, that we most need help today. After nearly a century of bitter conflict and steadily declining influence, there are signs that the tide of evangelical fortunes is turning at last. Numbers of young people are joining evangelical communities, and a new interest in the old paths of evangelical theology has arisen, For this we thank God. But it appears that evangelical zeal today is not wholly according to knowledge. Our understanding of our own faith has become defective at point after point. This seems due partly to the pressure of prolonged controversy, which has had the effect of focusing attention on a few disputed doctrines (biblical inspiration, the atonement, etc.) to the virtual neglect of all others; partly to the jealousy with which we have maintained some questionable nineteenth-century emphases, under the mistaken impression that they formed a part of the authentic evangelical tradition. But, whatever the cause, the fact is undeniable. If we would see how far we have fallen, we have only to contrast the characteristic Puritan outlook with our own.

Comparisons are notoriously odious, and generalisations doubtless more so. However, the following broad statements, by and large, seem to be sufficiently warranted: (1) Whereas the Puritans demanded order, discipline, depth, and thoroughness in every department of the Christian life, the modern evangelical temper is rather one of casual haphazardness and restless impatience. We crave for stunts, novelties, and entertainments; we have lost our taste for solid study, humble self-examination, disciplined meditation, and unspectacular hard work in our callings and in our prayers. Our evangelicalism appears superficial, sophisticated, almost blasé—a sure sign that we have largely lost touch with spiritual reality, and are not in fact close to God. Nor is this surprising, in view of the second fundamental contrast which must be drawn. (2) Whereas the Puritan outlook had God and His glory as its unifying centre, and was in consequence a broad, balanced, biblically proportioned whole, its modern evangelical counterpart has a different centre. It revolves around the individual man, as if he were the real hub of the universe. (How Victorian! and how irreligious!) As a result, it is partial and lopsided at point after point. The fundamental falseness of our vaunted biblicism becomes apparent as again and again we are found putting asunder things which God has joined. Thus, we concern ourselves about the individual, but not about the church; about witnessing to men, but not about worshipping God; about the "devotional," "practical" significance of Scripture, but not about its doctrinal teaching (as if the former were not just the application of the latter!). And then we make a virtue of this ungodly one-sidedness, as if it were really a case of putting first things first! Then, in evangelising, we preach the gospel without the law, and faith without repentance; we highlight the gift of salvation, and gloss over the cost of discipleship. And then we wonder that so many who profess conversion fall away entirely, and that so many of those who remain prove shallow, stunted, unstable Christians! Or again, in teaching the Christian life, our habit is to depict it as a life of thrilling feelings rather than of working faith. We stress supernatural experiences at the expense of rational righteousness. And even in dealing with Christian experience we are one-sided, for we dwell continually on the themes of joy, peace, happiness, satisfaction, and rest of soul with no balancing reference to the divine discontent of Romans 7, the fight of faith of Psalm 73, or any of the burdens and strains which the responsibility of living as a child of God brings with it. Thus the spontaneous jollity of the carefree extravert comes to be equated with healthy Christian living, so that jolly extraverts in our churches are encouraged to become complacent hypocrites, while saintly souls of less sanguine temperament are driven almost to distraction because they find themselves unable to bubble over in the prescribed manner. Whereupon they consult their pastor, and he perhaps has no better remedy than to send them off to a psychiatrist!

It is tragically clear that modern evangelicalism needs help. Our thinking is man-centred where it should be God-centred. As a result we have misunderstood our own message; we have lost the balance of truth; pastorally and evangelistically, we have become clumsy and inept. We need to humble ourselves and face this. It is no answer to the above indictment to point to the specialised counseling techniques which we have developed in recent years for pastoral and evangelistic purposes, and of which we tend to be so inordinately proud. Spiritual life is fostered, not by techniques, but by truth, and techniques evolved in terms of a defective notion of the message to be conveyed and the goal to be aimed at cannot make us better pastors than we were before; they can only increase our efficiency at being bad ones. If our message and way of thinking are wrong, the only cure is for them to be corrected. It is here that the Puritans are so uniquely qualified to help us, and the purpose of the "Puritan Conference" is to avail ourselves of the help which they can give.

The interests of the Conference; therefore, are practical and constructive, not merely academic. We look on the Puritans as our fellow-Christians, now enabled to share with us, through the medium of their books, the good things which God gave them three centuries ago. We study their teaching on the topics which took first place in their own thoughts and writings—the doctrines of God, of man, of sin, of grace; of Christ, the covenant, and the Spirit; of the church, the sacraments, and the ministry; of the life of faith, the war with Satan, the pilgrim's progress from this world to the next. We study the history of their doings as a commentary upon their convictions. And the question which we ask is not simply the historical one: What did they do and teach? (though, of course, that is where we start); our questions are rather these: How far is their exposition of the Scriptures a right one? and What biblical principles does it yield for the guiding of our faith and life today? The second half of each session of the Conference is devoted to discussing the contents of the paper that has been read from the standpoint of these two questions.

Inevitably, the attempt to bring Puritan principles to bear on the present-day Christian situation involves polemics. But note why. These are not the negative, disinterested polemics of pure scholarship, which regard the exposure of inaccuracy as an end in itself, but the positive, pastoral polemics in which all who seek the edification of Christ's church are sooner or later involved: polemics, that is, whose purpose is to clear away the rubbish of error in order to make room for truth. Polemics of this kind arise in carrying through any teaching programme in the church, for theological error is the natural inhabitant of the fallen human minds to which God's truth is addressed. In this case, when we seek Puritan help for our correction and direction today, such polemics are quite unavoidable. Indeed, they become our duty; for if Puritan teaching challenges—as it does—things which modern evangelicalism takes for granted, or even views as signs of its own superior enlightenment, and Scripture is found to sustain the Puritan position, then, as an act of Christian duty and loyalty to God, we must say so, and make this fact known to those who are unaware of it. And if some react like querulous invalids, protesting that they are perfectly all right in their present routine and no new treatment can possibly do them any more good, that might well confirm the suspicion that they are in fact theological invalids, whose grousing should not be taken too seriously.

Again let it be said: The aim of the Conference is to make a constructive application of what is learned to our own situation. There is, indeed, nothing more contrary to the Puritan spirit than burking the issue of a positive contemporary application of divine truth. The purpose of such an application is not merely to find out what we should not do; that would be to encourage in ourselves the hyper-Calvinist mentality, which is perpetually discovering that, after all, it is sufficient, and most honouring to God, to do precisely nothing. Our purpose in considering the application is rather to make clear to ourselves what we should do; and if this involves a critique of some common practices, it is only in order that we may learn to eschew the doubtfully good and so set ourselves free for what is certainly better. In the 1958 Conference, for instance, Mr. Cook's paper led to a lively discussion of what is and is not needed in the way of theological training if ministers of the Puritan stamp are to be made today. Dr. Gruffydd's paper prompted a heavy barrage of criticism against Morgan Llwyd's eccentricities, but Llwyd's story was recognised to be a most instructive cautionary tale, warning against the perils of the mystical mentality. Why, it was asked, should men of vivid interior experiences find it so tempting to go outside Scripture and hitch their theological wagon to the speculative stars of mystical fancy, as Llwyd, and after him, William Law and Alexander Whyte, did by invoking the teaching of Boehme? Llwyd's history, it was suggested, indicates the answer. Having enjoyed what seemed to him so luminously God-given an experience, he fell into the trap of making the experience itself the subject and source of his subsequent teaching. Wishing to explain and preach his experience, and to see all things in the light of his experience—wishing, that is, to treat his own experience as the sum of divine revelation—he found the Bible insufficient (for the Bible relates everything to God Himself, and gives no help or encouragement to those who would idolise experiences and put them in God's place); therefore he turned elsewhere, and became captivated by Boehme, whom he rightly recognised as a kindred spirit, having the same aim as himself. The final verdict, however, must be that he was trying to do a fundamentally wrong thing; as so often and so easily happens, the gift had seduced him from the Giver. Mr. Mingard's paper, on the other hand, led to a discussion of principles for dealing with the modern "gospel hypocrite." Stress was laid on the dangers of "believism"; of letting kindheartedness lead to the real cruelty of giving immediate comfort and relief to convicted souls of whose change of heart there is still doubt; of cultivating a soothing "professional-pastor" manner, which helps folk to feel better though they are not better; of being too impatient to wait till the "law-work" of conviction is sufficiently done, not realising that by comforting too soon one makes hypocrites. One corollary drawn from this was that the kind of evangelistic mission which seeks to precipitate quick "decisions" is of questionable worth, for it is calculated to produce just this result. We quote these as typical specimens of the kind of discussions to which Conference papers give rise.

The Conference has become, through the blessing of God, a source of inspiration to hundreds during the nine years of its existence; and the mines of Puritan exposition are far from being worked out yet. It is our hope and prayer that this ministry will continue with equal fruitfulness for many years to come.

1

THE LIFE AND WORK
OF A MINISTER
ACCORDING TO THE PURITANS

Paul Cook

Introduction: Puritanism and the Ministry

Historically, Puritanism began as a clerical movement of religious reform, reacting against, among other things, a corrupt
ministry; and one of the ideals which united the members of the
Puritan brotherhood throughout the whole period from the
movement's emergence under Elizabeth to its suppression a century later was a common high view of the minister's calling. This
never varied, and it was this as much as anything which held them
together. Their faith was a dynamic Calvinism; they shared Paul's
passion for personal holiness and for the glory of Christ within
His church; and their constant and uniting purpose was to promote spiritual preaching and seek the reviving of the ministry.

I. The Office of a Minister

Puritan thought on this, as on all other religious matters, was consciously based on and controlled by the Bible. It is essential for a right appraisal of the Puritans to realise that, for all their often immense learning, they depended for their guidance wholly upon the infallible revelation of God's will recorded in the Scriptures.

(a) The Nature of the Office

From the time of Thomas Cartwright, who attacked Elizabethan episcopacy as being rooted in human traditions and needing reformation by Scripture, the Puritans devoted much thought to elucidating the ministerial office as the Bible depicts it. Thomas Goodwin, though an Independent, is fairly representative here. A minister or "pastor" (his usual word), is appointed to rule and teach Christ's flock. He must be set over one flock (local congregation) and one only. If he has more, he cannot fulfil his duties to them all; if, like a diocesan bishop, he has none, he is a mere figurehead, not really a pastor at all (see *Works*, 11:221–31). He is appointed by a special, supernatural "call," which originates from God and is sealed to him by the Holy Spirit through the agency of the local church. Owen insists that the ministerial office was not created by man, but instituted by Christ for the continuance of His church. Ministers therefore occupy their office by His authority and are responsible to Him for the flock which He has committed to their care. He, for His part, grants them special grace for their special tasks.

To be a minister is a solemn responsibility. The Puritans echo Paul—"Woe unto me if I preach not the gospel!" To be entrusted with the dispensing of the gospel is a solemn thing, for "men cannot hear and disobey it, but under an extraordinary curse" (Goodwin, 5:6). Yet, Goodwin tells us, the pastoral ministry "is the best calling in the world" (6:415). It carries a special reward: "a poor minister shall have a personal glory for his personal holiness as a Christian, and a super-added glory as a minister" (9:368).

(b) Qualifications for the Office

When Puritanism emerged, the clergy were ignorant, uncouth, undisciplined, and corrupt. Preaching before Elizabeth in 1570, Edward Dering described them thus: "blind guides and can not see . . . dumb dogs and will not bark . . . The Parson against the Vicar, the Vicar against the Parson, the Parish against both, and one against another, and all for the belly" *(Works,* p. 12). Dering expressed the general Puritan sentiment in pleading for a learned and godly ministry.

Some, over-reacting, thought that godliness without learning would be sufficient. William Dell, a left-wing Puritan of Commonwealth times, attacked the practice of "making universities the fountains of the ministry . . . For human learning hath its place and use among human things, but hath no place nor use in Christ's kingdom" *(Select Works,* p. 583, cf. p. 655). With this depreciation of ordinary education as part of a minister's training went in some quarters a corresponding depreciation of the preparing of sermons, as a violation of the liberty of the Spirit. The assumption was that the Spirit would supply the message to the preacher as he rose to speak, but that He could not or would not do this at any earlier stage. This was not, however, the general Puritan attitude. "Whereas some men are for preaching only extempore and without study," says Goodwin (9:378), "Paul bids Timothy meditate and study . . ." The Puritans believed that true and sound learning was a necessary part of a minister's equipment. They were in consequence great advocates of education; the importance of university education was stressed under the Commonwealth, and when they were excluded from the universities at the Restoration they founded their own academies— twenty by 1688, fifty by 1750. Learning, they insisted, is a gift from God, which, rightly used, helps to make a minister. They did not overvalue learning or give it a false prominence; they never forgot that without the Spirit's help no man could minister to any purpose. But "if we give to reason, memory, study, books, methods, forms, etc., but their proper place, in subordination to Christ and to His Spirit, they are so far from being quenchers of the Spirit, that they are necessary in their places, and such means as we must use, if ever we will expect the Spirit's help" (Baxter, *Works*, 5:567).

What gifts mark a man out as called to the ministry? Owen (in *The True Nature of a Gospel Church*) lists five: (1) Spiritual gifts— "knowledge, wisdom, understanding and utterance for prayer and preaching." (2) Compassion and love. (3) Watchfulness of the flock of Christ. (4) Zeal for the glory of God. (5) "Some degree of eminency above others" in Christian character and holiness of life.

II. The Personal Life of a Minister

Horrified by current abuses, the Puritans re-examined every aspect of ministerial life and work in the light of Scripture and formulated one of the loftiest conceptions of this subject ever held in the Christian church.

Consistency, they held, was vital. A minister's life must be of a piece with his faith, and must be exemplary to his flock. Baxter's *Reformed Pastor* develops this powerfully: "Take heed to yourselves, lest you live in those actual sins which you preach against in others; and lest you be guilty of that which you daily condemn." Commenting on Paul's "Take heed therefore unto yourselves" (Acts 20:28), Baxter insists that a minister must (1) see that the work of saving grace is thoroughly wrought in his own soul; (2) take care to keep his Christian graces in vigilant and lively exercise, preaching first to himself all that he intends to preach to others, and watching constantly over his heart; (3) take heed lest his example contradict his doctrine; (4) take heed that he is not lacking the qualifications needed for his work. The minister must be a ruthless realist in dealing with himself and fighting the inner battle of the spiritual life against the world, the flesh, and the devil. He must therefore examine himself regularly and thoroughly; every Christian must, but the minister particularly. It should be clearly understood that the Puritan insistence on self-examination was not a summons to morbid and moody introspection, but to a practical discipline of measuring oneself in the sight of God by the standard of God for the glory of God—in order that, knowing oneself better, one might oppose one's sins more realistically and effectively. Baxter gives eight reasons why ministers should examine themselves: "(1)You have heaven to win or lose yourselves . . . A holy calling will not save an unholy man . . . (2)You have sinful inclinations as well as others . . . (3)(Ministers) have greater temptations than most men . . . (4)The tempter will make his first and sharpest onset upon you. If you will be leaders against him, he will spare you no further than God restrains him . . . (5)Many eyes are upon you, and therefore there will be many to observe your falls . . . (6)Your sins are more aggravated than those of other men. They have more of hypocrisy in them, and are more detrimental to the cause of religion . . . (7)The honour of your Lord and Master, and of His holy truth, doth lie more on you than other men . . . (8)The souls of your hearers and the success of your labours, do very much depend upon your self-examination." The preaching of one who does not live as he preaches will be disregarded. All that a minister does is a kind of preaching.

Daily repentance and confession of daily sins, the natural outcome of daily self-examination, was a necessary discipline, the Puritans held, in any man's Christian life, more especially a minister's; for only thus is the fulness of the Spirit and assurance of salvation preserved. God would not much regard a lazy man who was so little concerned about his sins that he would not take the trouble to examine his life and confess them one by one. The diaries of Richard Rogers and Samuel Ward (published by M. M. Knappen, *Two Elizabethan Puritan Diaries)* were kept as aids to this daily discipline: the diarists "note and lament their lapses so that they will be ashamed to repeat them" (p. 3). Matthew Henry, we are told, regularly reviewed and confessed his failures and lost opportunities at the end of each day, using a pencil and paper to record them. These practices were typical, and the importance of this daily discipline of self-examination and confession in moulding the Puritan pastors' lives can hardly be exaggerated.

The Puritans laboured to subject all parts of their life to the will of God: "they proposed, that is, within the church and under the conditions of society around them, to try the experiment of living according to the self-imposed discipline which they derived from Paul, Augustine and John Calvin" (W. Hailer, *Rise of Puritanism*, p. 25). Simplicity and order were the marks of their daily routine. Doubtless it was no harder, as it was certainly no easier, for them to live lives thus disciplined in their day than it would be for us in ours.

The Puritans said much of the special temptations which ministers face. Their task is so onerous as to be literally killing: "The minister's work debilitates nature; like the candle, he wastes while he shines" (Gurnall, *The Christian in Complete Armour*, p. 791). The devil opposes him in the study and the pulpit, "disturbs him with passion and leavens his zeal into sourness and unmercifulness" (ibid.). Baxter mentions three peculiar sins always dogging ministers: pride of office, applause, and appearance; negligence of study and inadequate preparation; worldly temporising, so that one grows afraid to speak one's mind. Also, if he is faithful, the minister can expect abuse and slander from a wrathful world, which he must learn to bear meekly. Truly he needs his people's prayers!

The minister must be holy, humble, and reverent in his handling of holy things. "The . . . preacher that speaks as if he saw the face of God doth more affect my heart though with common words, than an unreverent man with the most exquisite preparations" (Baxter). He must learn to abhor and eschew all sins, even the smallest, for no sin is really small when it affronts a great God; and he must learn (indeed, if he walks with God he cannot but feel) a great compassionate sorrow for those who let unrepented sin come between themselves and God. " 'A minister,' saith Chrysostom, '. . . should be still lamenting his own sins and the sins of his people.' The office of a minister is the office of a mourner" (Thomas Adams, *Works*, 1:365).

Prayer was a constant activity with the Puritan pastor. "Pray often," said Bunyan, "for prayer is a shield to the soul, a sacrifice to God, and a scourge of Satan" *(Works,* 2:1297). Regular times were set apart for prayer, both in private and with the family.

The pastor's home radiated a simple godliness. His family life was ordered as an example to his people for good. Morning and evening prayers, conducted by the minister as head of the house, were the rule. The highest ambition of the minister, as of every Puritan parent, for his children was that they might adorn the doctrine of Christ with pure and humble lives.

III. The Work of a Minister

(a) Their Doctrine

What was the substance of the message which the Puritans declared and by which they lived? Generally, it was Calvinistic (though a few Puritans were not Calvinists—Milton and John Goodwin, for example—and some Calvinists were not Puritans: Whitgift, for instance, was a Calvinist). The Bible was their rule of faith; the centrality of God and His glory determined their approach to all things; and Paul's doctrine, especially as set out in Romans ("the quintessence and perfection of saving doctrine," Thomas Dr.axe, *Earnest of our Inheritance,* p. 1), was the essence of their gospel. God, sin, the law, election, salvation by grace through faith in Christ, and the life of the regenerate soul, were their staple themes. The minister's responsibility was held to include the defence of the gospel "against the craft of seducers from with-out, or the springing up of any bitter root of error among them-selves" (Owen, *True Nature of a Gospel Church,* p. 70); and therefore he has double need to study Scripture diligently and know the faith thoroughly.

(b) Their Preaching

In *The Faithful Shepherd,* Richard Bernard defines the preaching of God's word as "an open unfolding thereof by a public minister to the people's capacity, according to the analogy of faith, with words of exhortation applied to the conscience both to inform and reform, and where they be well, to confirm . . ." Preaching is solemn work, for the preacher speaks in God's name; one needs to prepare oneself by prayer and mount the pulpit with trembling. Said Daniel Cargill, the Covenanter, on the gallows ladder, "Lord knows I go up this ladder with less fear and perturbation than ever I entered a pulpit to preach."

184 ~ PAUL COOK

The Puritans preached solid doctrine, but they preached it in such a way as to be understood by the common man. Repudiating the fashion of pedantry and ostentation which governed most of the preaching of their day, they sought to be "plain and perspicuous," "spiritual," and "powerful." "Whereof comes it that there is so much preaching and so little learning? but because men preach high and delight to hear plausible novelities, to please the ear rather than the simple power of the word to please the heart" (Richard Greenham). The Puritans eschewed "plausible novelities" and sought only to be vehicles of the "simple power of the word," preaching central truths in a plain, serious, vivid, passionate, homely, yet dignified manner. They preached the law to drive men out of themselves, the power of God in saving the helpless to give them hope, and the gospel to draw them to Christ. The law must be preached in its place, for "the field is not fit for the seed to be cast into it, till the plough hath broken it up! nor is the soul prepared to receive the mercy of the gospel, till broken with the terrors of the law" (Gurnall). Man must first be made miserable if he is to be made truly happy. In selecting subjects for sermons, pride of place must be given to those that are most basic, necessary, and practically relevant: "first, fundamental truths, or . . . catechism points, that contain truths necessary to be known and believed . . . Secondly, those truths are oft to be preached which ministers observe to be most undermined by Satan, or his instruments, in the judgments or lives of their people . . . and thirdly, truths of daily use and practice" (Gurnall). The Puritans favoured series of sermons, in order to facilitate large-scale systematic instruction.

Preaching demands much of the minister: he must know God's truth, and he must enjoy some personal experience of the power of it, for "a man preacheth that sermon only well unto others, which preacheth itself in his own soul" (Owen). But the godly minister, conscious of his unworthiness and limitations, may yet mount the pulpit in confident expectation, for "Christ and the minister go into the pulpit together; a greater than man is there; Master and servant are both at work" (Gurnall). What sustains the preacher is his hope that the Spirit's power may be upon him, guiding him and working through him; without such a hope, preaching would be a heart-breaking enterprise indeed, for "let us weave our nets never so close, a cunning wicked man will find holes to get out at, except the Holy Ghost comes down and stops all . . . The hearts of men are very deceitful and cunning, and ministers have need of a great deal of wisdom to search out all their windings and turnings; and this they never can do unless the wisdom of the Spirit of God assist them" (Goodwin). And to give the Spirit full liberty Bernard advises the preacher to be free from his manuscript if possible, and to be ready to alter the course of his sermon if circumstances demand it.

Preachers are tempted to moral cowardice more almost than to any sin. Too many ministers, says Bernard, are "men pleasers, not the servants of Christ. This is the cause why many weigh every word, as in a balance, for weight and turnable measure, for fine pronouncing, to delight the ear, more for a plaudite, than to convince conscience, or to remove impiety; they glance at sin sometimes but fair and far off, for fear of hitting." But the Puritans, because they feared God, were fearless of men's faces. A man who fears God, says Gurnall, will be bold "first, in asserting the truths of the gospel . . . and secondly, in reproving sin, and denouncing judgment against impertinent sinners." He adds that boldness must be robed in a wise, meek, and humble spirit, but there must be no compromise, for he that fears his people's faces is the man that is most likely to murder their souls."

The pulpit is no place for flippancy and jocularity, but for the most serious urgency. Baxter found himself "despising . . . wittiness (in the pulpit) as proud foolery which savoureth of levity, and tendeth to evaporate weighty truths and turn them all into fancies and keep them from the heart." The preacher, he maintained, should preach "as a dying man to dying men." With this all the Puritans would have agreed.

(c) Their Praying

Some Puritans used a set form for public prayer, some did not; but there was a general feeling among them that a set form, solely and invariably used, imposed an undue restraint on the minister and made it hard for him to relate public prayers to the changing needs of his congregation. Many Puritans, Baxter among them, agreed with Calvin that liturgical forms and free prayer might ideally be combined in the same service. In general, the Puritans were tolerant here. Gurnall is typical when he observes that no definite commands or prohibitions of extempore prayer are found in Scripture, and goes on to comment, "Alas! the evil is not in form, but formality." The Puritans all held that public prayer must in any case be comprehensible to the congregation (not offered inaudibly, therefore, or in Latin) and that the congregation should "testify by their hearty 'Amen' at the close" their willing association with the prayer that has been offered in their name.

(d) Their Study

The Puritans were great students, both of Scripture itself and of other subjects insofar as they believed these would help them to understand Scripture better. Their motive in study was not selfish intellectual gratification, but the glory of God and the service of their people. They demanded constantly that all ministers should be diligent and disciplined in study. "Remember this," says Cotton Mather, "there never was an eminent, who was not an industrious man." Mather perceptively warns ministers against being too taken up with contemporary writing and theological thought, for the ruminations of a single passing age—even our own—may reflect a general deficiency in some article of faith, and represent a real declension from what has gone before. All study of divine things is in any case vain and fruitless without illumination from above. "There must be Spirit in me as there is a Spirit in the Scripture, before I can see anything," says Richard Sibbes.

(e) Their Visitation

The Puritans left a lasting mark on the home life of Britain. Says Trevelyan, "It was only by the sustained personal efforts of Puritans in every part of the island, during the period when they were still within the official church, that family prayers and Bible reading became at all customary. These habits, which remained the staple of English education for generations . . . were being slowly established during the reigns of James and Charles I by the patient work of exhortation and instruction carried on by thousands of zealous men . . ." *(The Stuarts)*. The ministers produced this effect by being regularly in their people's homes. Their visits were not social formalities; they went to catechise and teach. Baxter's *Reformed Pastor*, which describes the system of visitation and catechising which Baxter himself had used with great success at Kidderminster (a system whereby he and his two assistants dealt with eight hundred families each year), did much to encourage work of this kind elsewhere.

(f) Their Counseling

"All Christians are bound to teach or help each other in charity, but Christian ministers are set in the Church to do it by office, and therefore must be qualified above others for it" (Baxter). The minister must have the biblical knowledge, diagnostic discernment, and prescriptive skill to act as physician to the souls of his people. "Ministers," says Thomas Adams, "are physicians under Christ, sent only with His physic in their hands, and taught to apply it to our necessities." The requisite understanding of spiritual health, malaise, and proper treatment can be obtained, says Owen, only "by diligent study of the Scriptures, meditation thereon, fervent prayer, experience of spiritual things, and temptations in their own souls, with a prudent observation of the manner of God's dealing with others and the ways of opposition to the work of His grace in them."

The Puritan approach to distressed souls may be briefly outlined. The pastor would consider first whether the person with whom he was dealing was truly converted, for he knew that there was much self-deception here. To decide this question, he would look for a sense of sin and love of God. If he found reason to doubt the person's conversion, he would deal with him as an unbeliever. If, however, he was satisfied on this score, he would then consider the possibility that the enquirer's distress was due to non-spiritual factors ("melancholy"). If it seemed genuinely spiritual, he would then seek its cause in either (1) an attack of Satan, or (2)unrealised or unconfessed sin, or (3)a God-given state of temporary spiritual desertion. On the basis of the axiom that all God's children are in His hands and under His care, the pastor would then try to help the enquirer understand his own condition and God's purpose in it, and teach him what his behaviour under it ought to be.

IV. Practical Results of a Puritan Ministry

The Puritans raised ministerial standards. Baxter pointed out the vital strategic importance of doing this in his *Reformed Pastor:* "If God would but reform the ministers and set them on their duties zealously and faithfully the people would certainly be reformed. All churches either rise or fall as the ministry doth rise or fall (not in riches and worldly grandeur but) in knowledge, zeal and ability for their work." Under God, a generation of Reformed pastors grew up in England during the Puritan ascendancy; it was a major tragedy that in 1662 so many of them were driven out of their livings and separated for ever from the congregations they had laboured to serve. But in the days when they were free to minister they accomplished much. Not merely did they re-establish the dignity of the ministry in the eyes of the people; they built up churches and influenced whole communities towards a more godly way of life. "This have I made good observation of," declared Samuel Ward of Ipswich, "that where God hath raised up zealous preachers, in such towns this serpent (Satan) hath no nestling, no stabling or denning." Preaching the truth in public and private in a homely, pointed, loving way, the Puritans wrought wonders. When Baxter first arrived in Kidderminster, for instance, he found "there was about one family in a street that worshipped God and called upon His name, and when I came away there were some streets where there was not past one family in the side of the street that did not so." During that time—under fifteen years—hundreds had been converted and the church had had to be enlarged to hold the crowds. And Baxter was only one among many. Is it not, then, reasonable to suppose that their theology, which produced so much true godliness, must have been in close accord with divine truth? And is it not worth our while to labour to re-think, re-state and re-apply this same scriptural teaching in our own day?

Selected Bibliography

(i.) *Historical:* G. R. Cragg, *From Puritanism to the Age of Reason; Puritanism in the Period of the Great Persecution;* W. Haller, *The Rise of Puritanism.*

(ii.) *Puritan:* Thomas Adams, *Works,* vol.1; Richard Baxter, *The Reformed Pastor;* Richard Bernard, *The Faithful Shepherd, The Shepherd's Practice;* Thomas Goodwin, *Works,* vols. 5, 6, 9, 11; William Gurnall, *The Christian in Complete Armour;* Cotton Mather, *Student and Pastor;* John Owen, *True Nature of a Gospel Church.*

2

THE PURITANS AS INTERPRETERS OF SCRIPTURE

J. I. Packer

We introduce our study by reproducing John Howe's account of an episode described to him by Dr. Thomas Goodwin. During his student days, said Howe, Goodwin, "having heard much of Mr. Rogers of Dedham" (an early Puritan Boanerges) "took a journey . . . to hear him preach on his lecture day . . . Mr. Rogers was . . . on the subject of . . . the Scriptures. And in that sermon he falls into an expostulation with the people about their neglect of the Bible; . . . he personates God to the people, telling them, 'Well, I have trusted you so long with my Bible; you have slighted it, it lies in such and such houses all covered with dust and cobwebs; you care not to listen to it. Do you use my Bible so? Well, you shall have my Bible no longer.' And he takes up the Bible from his cushion, and seemed as if he were going away with it and carrying it from them; but immediately turns again and personates the people to God, falls down on his knees, cries and pleads

191

most earnestly, 'Lord, whatever thou dost to us, take not thy Bible from us; kill our children, burn our houses, destroy our goods; only spare us thy Bible, only take not away thy Bible.' And then he personates God again to the people: 'Say you so? Well, I will try you a while longer; and here is my Bible for you. I will see how you will use it, whether you will love it more . . . observe it more . . . practice it more, and live more according to it.' By these actions (as the doctor told me)he put all the congregation into so strange a posture that . . . the place was a mere Bochim, the people generally . . . deluged with their own tears; and he told me that he himself, when he got out . . . was fain to hang a quarter of an hour upon the neck of his horse weeping before he had power to mount; so strange an impression was there upon him, and generally upon the people, upon having been expostulated with for the neglect of the Bible" (Howe, *Works,* 1832, p. 1084).

This anecdote takes us to the very heart of Puritanism. The congregation's reaction shows that Rogers was touching their conscience at its most sensitive point. For Puritanism was, above all else, a Bible movement. To the Puritan the Bible was in truth the most precious possession that this world affords. His deepest conviction was that reverence for God means reverence for Scripture and serving God means obeying Scripture. To his mind, therefore, no greater insult could be offered to the Creator than to neglect His written word; and, conversely, there could be no truer act of homage to Him than to prize it and pore over it, and then to live out and give out its teaching. Intense veneration for Scripture, as the living word of the living God, and a devoted concern to know and do all that it prescribes, was Puritanism's hallmark.

Our present task is to study the principles and methods, and to assess the quality, of Puritan biblical interpretation. Source material, consisting of both hermeneutical directories and sermons, treatises and commentaries, is abundant. We may draw on these sources indiscriminately, for on all the matters we shall discuss we find the Puritans to be virtually unanimous.

Two presuppositions governed their approach to interpretation; six rules sum up their method.

(1) Presuppositions of Interpretation

The first presupposition concerns *the nature of Scripture.* To the Puritans, Scripture, as a whole and in all its parts, was the utterance of God: God's word set down in writing, His mind opened, and His thoughts declared for man's instruction. The content of Scripture is God's eternal truth, for the historical process which the Bible records and interprets is just the temporal outworking of God's eternal plan, formed before the world was. In this sense, "what our Scriptures have set down and written, is all but extracts and copies taken out of the Scriptures in God's heart, in which they were written from everlasting" (T. Goodwin, *Works,* 1861, 9:28). That which was delivered by such a multiplicity of human authors, of such different backgrounds and characters, in such a variety of styles and literary forms, should therefore be received and studied as the unified utterance of a single divine mind, a complete and coherent, though complex, revelation of the will and purpose of God. To the Puritan Bible student, it was God who had uttered the prophecies, recorded the histories, expounded the doctrines, declared the praises, written the visions, of which Scripture was made up; and he knew that Scripture must be read, not merely as words which God spoke long ago, in the actual inspiring of the biblical books, but as words which God continues to speak to every reader in every age. "Think in every line you read that God is speaking to you," says Thomas Watson *(Body of Divinity,* 1890, 1958, p. 25)—for in truth He is. What Scripture says, God is saying.

Just as God's mind is unfathomable, so there are illimitable depths in Scripture: "the stores of truth laid up in it are inexhaustible" (J. Owen, *Works,* ed. Russell, 1826, 3:477). It is always the case that, in the famous words ascribed to John Robinson, "the Lord hath more truth yet to break forth out of his holy word." As interpreters, we never reach the end of God's thoughts, and must not permit ourselves to imagine otherwise. "Never think you have knowledge enough; study the word more fully . . ." (Goodwin, 5:537). God safeguards our humility by keeping us "in continual dependence on him for teaching and revelations of himself out of the word, never in this world bringing any soul to the utmost of what is from the word to be made out and discovered" (Owen, 7:409). The Puritans often echo Augustine's remark that, just as there are shallows in Scripture where a lamb may wade, so there are depths in Scripture where an elephant may swim—depths which the most learned and godly have yet to plumb. All Christians, therefore, should approach their study of Scripture knowing that they know but little, longing to learn more and looking to God Himself to open to them His own word.

This brings us to the second presupposition, which concerns *the subject matter of Scripture.* "What do the Scriptures principally teach?" is the third question of the Shorter Catechism, and the answer is: ". . . what man is to believe concerning God, and what duty God requires of man." Consider the implications of this answer. First, Scripture teaches us what to believe about God—that is, it sets before us spiritual truths concerning spiritual realities, truths beyond the grasp of fallen reason which only the Holy Spirit can enable us to discern. Therefore we must distrust ourselves, confess our natural inability and blindness in this realm, and invoke the aid of the Spirit to interpret Scripture to us. "It was the Spirit that wrote that word," says Goodwin, ". . . therefore . . . no man's or men's private understandings, without the aid of that public secretary of heaven, can understand them . . . he only hid the treasures of knowledge in that field, and he only knows where they lie; what an advantage is it then by prayer to unlock God's breast, obtain the key of knowledge that unlocks God's study, and can direct to all his notes and his papers!" (4:302). Less quaintly, but more categorically, Owen makes the same point: "I suppose . . . this may be fixed on as a common principle of Christianity; namely, that constant and fervent prayer for the divine assistance of the Holy Spirit, is such an indispensable means for the attaining the knowledge of the mind of God in the Scripture, as that without it all others will not be available (will not avail)" (3:474). "Before and after you read the Scripture," says Baxter, "pray earnestly that the Spirit which did indite it, may expound it to you, and lead you into the truth" *(Works,* ed. Orme, 1830, 4:265).

Also, Scripture teaches us our duty. Its instruction is for practice. It must be studied, therefore, for the purpose of setting our lives in order. And God will only prosper our study if we continually exercise ourselves to live by what we learn. Then our knowledge will deepen and expand; but otherwise it will run out into sterile verbiage and mental error. "The true notion of holy evangelical truths will not live, at least not flourish, where they are divided from a holy conversation," says Owen. As we learn all to practise, so we learn much by practice . . . "And herein alone can we come unto the assurance, that what we know and learn is indeed the truth. So our Saviour tells us, that 'if any man do the will of God, he shall know of the doctrine whether it be of God' (John 7: 17) . . . And hereby will they be led continually into farther degrees of knowledge. For the mind of man is capable of receiving continual supplies in the increase of light and knowledge whilst it is in this world, if so be they are improved unto their proper end in obedience unto God. But without this the mind will be quickly stuffed with notions, so that no streams can descend into it from the fountain of truth" (3:478).

He who would interpret Scripture aright, therefore, must be a man of a reverent, humble, prayerful, teachable, and obedient spirit; otherwise, however tightly his mind may be "stuffed with notions," he will never reach any understanding of spiritual realities.

We turn now to the Puritan approach to the task of interpretation itself. Their governing principles may be summarized under the following heads:

(i) Interpret Scripture Literally and Grammatically

The Reformers had insisted, against the Mediaeval depreciation of the "literal" sense of Scripture in favour of the various "spiritual" (allegorical) senses, that the literal—i.e., the grammatical, natural, intended—sense was the only sense that Scripture has, and that it was this sense that must be sought in exposition through careful attention to the context and grammar of each statement. The Puritans fully agreed. "If you would understand the true sense . . . of a controverted Scripture, then look

196 ∾ J. I. PACKER

well into the coherence, the scope and the context thereof" (W. Bridge, *Works*, 1845, 1:454). "There is no other sense in it (Scripture) than what is contained in the words whereof materially it doth consist . . . In the interpretation of the mind of anyone, it is necessary that the words he speaks or writes be rightly understood; and this we cannot do immediately unless we understand the language wherein he speaks, as also the idiom of that language, with the common use of and intention of its phraseology and expressions . . . And what perplexities, mistakes and errors, the ignorance of the original languages hath cast many expositors into . . . especially among those who pertinaciously adhere unto one translation . . . might be manifested by instances . . . without number" (Owen, 3:489).

Of course, there might be places in Scripture where the literal sense was itself allegorical. The Puritans all regarded the Song of Solomon as a case in point, and James Durham has some interesting remarks on the subject. "I grant it hath a literal meaning; but I say, that literal meaning is not . . . that which first looketh out, as in historical Scriptures . . . ; but that which is spiritually . . . meant by these allegorical and figurative speeches, is the literal meaning of this Song . . . for a literal sense (as it is defined by Rivet out of the school-men) is that which floweth from such a place of Scripture, as intended by the Spirit in the words, whether properly or figuratively used, and is to be gathered from the whole complex of expressions together . . . as in the exposition of parables, allegories and figurative Scriptures is clear." But, Durham notes, this is quite different from the illegitimate allegorizing of which the Mediaevals were guilty; for "there is a great difference between an allegorical exposition of Scripture and an exposition of allegorical Scripture" (*Exposition of the Song*, 1840 ed., p. 28). Durham expounds allegorically only when he has reason to think that it is an allegory that he is expounding.

(ii) Interpret Scripture Consistently and Harmonistically

If Scripture is God's word, the expression of a single divine mind, all that it says must be true, and there can be no real contradiction between part and part. To harp on apparent contradictions, therefore, says Bridge, shows real irreverence.

"You know how it was with Moses," Bridge continues, "when he saw two men fighting, one an Egyptian, and another an Israelite, he killed the Egyptian; but when he saw two Hebrews fighting, now, saith he, I will go and reconcile them, for they are brethren; why so, but because he was a good man, and gracious? So also it is with a gracious heart; when he sees the Scripture fighting with an Egyptian, an heathen author, or apocryphal, he comes and kills the heathen . . . the Egyptian, or the apocrypha; but when he sees two Scriptures at variance (in view, though in truth not), Oh, saith he, these are brethren, and they may be reconciled, I will labour all I can to reconcile them; but when a man shall take every advantage of seeming difference in Scripture, to say, Do ye see what contradictions there are in this book, and not labour to reconcile them; what doth this argue but that the corruption of a man's nature is boiled up to an unknown malice against the word of the Lord; take heed therefore of that" (1:459). It is a striking thought and an acute diagnosis.

Since Scripture is the unified expression of a single divine mind, it follows that "the infallible rule of interpretation of Scripture is the Scripture itself, and therefore, when there is a question about the true and full sense of any Scripture . . . it must be searched and known by other places that speak more clearly" (*Westminster Confession,* 1.9). Two principles derive from this. (i) What is obscure must be interpreted by the light of what is plain. "The rule in this case," says Owen, "is that we affix no sense unto any obscure or difficult passage of Scripture but what is . . . consonant unto other expressions and plain texts. For men to raise peculiar senses from such places, not confirmed elsewhere, is a dangerous curiosity" (3:468). (ii) Peripheral ambiguities must be interpreted in harmony with fundamental certainties. No exposition of any text, therefore, is right which does not "agree with the principles of Religion, the points of Catechism set down in the Creed, the Lord's Prayer, the Ten Commandments, and the doctrine of Sacraments" (R. Barnard, *The Faithful Shepherd,* 1607, p. 28). These two principles together comprised the rule of interpretation commonly termed "the analogy of faith," a phrase borrowed—probably not in the apostle's sense—from Romans 7:6.

Both the foregoing rules concern the form of Scripture; the next four have to do with its matter and content.

(iii) Interpret Scripture Doctrinally and Theocentrically

Scripture is a doctrinal book: it teaches us about God and created things in their relation to him. Bridge brings this out in a passage where he develops James' image of Scripture as a looking-glass. "When ye look upon a looking-glass, ye see three things, the glass, yourself, and all the other things, persons, stools or pictures that are in the room. So in looking upon Scripture . . . ye see the truths that are therein contained concerning God and Christ. There is God seen especially, and Christ seen; there also you see yourself, and your own dirty face; there also you see the creatures that are in the room with you, and their emptiness . . ." (1:411). Also, Scripture teaches a theocentric standpoint: whereas fallen man sees himself as the centre of the universe, the Bible shows us God as central, and depicts all creatures, man included, in their proper perspective—as existing through God, and for God. One of the points at which the Puritans can help us most is in the recovery of this God-centred standpoint of Scripture, which they themselves grasped so firmly.

(iv) Interpret Scripture Christologically and Evangelically

Christ is the subject matter of Scripture: all was written to bear witness to Him. He is "the sum of the whole Bible, prophesied, typified, prefigured, exhibited, demonstrated, to be found in every leaf, almost in every line, the Scriptures being but as it were the swaddling bands of the child Jesus" (T. Adams, *Works*, 1862, 3:224). Therefore, "Keep still Jesus Christ in your eye, in the perusal of the Scriptures, as the end, scope and substance thereof: what are the whole Scriptures, but as it were the spiritual swaddling clothes of the holy child Jesus? 1. Christ is the truth and substance of all the types and shadows. 2. Christ is the substance and matter of the Covenant of Grace, and all administrations thereof; under the Old Testament Christ is veiled, under the New Covenant revealed. 3. Christ is the centre and meeting place of all the promises; for in him the promises of God are yea and Amen. 4. Christ is the thing signified, sealed and exhibited in the Sacraments of the Old and New Testament. 5. Scripture genealogies use to lead us on to the true line of Christ. 6. Scripture chronologies are to discover to us the times and seasons of Christ. 7. Scripture-laws are our schoolmasters to bring us to Christ, the moral by correcting, the ceremonial by directing. 8. Scripture-gospel is Christ's light, whereby we hear and follow him; Christ's cords of love, whereby we are drawn into sweet union and communion with him; yea it is the very power of God unto salvation unto all them that believe in Christ Jesus; and therefore think of Christ as the very substance, marrow, soul and scope of the whole Scriptures" (Isaac Ambrose, *Works,* 1701, p. 201). How richly the Puritans applied this evangelical principle of exegesis can only be appreciated by those who dig into the expository writings of such authors as Owen, Goodwin, and Sibbes.

(v) Interpret Scripture Experimentally and Practically

The Bible is, from one standpoint, a book of spiritual experience, and the Puritans explored this dimension of it with unrivalled depth and insight. *Pilgrim's Progress* serves as a kind of pictorial index to the themes which they handled under this head—faith, doubt, temptation, despair, fear, hope, the fight with sin, the attacks of Satan, the peaks of spiritual joy, the dry wastes of spiritual desertion. Equally the Bible is a practical book, addressing man in a concrete situation—as he stands before God, guilty, vile, helpless—and telling him in that situation what he must believe and do for his soul's health; and the Puritans recognised that this practical orientation must be retained in exposition. Doctrines must be taught from the standpoint from which, and applied for the purpose for which, Scripture itself presents them. Owen makes this point as he embarks on his analysis of the doctrine of justification. "It is the practical direction of the consciences of men, in their application unto God by Jesus Christ, for deliverance from the curse due unto the apostate state, and peace with him . . . that is alone to be designed in the handling of this doctrine . . . And whereas we cannot either safely or usefully treat of this doctrine, but with respect unto the same ends for which it is declared, and whereunto it is applied, in the Scripture, we should not . . . be turned aside from attending unto this case and its resolution, in all our discourses on this subject. For it is the direction, satisfaction, and peace of the consciences of men, and not the curiosity of notions or subtlety of disputations, which it is our duty to design" (11.6.12). Neglect of this rule by many in the Puritan age led to much irresponsible, doctrinaire handling of Holy Scripture; but the great Puritan pastors consistently observe it, and their writings are in consequence "practical and experimental" (their own regular phrase) in the best and most edifying sense.

(vi) Interpret Scripture with a Faithful and Realistic Application

The application comes out of Scripture; the indicating of the "uses" of doctrine is therefore part of the work of expounding Scripture. Interpretation means making Scripture meaningful and relevant to those whom one addresses, and the work is not finished till the relevance of doctrine for their "reproof, correction, instruction in righteousness" (2 Tim. 3:16) has been shown. The standard "uses" (types of application) were: the use of information, whereby the point of doctrine under review was applied, and its implications drawn out, to mould men's judgments and outlook according to the mind of God; the use of exhortation, summoning them to action; the use of comfort, whereby the doctrine was shown to be the answer to doubts and uncertainties; the use of trial, of self-examination, a call to measure and assess one's own spiritual condition in the light of the doctrine set forth (the marks of a regenerate man, perhaps, or the nature of some Christian privilege or duty). The application must be realistic: the expositor must watch that the Bible is made to address men where they are. Yesterday's application may not speak to their condition today. "It is but a cheap zeal that declaimeth against antiquated errors, and things now out of use and practice. We are to consider what the present age needeth" (T. Manton, *Works,* 1871, 5:103). For an expositor to make a truly relevant, searching, edifying application of Scripture (as distinct from a clumsy, inappropriate, confusing one) is, no doubt, "a work of great difficulty to himself, requiring much prudence, zeal and meditation, and to the natural and corrupt man will be very unpleasant" (which consideration will sorely tempt God's messenger to pull his punches, for no normal man likes causing offence); "yet he is to endeavour to perform it in such a manner, that his auditors may feel the word of God to be quick and powerful, and a discerner of the thoughts and intents of the heart; and that, if any unbeliever or ignorant person be present, he may have the secrets of his heart made manifest, and give glory to God"*(Westminster Directory).* To apply Scripture realistically, one must know what is in men's heads as well as in their hearts, and the Puritans insisted that the would-be expositor needs to study people as well as the Bible.

Such were Puritan principles in the matter of biblical interpretation. To them, no discipline was so exacting, and no labour so rewarding. The soundness of their method is unquestionable; we shall do well to follow in their footsteps. That will mean asking six questions of each passage or text that we seek to expound:

(1) What do these words actually mean?
(2) What light do other Scriptures throw on this text? Where and how does it fit into the total biblical revelation?
(3) What truths does it teach about God, and about man in relation to God?
(4) How are these truths related to the saving work of Christ, and what light does the gospel of Christ throw upon them?
(5) What experiences do these truths delineate, or explain, or seek to create or cure? For what practical purpose do they stand in Scripture?
(6) How do they apply to myself and others in our own actual situation? To what present human condition do they speak, and what are they telling us to believe and do?

3

WILLIAM GUTHRIE ON THE TRIAL OF A SAVING INTEREST IN CHRIST

D. Mingard

"Since there are so many people living under the ordinances, pretending, without ground, to a special interest in Christ . . . And since many who have good ground of claim to Christ, are not established in the confidence of His favour, but remain in the dark, without comfort, hesitating concerning the reality of godliness in themselves, and speaking little in commendation of religion to others . . . I shall speak a little respecting two things of the greatest concern. The one is, How a person may know if he doth lay just claim to God's favour and salvation. The other is, In case a person fall short of assurance in this trial, what course he should take. . . ."

So opens Guthrie's little classic, *The Christian's Great Interest*— a book which Chalmers once called "the best book I ever read." John Owen said of Guthrie, "That author I take to have been one of the greatest divines that ever wrote"; and of his book, "I have written several folios, but there is more divinity in it than in them all." John Macleod *(Scottish Theology,* p. 91) affirms, "He (Guthrie) is remarkable for the soundness of his judgment, and the tenderness with which he deals with Christian experience . . . If we except *The Fourfold state* of Thomas Boston, we are safe in saying that no work of divinity in Scotland has had a wider circulation or has exercised a better influence than this one from William Guthrie's pen."

What relevance has this book for us today? Look again at the introduction. Guthrie addresses two groups of people. The first are hypocrites, who claim a saving relationship to Christ on insufficient grounds. Guthrie quotes Matthew 7:22; 25:11; and Luke 13:24 as picturing them. The second are regenerate persons lacking assurance. These are, perhaps, rare nowadays, being found, generally speaking, only where the gospel is preached in an unduly experimental way, or where the dangerous position of the hypocrite is overly stressed. But the first group seems very prevalent in evangelical churches, in consequence of the shallow believism, divorced from repentance and bolstered by a too-easy assurance, that has disfigured much modern evangelism. Guthrie can help us wisely to urge such people to examine the grounds of their assurance, for his address to them is a model of balance. He clearly shows how the true believer's experience differs from that of the conscientious hypocrite, while resisting the temptation to raise the minimum standard of experience necessary for making out a true interest higher than Scripture does. This is the theme of the first part of his book entitled, "The trial of a saving interest in Christ," to which we shall confine our attention in this paper.

Guthrie naturally maintains "that (for) a man (to) be savingly in covenant with God is a matter of the highest importance," and rebukes those who will not take pains to discover their true position. Quoting 2 Corinthians 13:5 and 2 Peter 1:10, he continues: "Be ashamed, you who spend so much time in reading of romances, in adorning your persons, in hawking and hunting, in consulting the law concerning your outward state in the world, and it may be in worse things than these . . . Be ashamed, you that spend so little time in search of this, whether ye be an heir of glory or not?

Whether you be in the way that leadeth to heaven . . . ? You who judge this below you, and unworthy of your pains . . . it is probable, in God's account, you have judged yourselves unworthy of everlasting life . . ." (Free Presbyterian Church of Scotland, 6th ed., p. 17).

But how can we tell whether a person has a valid title to life eternal? There are various characteristics peculiar to the children of God, says Guthrie; and he selects for consideration "two great and principal marks" from among these: justifying faith and personal renewal in holiness.

Before dealing with these, however, he pauses to discuss the *"law-work"* which, he says, "the Lord usually uses in preparing His own way in men's souls." Not all experience it. Some are called from the womb (as John the Baptist) or in early childhood (as Timothy). Others "are brought to Christ in a sovereign gospel way . . . by some few words of love . . . as . . . Zacchaeus, and others who, upon a word spoken by Christ, did leave all and follow Him: and we hear nothing of a law-work dealing with them before they close with Christ Jesus" (p. 26). All these, however, are deeply convicted of sin after coming to faith, as Zacchaeus' case shows. Others, again, are called on their deathbeds; but "there be few at all saved . . . and fewest saved this way." Ordinarily, however, a clear and discernible "law-work" of conviction and humiliation precedes faith.

This work may be violent, as in the case of Paul and the Philippian jailer "on whom Christ did break in at an instant, and fell on them as with fire and sword, and led them captive terribly" (p. 31). But, says Guthrie, "the Lord sometimes carries on this work more calmly, softly and gradually, protracting it so that the several steps of man's exercise under it are very discernible" (p. 33). He is convinced first of certain particular sins, then of more sins and of sin itself, and of his own unbelief and real ungodliness. He is now preoccupied with the quest for salvation. He is frightened of dying unsaved. He may be tormented with fear of having committed the unpardonable sin, and be tempted even to suicide; but God upholds him, "quietly and underhand supporting him; and this by infusing into his mind the possibility of his salvation" (p. 36). He seeks salvation by his own works (Romans 10:3); but hereupon "the Lord makes a new assault upon him," convincing him yet more thoroughly of the spirituality of the law, his own utter corruption, and the filthiness of his fancied righteousness. He withdraws from company to seek God; in self-abhorrence and despair, and grief for his past contempt of true Christians and abuse of the merciful long-suffering of God, he begins to pray. "Now," says Guthrie, "it is about the dawning of the day with the man" (p. 43).

Guthrie reaffirms that this preparatory "law-work" is not experienced by all, nor by all who do experience it to the same degree of intensity, or for an equally long period. "The main thing that we are to look unto in these legal awakenings . . . is, if the Lord reach those ends for which usually these stirrings and convictions are sent into the soul" (p. 48): namely, self-despair, fear of sin, a high valuation of Christ and the gospel, and a readiness patiently and thankfully to submit to His saving lordship. "If the Lord have driven thee out of thyself, and commended Christ to thy heart above all things, and made thee resolve in His strength to wage war with every known transgression, and thou art in some measure as a weaned child, acquiescing in what He doth unto thee . . . then thy conviction of sin and misery . . . is . . . sufficient" (p. 51). Evidently, however, it is no sufficient test of a profession of faith to enquire into the nature of the "law-work," if any, which preceded it; for a prolonged preliminary law-work is not a necessary condition of true faith.

Guthrie now turns to the first of his two "principal marks" of an interest in Christ, and explains what it is that constitutes *evidence of a believing state.*

Faith, he argues, is discernible in two ways: by the heart's closing with Christ in the gospel, and by the heart's satisfaction with God's plan of salvation through Christ. Faith is not a "difficult, mysterious thing, hardly attainable": "if men have but an appetite, they have it; for they are 'blessed that hunger after righteousness' (Matt. 5:6) . . . Is it a matter of such intricacy and insuperable difficulty, earnestly to LOOK to that exalted Saviour . . . (Isaiah 45:22): And to receive a thing that is offered, held forth, and declared to be mine, if I will but accept and take it, and in a manner 'open my mouth' and give way to it . . . (Psalms 81:10)?

Such a thing is faith" (p. 57)—a thing "more easy than men do imagine" (p. 55). Faith is a matter of the heart as well as of the understanding; of accepting Christ, as well as of acquiescing in the truth about him. It may be weak, but the weakest faith is saving, and may be known to exist: for "a man may clearly know, if from known distress in himself, upon the report and fame of Christ's fulness, his heart is pleased with God's device in the new covenant: if it goeth after Christ in that discovery and approveth Him as Lord of the life of men, terminating and resting there, and nowhere else, acquiescing in that contrivance with desire and complacency. This is a discernible thing . . ." (p. 69).

Guthrie now moves on to his second "principal mark," and shows what constitutes *evidence of a renewed state.*

A man in Christ is a "new creature" (2 Corinthians 5:17); he has put on the "new man," and consequently "is renewed in some measure every way" in the image of Christ (Colossians 3:10) (p. 75). His understanding is renewed, so that he recognises the gospel to be the wisdom of God, and discerns the reality of the things of God. His heart and affections are renewed; the law of God is written within him, so that he loves God and God's image in His saints, and hates sin and all that robs God of His glory. With this, "the very outward members of the man are renewed . . . the tongue, the eye, the ear, the hand, and the foot so that those members which once were abused . . . are now improved as weapons of righteousness unto holiness (Romans 6:19)" (p. 79). The proof of renewal appears

(i) in his *interests;* for now his supreme concern is to be found in Christ and to obey Him (Philippians 3:9);
(ii) in his *worship;* for now he seeks to worship "in the newness of the Spirit . . . doing and saying TRULY AND NOT FEIGNEDLY when he worshippeth," "and doth not much reckon that worship which is not so performed unto God" (p. 80);
(iii) in his *calling;* for now he does his work diligently, "as unto the Lord," and seeks to keep up some intercourse with God as he does it;

(iv) in his *relationships;* for now he becomes more dutiful as a
husband, father, brother, master, servant, neighbour;

(v) in his *use of lawful liberties;* for now "he studies to make use
of meat, drink, sleep, recreations, apparel, with an eye to
God, labouring not to come under the power of any lawful things . . . nor to give offence to others in the use of
these things . . . 'doing all to the glory of God'"(pp. 82f.).

Guthrie equates this renewal of life with the " 'holiness without which no man shall see the Lord' (Heb. 12:14)" (p. 83). For
proof that it is discernible in those who have it he quotes 1 John
2:3 and 3:19–21.

Guthrie outlines some limitations in the application of these
tests. We may not observe a high degree of every change listed,
but it is necessary that some measure of change appear throughout the whole man. He thinks it vital that there be "such a respect
unto God's known commands, that a man do not allow peaceably
any known iniquity to dwell in him" (p. 87). However, where, despite himself, and to his own displeasure and distress a man is
overcome by particular sins of infirmity, we must not thence conclude him unrenewed.

Such are the tests which Guthrie would apply for the making
out of a true interest in Christ. We turn now to what he says about
the hypocrite, who may to a certain extent have in himself a coun-
terfeit of all these marks: great stirrings of conscience about sin,
a sort of faith, and a real change in his manner of life. Guthrie
has much to say about the difference between the experience of
the hypocrite and of the true believer at each point.

(a) *The hypocrite's conviction.* Guthrie recognises the difficulty
of giving sure distinctions here; what follows the conviction is a
surer test of its character. But he mentions three things *rarely*
found in the stirrings of reprobates but *generally* found in the person who becomes a true believer.

(i) Hypocrites' convictions are usually either of a few gross
transgressions only (as Saul admits no more than persecuting
David, or Judas than betraying innocent blood), or else of sinful-

ness in general without any specific sins; but the law-work which has a gracious ending comprehends both (cf. 1 Timothy 1:13).

(ii) Hypocrites' convictions seldom reach the recognition of inner corruption, inability, and helplessness; so that they still "go about to establish their own righteousness" (Romans 10:13) by works.

(iii) Hypocrites' convictions are often put right out of mind by other matters (Cain goes and builds a city and no more is heard of his conviction; Felix waits till a more convenient time and we hear no more of his trembling). Or, if conviction grows, it produces utter despair of relief (thus Judas hanged himself).

(b) *The hypocrite's faith.* Hypocrites may reach a kind of faith; but

(i) They never abandon works, forsaking every other ground of confidence to close with Christ alone.

(ii) They never receive Christ "as anointed to be a King, to rule over a man in all things; a Priest to procure pardon and to make peace upon all occasions; a Prophet, to be wisdom, and a teacher and counsellor in all cases to man: so they do not receive Christ, especially in the first and third offices" (p. 12).

(iii) They are seldom prepared to accept all the inconveniences that result from following Christ, but shy back at certain points.

(c) *The hypocrite's reformation.* Hypocrites may appear changed men, having much knowledge (Hebrews 6:4), receiving the word with joy (Matthew 8:20), eschewing the practice of many sins and giving themselves to religious duties (like the Pharisees, Luke 18:11), and approving in some measure the things of God (John 7:46). They "may have a great deal of profession," talking of the law and the covenant (Psalms 50:16), confessing their sins (1 Samuel 26,21), humbling themselves (1 Kings 21:27), giving much, perhaps all of their goods to God and to the saints (Acts 5:2, 1 Corinthians 13:3), and submitting even to martyrdom (1 Corinthians 13:3). They may have great convictions, tremble at the word, and find peace and quiet in the hope of Christ's return

(Matthew 25:1); and they may enjoy striking experiences and "tastings of the good word of God" (Hebrews 6:4), the powers of the world to come, working powerfully on them, with some flashes of joy arising thence (p. 93). They may have something very like the saving graces of the Spirit—a kind of faith (Acts 8:13), great fear of God, like Balaam, a sort of hope (Job 13:13), some affection for the godly (Mark 6:26): indeed, "they have counterfeits of all saving graces" (p. 93). But, says Guthrie, invariably "they want the three great essentials of religion and true Christianity: (i) They are not broken in heart, and emptied of their own righteousness, so as to loathe themselves . . . (ii) They never took up Christ Jesus as the only treasure and jewel that can enrich and satisfy . . . (iii) They never in earnest close with Christ's whole yoke without exception . . . Therefore, whoever thou art, who can lay clear and just claim to these things, thou art beyond the reach of all atheists, hypocrites and reprobates, as having answered the great ends and intents of the law and gospel" (p. 97).

In concluding, may I venture to offer some application of this to the present situation?

Many in our churches have been encouraged to profess Christ after little, if any, preparatory law-work. Of these, some have come to know their sinfulness later; others, however, continue in danger of falling away when a crisis tests their faith and exposes its shallow character. But most of these people have no doubt about their salvation. They have been given some psychological assurance, based on a bare inference from such verses as John 1:12 and 5:24, told to mistrust their feelings and led to believe that all uncertainty about the validity of their "decision" shows lack of faith in God. Such persons have a stifling and deadening effect on the worship and witness of our churches, for they have no interest in anything truly spiritual, but take great delight in that which appeals to carnal nature, such as are many of the practices often regarded today as necessary aids to the preaching of the gospel. In this context, we need to reintroduce the scriptural teaching concerning hypocrites, and deliberately to eschew all methods tending to produce this kind of convert. The very withdrawal of such methods will help some hypocrites: it will make them realise how little true spirituality they really have. And, alongside this, we must preach with due seriousness the true nature of a saving interest in Christ. Some will be enlightened and come to true faith in Christ at last. Others will be grossly offended, and their reaction will reveal the rebellious nature of their unregenerate hearts. They will hark back to the "old-fashioned gospel," meaning the shallow evangel in which they were nurtured. They may leave to join another church, where they consider the minister more "loving" (because he does not preach hell) and more truly "evangelistic" (because he shows films, makes "appeals," etc.). But this sifting will transform the life of the local church. Believers, charged to "make their calling and election sure," will lay aside lethargy. Their appetite for spiritual things will grow now that they are denied the enervating palliative of carnal amusement. Having seen the fallacy of inferential assurance, they may now be led not only to an experimental discerning of their standing in grace, but further to that immediate sensible witness of the Spirit who assures sinners that they are children of God; to that "glorious divine manifestation of God into the soul, shedding abroad God's love in the heart . . . a thing better felt than spoken of . . . no audible voice, but . . . a ray of glory filling the soul with God" (p. 115). May God grant to us the joy of seeing many who now rest their salvation upon false hopes entering thus into "that honourable company of the first-born: that stately troop of kings and priests, whose glory it shall be to have washed their garments in the blood of that spotless Lamb, and whose happiness shall continually flourish in following Him whithersoever He goeth" (pp. 222f.).

4

DIVINE SOVEREIGNTY
IN THE THOUGHT OF
STEPHEN CHARNOCK

F. K. Drayson

"The Puritans," wrote Macaulay, "were men whose mind had derived a peculiar character from the daily contemplation of superior beings and eternal interests . . . . Not content with acknowledging, in general terms, an over-ruling providence, they habitually ascribed every event to the will of the great Being for whose power nothing was too vast, for whose inspection nothing was too minute." Of none was this more true than of Stephen Charnock. He may lack the monumental erudition of Owen, or the metaphysical brilliance of Howe, or the awful earnestness of Baxter, but nevertheless his writings are of the highest class, and Toplady wrote of his *Existence and Attributes of God*, "I have met with many treatises on the divine perfections; but with none which in any way equals that of Mr. Charnock. Perspicuity and

214 ∽ F. K. Drayson

depth; metaphysical sublimity and evangelical simplicity; immense learning and plain, but irrefragable reasoning; conspire to render that performance one of the most inestimable products that ever did honour to the sanctified judgment and genius of a human being."

Of Charnock's life little is known. Born in London in 1628, he graduated at Emmanuel College, Cambridge; obtained a fellowship at New College, Oxford, in 1650; and in 1656 moved to Ireland, where he was chaplain to the Governor, Henry Cromwell, the Protector's son. For fifteen years after the Restoration he lived in obscurity; then, in 1675, we find him again in a pastoral charge, sharing the pulpit of Crosby Hall, London, with Thomas Watson, the ejected minister of St. Stephen's, Walbrook, and author of A *Body of Divinity*. Charnock died in 1680, aged 52.

Almost all his works were published posthumously by his friends. *A Discourse on Divine Providence* appeared within a few months of his death in 1680, followed by his *Existence and Attributes* in 1682 and other works after a longer interval. The theme of divine sovereignty runs through them all. This study, however, will be confined mainly to what is contained in the *Discourse on Providence* and the *Existence and Attributes*—in the latter work, in the Discourses on God's Power and Dominion especially.

Charnock's teaching on this subject might well be summarised by quoting the Westminster Confession (3.1–2): "God from all eternity did, by the most wise and holy counsel of his own will, freely and unchangeably ordain whatsoever comes to pass; yet so, as thereby neither is God the author of sin, nor is violence offered to the will of the creatures, nor is the liberty or contingency of second causes taken away, but rather established. Although God knows whatsoever may or can come to pass upon all supposed conditions; yet hath he not decreed anything because he foresaw it as future, or as that which would come to pass under such conditions." It is noteworthy that this statement links God's sovereignty with His omnipresence and omniscience. Charnock does the same. "Let us have right notions of the omnipresence of God," he wrote *(Works*, 1864, 1:454). "Wheresoever we move, we are in God. As there is not a moment but we are under his mercy, so there is not a moment that we are out of his presence. Let us therefore look on nothing without thinking who stands by, without reflecting on him in whom it lives, moves and has its being." And he insists that God is all-knowing also. "No thought is hid, no lust is secret, but the eye of God beholds this, and that, and the other . . . We may exclude the sun from peeping into our solitudes, but not the eye of God from beholding our actions" (1:450). God knows the future as well as the present and past, and all things possible as well as all things actual; and this knowledge lies at the very root of His omnipotence, so that Charnock can say, "To deny God knowledge is to dash out the Scripture and demolish the Deity" (1:463).

This brings us to the subject of this paper proper—a subject which Charnock regarded as immensely important, for "the consideration of God as the supreme Lord is the foundation of all religion" (2:485). Again, "If God hath an extensive dominion over the whole world, this ought to be often meditated on, and acknowledged by us . . . We should bear a sense of this always upon our spirits, and be often in the thoughts of it in our retirements. We should fancy that we saw God upon his throne in his royal garb, and great attendants about him, and take a view of it, to imprint an awe on our spirits" (2:483).

Charnock analyses the notion of divine sovereignty into two strands: *power,* or *strength,* and *authority,* or *dominion.* These he distinguishes as follows: "We commonly mean by the power of God, the strength of God, whereby he is able to effect his purposes; by the authority of God, we mean the right he hath to act what he pleases. Omnipotence is his physical power, whereby he is able to do what he will; Dominion is his moral power, whereby it is lawful for him to do what he will" (2:407). Of the latter he writes, "There is a three-fold dominion of God: 1. Natural, which is absolute over all creatures, and is founded in the nature of God as creator. 2. Spiritual or gracious, which is a dominion over his church as redeemed, and (is) founded in the covenant of grace. 3. A glorious kingdom at the winding up of all, wherein he shall reign over all, either in the glory of his mercy, as over the glorified saints, or in the glory of his justice in the condemned devils and men" (2:407). Charnock develops the thought that God's dominion over His creation is founded upon His sovereignty as Creator. "The relation of an entire Creator induceth the relation of an absolute Lord; he that giveth being, life, motion, that is the sole cause of the being of a thing which was before nothing, that had nothing to concur with him, nothing to assist him, but by his sole power commands it to stand up into being, is the unquestionable lord and proprietor of that thing . . . And by this act of creation, which extended to all things, he became universal sovereign over all things" (2:411). As proprietor of His creation, it is His prerogative to make laws for His creatures. "God as a king enacts laws by his own proper authority, and his law is a declaration of his own sovereignty, and of man's moral subjection to him and dependence on him. His sovereignty doth not appear so much in his promises as in his precepts" (2:427). He has authority and power justly to punish those who transgress His laws, or alternatively to pass over in mercy offences against them; and both these activities are further declarations of His sovereignty.

God the Creator rules and governs all His creatures by His sovereign power. Of His rule over the inanimate and brute creation, Charnock writes, "It is one of his titles to be the preserver of beasts as well as men, Nehemiah 9:6. He is the great caterer for all creatures, Psalm 104:21. They attend on him for their daily portion, and what they gather and meet with in their pursuit is God's gift to them, v. 27, 28 . . . . He acts them by a commandment and imprinted law upon their natures . . . They observe their stations, the law God hath set them, as if they had a rational knowledge of their duty in their particular motions, Psalm 104:19. Sometimes he makes them instruments of his ministry to us, sometimes executioners of his judgments" (1:14). Things apparently fortuitous are all in reality ordained of God and directed by His wisdom. "Providence is the great clock, keeping time and order, not only hourly, but instantly, to its own honour" (1:17).

Naturally Charnock is most interested in the way in which God governs the affairs of men. Like all the Puritans, he believes that every thought and action of every man is with the concurrent knowledge and will of God. When a man sins, he does so by divine permission; God is able either to restrain his sin or to let him do the evil that is in his heart. Similarly, if a man does a right act, it is because God has moved him to do so. Thus every deed of man, and all his circumstances, are determined by the sovereign hand of God. This is true of all men, the ungodly and rebellious no less than the saints. "When the hearts of men are so numerous, their thoughts so various and different from one another, yet he hath a key to those millions of hearts, and with infinite power, guided by an infinite wisdom, he draws them into what channels he pleases for the gaining his own ends" (2:141). "God having a sovereignty over the will in the manner of its acting, causeth it to will what he wills, as to the outward act, and the outward manner of performing it" (2:451). "As a man manages a staff which is in his own power, so doth God manage wicked men for his own holy purposes, and they can go no further than God gives them licence. . . . How great is that power that curbs, bridles or changes as many headstrong horses at once and every minute, as there are sons of Adam on the earth!"(1:17). Charnock considers that some Scripture incidents, e.g., the events of the book of Esther (the one book of Scripture in which God's name is not even mentioned!), show God's sovereign overruling of wicked men so plainly that, even if Scripture did not declare it to be so, they could not reasonably be ascribed to anything but God's direct action.

Men's callings and stations in life are equally in God's hand: "If the hairs of every man's head fall under his sovereign care, the calling of every man, wherein he is to glorify God, and serve his generation . . . falls under his dominion . . . Though our callings are our work, yet they are by God's order, wherein we are to be faithful to our great master and ruler" (2:455). "His sovereignty is manifest in the bestowing much wealth and honour upon some, and not vouchsafing it to the more industrious labours and attempts of others. His right to dispose of the goods of every particular person is unquestionable. He doth no wrong to any man . . . if he gives or takes away, he meddles with nothing but what is his own more than ours" (2:447). And God rules the affairs of nations with the same absolute sovereignty as He does the private affairs of ordinary men: "All those changes in the face of the world, the revolutions of empires, the desolating and ravaging wars which are often immediately the birth of the vice, ambition and fury of princes, are the royal acts of God as governor of the world . . ." (2:451).

Consider now, against this background of God's rule over all nature, His redemptive sovereignty in grace. This sovereignty appears first in His forming and executing the plan of redemption in and through Christ. "The whole gospel," says Charnock, "is nothing else but a declaration of God's sovereign pleasure concerning Christ, and concerning us in him; it is therefore called the 'mystery of his will,' Ephesians 1:9; the will of God as distinct from the will of Christ, a purpose in himself, not moved thereunto by any; the whole design was framed in the deity, and (is) as much the purpose of his sovereign will as the contrivance of his immense wisdom" (2:457). Sovereignty appears in God's appointment of His Son to redeem: "as God was at liberty to create or not to create, so he was at liberty to redeem or not to redeem, and at liberty whether to appoint Christ to this work, or not . . . "(2:458). Sovereignty further appears throughout the Redeemer's earthly existence: in the circumstances of His birth, His life, the manner of His death, and most especially in His resurrection. We see it in the transference of our sins to His head. Moreover, "the sovereignty of God appears in exalting Christ to such a sovereign dignity . . . to obscure his own authority in a sense, and take into association with him, or vicarious subordination to him, the human nature of Christ as united to the divine, not only lifting it above the head of all the angels, but giving that person in our nature an empire over them, whose nature was more excellent than ours . . . The sovereignty of God is paramount in all that Christ has done as a priest, or shall do as a king" (2:460).

We see God's sovereignty also, Charnock tells us, in the content of the gospel—incarnation, atonement, mercy contrary to merit without violation of justice; all doctrines wholly contrary to the world's wisdom—and in the manner of its propagation. God sent out ignorant man to preach it, the weak of this world to confound the mighty in order to show that excellency of the power was of Himself. "They used no weapons but the doctrine they preached. . . . No less than a supernatural power could conduct them in their attempt, with such weak methods in human appearance" (2:156). "How great a testimony of God's power is it, that from so small a cloud should rise so glorious a sun, that should chase before it the darkness and power of hell, triumph over the idolatry, superstition and profaneness of the world" (2:158).

God's sovereignty appears further in the application of redemption to sinful men. This is a fruit of sovereign election, free and unconditional. "He hath set apart some from eternity, wherein he will display the invincible efficacy of his grace, and thereby infallibly bring them to the fruition of glory, Ephesians 1:4. Why doth he write some names in the book of life, and leave out others? . . . The apostle tells us, it is the pleasure of his will" (2:433). "It could not be any merit in the creature that might determine God to choose him" (2:434), for the creature had none; "nor could it be any foresight of works to be done in time by them, or of faith" (2:435), since both the latter were of his enabling. "Election is the cause of faith, and not faith the cause of election . . . men are not chosen because they believe, but they believe because they are chosen . . . Well, then, there is no possible way to lay the original foundation of this act of election and preterition in anything but the absolute sovereignty of God" (2:435). God's sovereignty is seen, too, in His dealings with Jews and Gentiles. His long-continued limitation of mercy to the Jews, "leaving the rest of the world as a barren wilderness, can be placed on no other account originally than that of the unaccountable sovereignty of his love to them." Through Israel's fall, the Gentiles were enriched, but again not through any merit, for if the Jews were bad, the Gentiles were worse, steeped in idolatry. "There is something of justice in the case of the Jews' rejection, nothing but sovereignty in the Gentiles' reception into the Church" (2:442).

The sinner's regeneration and conversion, in accordance with God's electing purpose, is equally an act of sovereignty. "It is resembled to the most magnificent act of divine power that God ever put forth, viz., that in the resurrection of our Saviour, Ephesians 1:19, wherein there was more than an ordinary impression of might" (2:159). Conversion is a divine act of extraordinary might, for, "there is in every natural man a stoutness of heart, a stiff-neck unwillingness to good, forwardness to evil. Infinite power quells this stoutness, demolisheth these strongholds . . . routs those armies of turbulent nature. To turn the floods of the sea is not such an act of power as to turn the tide of the heart." "As conversion is wrought against the inclinations of nature, so against a multitude of corrupt habits rooted in the souls of men . . . To dispossess man of his self-esteem and self-excellency, to make room for God in the heart where there was none but for sin, as dear to him as himself, to hurl down the pride of nature, to make stout imaginations stoop to the cross, to make desires of self-advancement sink under a zeal for the glorifying of God and an over-ruling design for his honour, is not to be ascribed to any but an outstretched arm wielding the sword of the Spirit" (2:161). Charnock describes the manner of conversion thus: "The power is so efficacious, that nothing can vanquish it, and so sweet, that none did ever complain of it. The almighty virtue displays itself invincibly, yet without constraint, compelling the will without offering violence to it . . . not forcing it, but changing it; not dragging it, but drawing it . . . "(2:162).

God's sovereignty appears also in His preservation of the regenerate in faith and grace. "As the providence of God is a manifestation of his power in a continued creation, so the preservation of grace is a manifestation of his power in a continued regeneration . . . God doth more magnify his power in continuing a believer in the world, a weak and half-rigged vessel in the midst of so many sands whereon it might be split, so many rocks whereon it might dash, so many corruptions within, and so many temptations without, than if he did immediately transport him into heaven . . ." (2:163). God exhibits His sovereignty by over-ruling all circumstances for His people's good, so that "that which in its own nature is an injury, by God's ordering puts on the nature of a mercy; and what is poison in itself, by the almighty art becomes a sovereign medicine" (1:71). Persecutions would naturally tend to the church's detriment, but God orders them otherwise, so that in the event "God's vine thrives the better for pruning" (1:78). Afflictions are used to teach a man to love, trust, and pray to God more; to despise the things of this world and set his heart on things above. Thus "they can no more be said to be evil than the fire which refines the gold, and prepares it for a prince's use" (1:36). Even a believer's lapses into sin are made a blessing to him: "God, by permitting the lapses of men, doth often make them despair of their own strength to subdue their enemies, and rely upon the strength of Christ, wherein God hath laid up power for us, and so become stronger in that strength which God hath ordained for them" (2:38).

So much for the positive aspects of Charnock's teaching. Let us now see how he answers five objections, raised then as now, against this doctrine of the absolute sovereignty of God.

The first is that it represents the rule of God as an arbitrary and unprincipled tyranny. Charnock replies by refusing to accept the separation of God's attributes which the objection assumes. "Since he is his own rule, and his nature is infinitely wise, holy and righteous, he cannot do a thing but what is unquestionably agreeable with wisdom, justice and purity" (2:418). Again, "you may as soon dash in pieces his throne, as separate his goodness from his sovereignty" (2:422). If his acts seem unwise or unjust, that is because in our finitude and dulness we have failed to fathom them, and missed their true rationale.

The second objection appeals to the unequal distribution of God's gifts to man: if this is sovereignly willed, is not the Sovereign unjust? Charnock's reply is an application of the principle just stated to this specific case. To judge God's providential action is presumptuously to question His wisdom, and to impugn His deity: may He not do what He will with His own? Also, the inequalities are less than might at first appear. Great possessions do not always bring great happiness, as the rich young ruler found. Nor is it all ill with the righteous under affliction; affliction, as we saw, may profit them, and the eternal blessings which God gives them far outweigh any temporary temporal advantages enjoyed by worldly men at present.

The third objection is stated as a question: "If God's providence orders all things . . . how will you free God from being the
author of sin?" In reply, Charnock reaffirms as axiomatic that
"God hath a hand about all the sinful actions in the world"
(1:25)—i.e., all human actions whatsoever, for none are sinless—
but insists that His permission of them as acts does not imply either His causing or His approving of them as sins. Of God's secret
will to allow sin to enter the world, he writes, "He doth not properly will it, but he wills not to hinder it, to which by his omnipotence he could put a bar" (2:222). Of sins themselves, he has this
to say: "God supports the faculties wherewith a man sinneth, and
supports a man in that act wherein he sinneth, but concurs not
to the sinfulness of that act." It is man's evil intention that makes
an act sinful, and for this man is responsible; God enables man to
do what his evil nature prompts him to do, but is not pleased with
it. "God wills the permission of sin. He doth not positively will sin,
but he positively wills to permit it. And though he doth not ap-
prove of sin, yet he approves of that act of his will whereby he permits it." "This act of permission," Charnock adds, "is not a mere
and naked permission, but such a one as is attended with a certainty of the event"—i.e., an act of foreordination: for "though
the will of God about sin was permissive, yet the will of God about
that glory he would promote by the defect of the creature was
positive . . . and therefore he did wisely and righteously order all
things to the accomplishment of his great and gracious purposes"
(2:223).

The fourth objection is as follows: If God concurs in the commission of every sin, and could if He so willed prevent it, and if
none can repent and believe unless He draw them, is He not unjust to punish for sin? No, says Charnock; for it is not God's permission of sin that causes sin, but the sinner's own corruption.
God never commands, inspires, or necessitates man to sin. The
most He does is to withdraw restraining grace from those who
first withdraw from Him. "Who will blame the physician for de-
serting the patient who rejects his counsel, will not follow his prescriptions, but dasheth his physic against the wall? No man will
blame him, no man will say that he is the cause of the patient's

death . . . And who can justly blame God in this case, who never yet denied supplies of grace to any that sincerely sought it at his hands?" (2:240).

The fifth objection is that the doctrine stultifies prayer. If all is predetermined by God from the beginning, what effect can our prayers have? Why pray at all? Charnock's answer is that the doctrine, so far from inhibiting prayer, should prompt it. "Let us learn to have adoring thoughts of, not murmuring fancies against, the sovereignty of God; to acknowledge it with thankfulness in what we have, to implore it with a holy submission in what we want. To own God as a sovereign in a way of dependence, is the way to be owned by him as subjects in a way of favour" (2:445). Prayer is an expression of desire, an acknowledgment of need, a profession of dependence, and a recognition that the remedy is of God's hand alone. God "is pleased with prayer, which is an acknowledgment of his dominion . . . for prayer, in the notion of it, imports this much: that God is the rector of the world, that he takes notice of human affairs, that he is a careful, just, wise governor, a storehouse of blessing, a fountain of goodness to the indigent, and a relief to the oppressed. What have we reason to fear, when the Sovereign of the world gives us liberty to approach to him, and lay open our case?" (2:482). And our prayers have a necessary place in the outworking of God's purposes: for "when God would do any mighty work in the world, he stirs up his people to pray for it; and their prayers by his own appointment have a mighty influence upon the government of the world" (1:92).

This brings us to the "uses"—practical applications—which Charnock draws from his exposition of the sovereignty of God. "This doctrine," he declares, "hath an influence upon our whole course; there is nothing we meet with but an act of providence, and there is no act of providence but calls for some particular duty. Is there any good we want? We must seek it at his hands, we must depend on him for it; we must prescribe no methods to him, but leave the conduct of it to his own wisdom. Is it a cross-providence, and contrary to our desires and expectations? Murmur not at it. Is it either good or bad, and present? We must study to understand it. Is it a good and present? Give God the glory of it" (1:54). The doctrine assures us that in affliction "our evils can never be so great to oppress us as his power is great to deliver us" (2:180); and that in temptation, "though Satan's power be great, yet God suffers him not to tempt as much as his diabolical appetite would . . . and the divine power tempers the other's malice and gives the creature victory" (2:140). Thus the doctrine affords firm ground for present confidence and future hope. God is able to perform all that He has promised. He who purposed from all eternity the salvation of the elect will not lose them now. "Our keeping is not in our own weak hands, but in the hands of him who is mighty to save" (2:181).

Above all, however, the sovereignty of God is a doctrine to humble us, to give us a true view of the divine majesty and of our own nothingness, to teach us awe and reverence. "The greatness of God claims an awful and inviolable respect from his creatures, in what way soever he doth dispose of them" (2:499). Reverence before God was the heart of the Puritan temper, and it is this, more than anything, that imparts to Puritan writings, Charnock's as much as any, their peculiar nobility and unction. It is in such matters as this that the Puritans have most to teach us; may God enable us to learn from them, to our profit and to His glory.

5

RICHARD BAXTER'S SOCIAL AND ECONOMIC TEACHING

D. R. Wooldridge

I. Baxter as a Teacher

Richard Baxter was born in 1615 and converted at 14. For over 13 years he ministered to a very large congregation at Kidderminster, and under God altered the whole character of the town before being ejected in 1662, along with some 2,000 other Puritan clergy, for refusing to conform. Thenceforth he lived in and around London, preaching occasionally and writing voluminously, till his death in 1691. The following summary of his social and economic teaching is drawn from a series of extremely practical discussions of these matters, notably in his *magnum opus, A Christian Directory*.

We begin by glancing briefly at Baxter's approach to the Christian life, for his emphases here are basic to his specifically economic teaching.

(a) *The beginning of the Christian life.* This must be by conversion: the unbeliever must give himself completely and unconditionally to the Lord and turn at every point from his past wickedness. Baxter urges this repeatedly. "Deliver up yourselves to the Lord Jesus, as the Physician of your Souls, that he may pardon you by his Blood, and sanctifie you by his Spirit . . . Do it speedily without delay . . . Do it unreservedly, absolutely and universally . . ." *(Works,* 1707 ed., 2:515a). This decisive self-surrender is man's entry into a covenant, or contract, with God, on the basis of God's promise to give pardon and life now and glory hereafter, to penitent believers; and this covenant obliges the Christian to continue in obedience as the condition of final salvation. Baxter therefore stresses the necessity of perseverance in good works, in conscious opposition to the loose antinomian tendency of some contemporaries. This emphasis adds urgency to his demand for Christian consistency in the world of business.

(b) *The continuance of the Christian life.* Baxter condemns all sinful self-indulgence and continually demands abstention from all forms of evil. He commends Bible reading and the study of other good books, public worship, private prayer, Christian fellowship, serious meditation on the life to come, and the choice of at least one Christian "bosom friend," as means to living a sanctified life. Holiness is "nothing else but the habitual and predominant devotion and dedication of soul, and body, and life, and all that we have to God; and esteeming, and loving, and serving, and seeking him, before all the pleasures and prosperity of the flesh" (1:7a)—and the perfecting of holiness must be the Christian's supreme concern. Christian virtue must be cultivated; love, honesty, kindness, and gentleness must become features of the believer's character, and he must be tireless in doing good. "Your lives must be laid out in doing God service, and doing all the good you can, in works of piety, justice and charity" (1:102b). "Do all the good that possibly you can" (1:103b). "Living and dying, let it be your care and business to do good" (1:439a). This thought returns again and again in his writings, and his constant aim is to show Christians what "doing good" means in every branch of life.

(c) *The culmination of the Christian life.* Baxter spent most of his life in acute suffering, supposing himself to be constantly at death's door. This taught him to direct his thoughts heavenward, and to live responsibly, as one whose time was short and who must soon give account of himself to God. Repeatedly he urges others to learn the same lesson. "Live as those that are going to the Grave . . ." (1:725a). "Spend every day in preparation for death; and in all your business remember whither you are going and where you must dwell for ever" *(Poor Husbandman's Advocate).* Daily life must be carried on *sub specie aeternitatis.*

In the light of these emphases, we now turn to examine Baxter's teaching on two main subjects—work and wealth.

II. Baxter's Teaching on Work

Baxter held the Reformed doctrine of the calling, which rests on the idea that secular work is as much a rendering of service to God as priestly ministry. He makes these points:

(i) *The Christian must have a calling.* All who can work in a calling must; only genuine disability can excuse one from so doing. This applies even to the rich, for while riches may excuse them from "sordid" work, they bestow no right to be idle. The minister may be excused "worldly labour" because he has "spiritual labour" to employ him, but the recluse is condemned for making his religion a pretext against doing good (1:106, 355b; 3:450).

(ii) *The Christian must carefully choose his calling.* His chosen employment should be that in which he can be most "serviceable to God," profiting both himself and others. It should be something which he finds agreeable and for which he is suited, and it should not be one which endangers his spiritual life. Some callings are better than others: e.g., those involving murder or gambling are definitely sinful; some are dangerous, e.g., that of vintner; others, like tobacco-selling and feather-making, should be avoided in favour of those of greater usefulness; a group including magistracy, schoolmastering, husbandry, tailoring, and the manufacture of clothes are recommended (1:357). Baxter's constant touchstone in judging callings is the public good. Employments which contribute to the public good (which includes one's personal welfare, both physical and spiritual) are lawful; and, of these, those which contribute most are the best.

(iii) *The Christian must work hard in his calling.* God means man to earn his daily bread by the sweat of his brow; if he does not work, he does not deserve his food. The fourth commandment, to rest on the seventh day, presupposes that "six days shalt thou labour . . ." God in Scripture commands and demands hard work. Baxter deals trenchantly with the "mischiefs of idleness," stressing the seriousness of this sin. Sloth, he tells us, destroys our faculties, robs God of His due service, robs ourselves and the commonwealth, destroys grace, spawns other sins, makes us the shame of creation, and disables us from doing good to others (1:358–361). Indeed, "Idleness is of the same kind with Fornication, Gluttony, Dr.unkenness, and other such beastley Sins; For all is but sinful Flesh-pleasing, or Sensuality" (3:641a).

It follows that Christians must "redeem the time"—"see that we cast none of it away in vain; but use every minute of it as a most precious thing and spend it wholly in the way of duty" (1:218b). All our time must be laid out for God; not only in meditating and praying, but also in working with the utmost diligence at our calling. Time must be put, not just to a good use, but to the best use; priorities must be observed. "He loseth his time, when he is getting a penny when he might get a pound, who is visiting his Neighbour, when he should be attending his Prince" (1:227a). Time wasters like excess of sleep, idle talk, needless sports, ungoverned thoughts, and useless reading must be renounced along with that "Master Thief . . . an unsanctified, ungodly heart" (1:227–228). "O spend your Time as you would hear of it in the Judgement!" (1:222a).

Now let us see what further specific advice Baxter has for three groups of people in particular callings—landowners, servants, and merchants.

(a) *Landowners.* Baxter was always a realist; his thoughts may have been fixed on heaven, but his eyes remained open to what was happening around him, and one of the crying abuses which

he saw as the seventeenth century wore on was the serious oppression of the poor tenant farmer by the rich landowner. Baxter
realised that the nation whose wealth was based on these yeoman
farmers was suffering, but he writes against this oppression
chiefly as a violation of justice and mercy from man to man.

First, he condemns high rents. He recognises that inflation
may embarrass the landlord with a fixed income and that he may
then have a just claim to raise the rent—indeed, when the tenant
is able to pay the increase and the lease permits it, he ought then
to do so. But in cases of great hardship mercy must come first,
even where the landowner is himself short of money.

Secondly, Baxter condemns extravagance, which he sees as a
root cause of high rents ("rack rents," as they were called). He rebukes landlords severely for love of money, hardness of heart,
and sensuality.

Thirdly, he pleads for charity. This would mean a lowering of
oppressive rents. Practical Baxter suggests also that landlords
should visit their tenants to learn first-hand the extent of their
needs and problems, so as to be able to help them effectively.

Baxter is also concerned for the spiritual welfare of the small
tenant farmers themselves, who, as things were, could only make
ends meet by toiling "like beasts." Having no time for anything but
work, they were ignoring "soul-concernes," and Baxter foresaw
the land degenerating into "Atheisme, Infidelity, and Bar-
barisme." Great poverty and excessive work were depriving the
poor husbandman of education and so preventing him from reading the Bible and other books which could lead him to God. (For
all this, see *The Poor Husbandman's Advocate,* ed. Powicke, 1926.)

To the rich who employ servants Baxter gives parallel advice.
Servants must be given neither so little work that they have time
for idleness, nor so much that they have no time for prayer, Bible
reading, and other spiritual exercises. Their master has a special
responsibility to care for their spiritual needs, in addition to
their temporal wants.

(b) *Servants.* In selecting employment and a master, servants
must not make ease, good wages, and pleasure their criteria, but
rather "the pleasing of God and the saving of your Souls." Find,

if you can, says Baxter, a godly family to serve, or, failing that, get a post where you can live under "a faithful, powerful, convincing Minister." "Neither a life of idleness, nor of excess of business should be chosen, if you have your choice" (1:386). Baxter in his practical way adds that if a servant wants the best master and the best job, he must try to be the best servant by excelling others in laboriousness, diligence, trustworthiness, and other menial virtues (1:387).

The servant must honour and obey his master, and work hard; for half-hearted work defrauds one's employer of labour for which he has paid, and thus amounts to theft. It is a sin to idle away time which belongs to someone else. Baxter reproves the servant who complains and is dishonest, and instructs him to bear hardship and admonition and to pray for his master (1:435–437; 4:208b).

(c) *Merchants*. Casuists of earlier ages had condemned the merchant's work as sinful, but Baxter, living in an age when the merchant was playing an increasingly important role, disagreed. The merchant's calling contributed to the "public good"; therefore Baxter judged it lawful (1:819a.).

Baxter provides general principles for business activities. All "bargaining and contracts" must be controlled by the twin axioms of religion and justice—love to one's neighbour and denial of oneself. Business life must be of a piece with religious life; commercial practice must be governed by the law of God. There can be no dual standard, and no compromise; life is not lived in watertight compartments. To the pragmatic objection, "It is taken for granted in the Market, that every Man will get as much as he can have," Baxter retorts, "It is not so among Christians, nor Infidels who profess either truth or common honesty." (See 1:805–23.)

In all transactions, therefore, the Christian must be exceptionally honest and always put the other person's interests first. Traders are advised on price fixing thus: Abide by the legal price requirement; observe the market price when selling there; estimate the true value of the goods in an equal contract, where the buyer can leave them if he wishes; do not take too large an advantage from one who has particular need of the goods. A relevant factor for determining prices is the financial position of the parties involved. There is no reason why a larger price should not be taken from a willing rich person than from a poor person. Price haggling is bad, for it encourages salesmen to mark up their goods at a dishonestly high level, whereas Christians should price goods at their true worth and "ask no more at all than a just gain."

"Window dressing" must not be used to enhance a commodity's value. The Christian should not pass on a faulty product by which he was deceived when he bought it. Generally, Baxter's rule is to sanction as much in the way of business enterprise as possible, as long as it does not violate truth, honesty, and the best interests of other persons. In cases of difficulty, Christian charity must guide and the rich help the poor.

Baxter's funeral encomium of his friend Henry Ashurst mirrors his ideal of a Christian tradesman: "God greatly blessed his honesty and liberality; and men knew that they might Trade with him without any danger of deceit, so that he grew up into a very considerable estate: And yet was never so intent upon his Trade, but he was ready for any service of God, and help to others or publick work" (4:909b).

III. Baxter's Teaching on Wealth

Baxter makes three points here.

(i) *Wealth is a reward of diligence.* Baxter did not regard poverty as an ideal, any more than does the Bible. To him, "success is God's ordinary temporal reward of diligence" (2:527a); legitimately gained wealth is a mark of God's blessing on the diligent. However, riches are not invariably a sign of God's blessing, and may prove a curse, as our next point shows.

(ii) *Wealth is a danger to salvation.* To seek gain for God's sake is right and good, but to aim at wealth for one's own benefit is covetousness, which is "a very denying of God and a perverting of the way of a man's life" (1:203a). Covetousness is idolatry, and turns labour into sin (3:627a). Wealth was never meant to be an end, but only a provision on the way. The Christian's heart must

D. R. WOOLDRIDGE

be in heaven, serving God, not on earth, enslaving itself to money. "Take heed lest the world or anything in it steal again into your hearts, and seem too sweet to you." "It is the love of money that is the root of all evil; and the love of this world that is the mortal enemy of the love of God" (1:488a). It is peculiarly difficult for the rich to be saved, because of the peculiar temptations which assault them at this point. Scripture teaches not merely that few will be saved, but that of the prosperous few among the few will find life: "Scripture speaketh in such general Language, as if Salvation had been almost appropriated to the Poor, and the Rich had been excluded, because of the rarity of their salvation" (4:474b).

(iii) *Wealth is a talent to be used.*

(a) *Wealth must not be wrongly used:* i.e., in personal extravagance. Baxter complains that "rich Men are not acquainted with the true use of Riches, nor think of the Account which they must make to God of all they have; They think that their Riches are their own, and that they may use them as they please" (1:294b). Wealth is a God-given stewardship; money should be employed for the glory of the Giver.

(b) *Wealth may be used for investment.* Baxter considers investment an essential part of economic life, in which Christians may lawfully partake. Indeed, lending is a duty when others' need so requires and prudence permits (1:816b); and there is no sin in expecting a reasonable rate of interest. Baxter proves the lawfulness of usury thus: First, it may greatly help the poor in the form of charitable endowments. Second, it is not forbidden by God: the Mosaic prohibitions forbid it only where it is an act of unkindness, and there is no positive law of Christ against it. Third, the "Law of Nature doth not forbid all Usury," for usury is not necessarily opposed either to piety, or to one's own welfare, or to one's neighbour's. Usury is sinful, however, when it is against justice or charity: e.g., it is wrong to charge interest when charity requires a loan interest-free.

Baxter wisely argues that wealth should not be allowed to depreciate by hoarding, but be used to increase its value and—more important still—to help others. It is this that glorifies God.

(c) *Wealth must be used sparingly on our own needs.* God is its "Chief Owner"; man must administer it faithfully as God's steward, and this means eschewing wastefulness and prodigality. Expensive eating and drinking, overdressing, and lavish outlay on sumptuous buildings and needless recreations must be ruled out (1:927ff.); though Baxter recognises that certain unavoidable expenses may be incurred in soberly maintaining one's appointed rank in society (1:372). Before the Christian devotes money to recreations and entertainments, he must reckon up how much he must spend on himself, his children, taxes, the poor, and church charges, according to the good which is likely to follow. Therefore he needs to keep accounts. Money should in any case be spent only on such "recreations" as are sinless and really recreate, i.e., promote the health of body and mind and make the Christian fitter for the service of God.

(d) *Wealth must be used to do positive good.* Baxter has a high view of the place of charity in the Christian life. Doing good in this way makes us like God; it pleases God; it shows our faith to be sincere; and it is commanded and commended in Scripture in the strongest terms. Therefore, "take it as the chiefest extrinsecal part of your religion to do good; and make it the trade and business of your lives; and not as a matter to be done on the by" (1:868a). And, he adds, do it now; good works should not be postponed to the indefinite future. This "doing as you would be done by" in meeting others' needs by charitable donation is a basic element in loving one's neighbour as oneself.

Baxter will not be legalistic in determining how much one should give to those in need. He lays down no fixed proportion; his only rule is "give as much as you can." On tithing, his judgment (in a letter to Thomas Gouge) is as follows: "Your proportion of the tenth part, is too much for some, and much too little for others, but for the most part, I think it as likely a proportion as is fit for another to prescribe in particular" (1:865b). He wants to see the Christian's money used for the conversion of the heathen, at home and abroad; for encouraging a "Godly ministry"; for building and endowing schools and hospitals; for helping poor children; and, of course, for relieving the poor. It seems that he himself gave almost half his own annual income to charitable causes of this kind.

IV. Conclusion

Thus Baxter shows us how God is to be glorified in our earning and in our spending. We must work with all our might in our calling; "we must endeavour after the most successful way, and pray for a just prosperity for our Labours; And when God doth prosper us with Wealth, we must take it thankfully (tho' with fear) and use it to his Service, and do all the good with it that we can" (3:658b). But we must not lose our heart to it. "Look up to Heaven men; and remember that there is thy Home, and there is thy Hope, or else thou art a man undone forever; and therefore it is for that that thou must care and labour" (1:206a).

6

MORGAN LLWYD

Geraint Gruffydd

Morgan Llwyd was born in 1619 in the farmhouse of Cynfal Fawr, Maentwrog, of an old and prosperous Merionethshire family. The head of the house during his youth was Huw Llwyd, a veteran of Queen Elizabeth's Netherlands campaigns, who had inherited Cynfal in 1623. Huw was a gifted amateur poet, and a faithful patron of the professional poets who at that time still toured gentlefolks' houses to sing elegies and eulogies and receive their due fees. Moreover, the parish clergy of Maentwrog were at that time men of letters: Edmwnd Prys, rector 1572–1623, had helped Bishop William Morgan to translate the Bible into Welsh; Huw Lewis, Prys's successor, had put into Welsh Wermuller's *Kleinot;* Dafydd Rowlands, Prys' curate, made an unpublished Welsh translation of Sutton's *Disce Mori.* In this environment, Morgan Llwyd became familiar early with the great literary tradition of Wales, and thus laid the foundations of his own superb prose style.

At about nineteen, Llwyd was sent away to school at Wrexham, then the largest town in Wales, and the home of a vigorous Puritan tradition since the early 1580s, when Christopher Goodman had been active in the adjoining diocese of Chester. The curate of the parish church at that time was the great Walter Cradock, who had already been expelled from the curacy of St. Mary's, Cardiff, for his Puritan nonconformity. Llwyd was converted through Cradock, and in 1639 followed him to Llanfair Waterdine in Shropshire, where Cradock had found refuge from the authorities under the patronage of Sir Robert Harley of Brampton Bryan. Here he met Vavasor Powell, another convert of Cradock's, and a lifelong friend thereafter. In November, 1639, Llwyd went with Cradock to help found the first Welsh independent church, at Llanfaches in Monmouthshire. There he met and married his wife Ann. When the Civil War broke out the church fled first to Bristol and then, in July, 1643, to London. Llwyd had already sent his wife and children home to his mother at Cynfal, and now he enlisted as a chaplain in the Parliamentary army. After active service in southern England, he was sent by Parliament in 1644 to North Wales as an itinerant preacher. He settled finally at Wrexham, in Brynyffynnon, a house belonging to his friend, Colonel John Jones, of Maesygarnedd, and remained in Wales almost uninterruptedly thereafter. His status was that of an itinerant minister, paid by Parliament. From 1650, as an Approver under the Act for the Better Propagation of the Gospel in Wales, it was also his duty to find fit ministers to replace the ejected clergy. In 1656 he was settled as minister of Wrexham parish with a salary of £100 per annum. Since 1647, however, he had been acting as pastor to the gathered church at Wrexham, now grown into a famous and influential congregation. He gave himself unsparingly to preaching far and wide, tending his flock and writing for the instruction of his fellow-countrymen till his death on June 3, 1659.

Such was his outward career. His inward development is less easily traced, for he was curiously reticent on the subject. However, there is a little evidence, and Llwyd himself provides a framework by a crucial note which he jotted down on a blank page in a holograph collection of his verse (Cardiff Central Library MS. 1:6, 65b, ca. 1654): 16 *Annis* (sic) *vixi in teneb. varijs,* 16 *postea in lucibus varijs* ("I lived for sixteen years in varying [degrees of] darkness, and for sixteen after that in varying [degrees of] light"). The first sixteen years cover his early life at Cynfal (1619–35). That this should be a time of "varying darkness" is perhaps not surprising, for the Welsh church of those days could offer her children little but elementary instruction in the forms of religion. Llwyd, however, seems to have come early under conviction of sin (in a poem he says he was long *dan fellt y gyfraith,* under the lightning of the law), and this may have been through reading one of the excellent books of devotion translated into Welsh since the Reformation—Dent's *Plain Man's Pathway to Heaven,* perhaps, or Bunny's *Resolution,* the book that awakened Baxter. The second sixteen years, 1635–51, begin with Llwyd's conversion. During this period, his views seem to have been those of a typical radical Puritan, as were Cradock's own: scepticism as to the importance of outward forms in religion, a strong antipathy to dogmatism about church order and church ordinances, and a marked tendency to evangelical antinomianism. Unlike Cradock, however, Llwyd became a fervent Fifth Monarchist, maintaining on the basis of various passages in Daniel and Revelation that Christ would soon return to earth to establish His kingdom, and that it was the saints' duty to prepare for this by political as well as spiritual means. Llwyd later renounced the political implications of this creed, but the hope which it enshrined never left him.

In 1651 (so the note quoted above implies) Llwyd received what seemed to him full light. A passage from Lazarus' testimony to his sisters in *Lazarus and his sisters Discoursing of paradise* (1655) may reflect his experience.

"I found myself full of thoughts, but very quiet, having no lust, or will, or motion of my own, but my mind breathed in God's own will all the while; I waited only for his pleasure in the quiet region of holy Angels, hearing (by an inward ear) the heavenly melody, and seeing (with the spirit of my mind) the unutterable wonders of the God-head."

238 ～ GERAINT GRUFFYDD

Llwyd's discovery of the writings of Jacob Boehme, the German Lutheran visionary, was in some way connected with this experience. All Boehme's works appeared in English between 1645 and 1662, and Llwyd, who in 1655 was able to introduce his own paraphrase of a passage in Boehme by writing, "I have seen more of the Lord Jesus by reading and considering nine words, then in many Books, Sermons and personal opinions," himself translated two parts of Boehme's *Der Weg zu Christo* into Welsh and published them in 1657. From 1651 onwards, Boehme was undoubtedly the dominant intellectual influence on Llwyd.

Llwyd expounded the complex and obscure metaphysical system which he worked out under Boehme's influence in nine works, six Welsh and three English: *Llythur ir Cyrnru cariadus* (A Letter to the loving Welshmen), London, 1653 [?]; *Gwaedd ynghymru yn wyneb pob Cydwybod* (A cry in Wales to every conscience), Dublin, 1653; *Dirgelwch I rai iw ddeall Ac i eraill iw watwar . . . Neu ARWYDD i annerch y Cymru* (A mystery for some to understand and for others to mock at . . . or a sign to confront the Welsh), London [1653] (these three summon Welshmen to prepare themselves for Christ's early return, an event presaged, Llwyd thought, by the summoning of the Saints' Parliament in 1653); *An Honest discourse between Three NEIGHBOURS*, London, 1655 (this reflects Llwyd's disillusionment after Cromwell dissolved the Saints' Parliament, and in effect urges Fifth Monarchists to prepare for their King's coming by spiritual rather than political means); *Lazarus and his sisters Discoursing of paradise*, London, 1655; *Where is Christ?*, London, 1655 (an anti-Quaker tract); *Gait o'r Gair* (A Word from the Word), London, 1656; *Cyfarwyddid ir Cymru* (Instruction for the Welsh), London, 1657; *Gwyddor vehod* (Heavenly science), London, 1657 (these last three are more in the nature of systematic expositions of Llwyd's metaphysics: the last is in verse, and uses current astrological ideas to give point to its message). In the five Welsh prose works, Llwyd shows himself one of the great masters of the language.

A fairly consistent doctrinal scheme appears in all his books, which may be summarized thus: The root and ground of all being is the immortal, unmeasurable, unsearchable, self-subsisting

God. At first, He was as nothing *(Dim)* in a condition of timeless, motionless existence. With Him was the Word (His Wisdom), the agent of His creative acts. Discerning in Himself His eternal thoughts, possibilities, and intentions, God expresses Himself in an act of creation, and His nature is revealed as a trinity of will, love, and power, which pervade all things. Endowed with will, His creatures depart from their root and become a dark, formless mass *(Diddim,* matter) from which the Four Elements emerge; God's mind, acting upon the Four Elements, then brings into existence all visible created things. Man is a unique case: his body is a compound of the Four Elements and is therefore dominated by a self-seeking principle or dark trinity alien to God; but he is also endowed with a spirit which derives directly from God through the word and in which the Holy Trinity itself dwells "substantially"; also, he possesses a soul, the intermediary between the body and the spirit, partaking of the nature of each and subject to the attractions of both. In the Incarnation, God expressed Himself a second time: the word became man in Jesus Christ, and by His perfect obedience and self-denial defeated and subjugated the dark trinity of this world; now He is become a Spirit who (in Llwyd's words) enlightens, searches, comprises, rules, quickens, and upholds all things. Finally, in the Last Day, God will express Himself a third and final time: the earth and all things earthly will be destroyed, time will be swallowed up by eternity, and a new heaven and earth come into being. The fate of the soul on that day will depend on whether she has chosen union with the spirit or enslavement by the body; if the first, her communion in the spirit with the Godhead will be made perfect and she will live for ever in joy and light; but if the second, she will not be destroyed with the body but will live for ever in darkness and deprivation. The soul can attach herself to the spirit by rejecting the claims of body and self-will, and obeying instead the dictates of conscience, through which the word in the spirit speaks.

This summary is undoubtedly over-simplified; but if we may tentatively accept it as substantially fair, two comments suggest themselves. First, much of this is pure uncontrolled speculation; second, certain features in it seem positively erroneous. This was pointed out in Llwyd's own day, most sharply by his old friend Vavasor Powell, who wrote in 1657, "It will be small joy to me and other saints to hear that beloved and blessed M(organ) L(lwyd) does degenerate so much in his doctrine as to hold many of the old Arminian and popish principles, as free will, perfection, or the Socinian d(octrine), as to enervate the power of Christ's death or intercession. I do not say you do, but look you to it." Powell's warning was justified. Llwyd did believe in free will and, it seems, in the possibility of Christian perfection (cf. C.C.L. MS. 1:6, p. 60: "Sinai & churches now bethinke/how all may strive for sin"). More seriously, his Behmenist doctrine of the word indwelling every man does in fact "enervate the power of Christ's death or intercession," undermining the centrality of the Incarnagion and atonement and gift of the Spirit to the church. If Christ already indwells all men, why need He have died at Jerusalem? And if He already teaches all men in their consciences, what need was there of an external revelation and a Bible? Though Llwyd directs a solemn admonition to the Quakers, who scoffed at the "Jerusalem Christ" and the "outward book," "be warned not to divide the Christ without, and the Christ within; it is the gulph of condemnation, a pit for self-conceited hearts; He that writeth hath seen the deceit . . . speak not reproachfully of the outward Bible" *(Where is Christ?)*, it is clear that the whole tendency of his own teaching was towards the Quaker position, and many of his own flock became Quakers after his death.

We can guess what happened to Llwyd. In the light of his 1651 experience, he saw that much current Puritan religion was intellectual only, an outward assent without any complementary inward experience of grace, exclusively and intolerantly concerned with a bare doctrinal correctness. Against this he reacted too far: not only did he tend to stress the inward aspects of Christian faith and life to the virtual exclusion of the outward, but he adopted as the basis of his teaching Boehme's "inward" mystical metaphysics. Not that his writings are therefore wholly unedifying, for he was surely a man of genuine, if fitful, spiritual insight; but we should perhaps do well to apply to his case Peter Sterry's caveat about Boehme himself.

"They that read him had need come to him well instructed in the mystery of Christ, with a heavenly newness of mind, by which they may be able to try what the good and acceptable word of God is."

I wish to record my great debt to the writings of Dr. E. Lewis Evans, our foremost authority on the thought of Morgan Llwyd. I should add, however, that Dr. Evans would certainly disagree forcibly with many of the views expressed above.

Part 4

How Shall
They Hear?

1959

INTRODUCTION

J. I. Packer

Most people today are out of touch with the Christian message. *How shall they hear?* Of all the problems that face our churches, this is surely the most insistent. The following five papers, which were read at the tenth Puritan and Reformed Studies Conference in December, 1959, the centenary year of the 1859 revival in Ulster and Wales and the quatercentenary of John Calvin's *Institutes,* are now published in this form in the belief that they point the way towards its solution.

How shall they hear? Each paper suggests part of the answer.

They will hear through the labours of men who, like John Calvin, give their lives unstintedly to spread and defend biblical truth; men who, with Paul, when faced with error, give place "by subjection, no, not for an hour; that the truth of the gospel might continue . . ."(Galatians 2:5).

They will hear through the preaching of a broad-based, God-centred gospel which confronts them with the glory of the Father and the Son, and in God's name commands their faith and repentance.

They will hear through the witness of churches which are notorious for their consistent godliness, which are intolerant of sin within their ranks, and walk humbly in the fear of the Lord.

They will hear through the outpouring of the sovereign Spirit of God in revival.

Apart from these things, they will not hear. If then, we desire that they should hear, it is for these things that we must work and pray.

L. Lupton's paper on *The Geneva Bible* has been omitted, since it formed part of a book which, it is hoped, will in due course be published separately. Some of Dr. Hughes' material, not reproduced here, will be found in the essay, "The Pen of the Prophet," which he contributed to the quatercentenary symposium, *John Calvin, Contemporary Prophet* (Baker, Grand Rapids, 1959).

1

JOHN CALVIN: THE MAN
WHOM GOD SUBDUED

P. E. Hughes

Who is this man John Calvin? Did he not invent an inhuman doctrine of theological fatalism, otherwise known as predestination? Was he not the intolerant tyrant over an unwilling city-state? and the heartless burner of any unfortunate individual who had the temerity to disagree with him on some abstruse point of theology? Or is it after all possible that a man who died nearly four hundred years ago may really have something to say to our modern generation? Increasingly in these days our Western world is becoming aware that John Calvin is still very much a man to be reckoned with—a man in fact who, so far from being dead and done with, has exerted and continues to exert an influence, not just in a few narrow circles, but throughout the world. Indeed, his influence has proved to be one of the great dynamic and formative forces in modern history. "Calvinism," it is true, is still a term of abuse, a swear-word for the use of theologians and clerics, intended to damn all unfortunate souls against whom it is huffed. But the time has come for those who use the term in this manner to reconsider their prejudices, and to ask whether it may not be themselves they are condemning by the passion of their ignorance.

Calvin was born in France, in the town of Noyon, on July 10, 1509. In an autobiographical passage of considerable interest, found in the preface of his commentary on the book of Psalms, he tells us that when he was still a very little boy he had been destined by his father for the study of theology; but that afterwards his father put him to the study of law, having concluded that the legal profession offered better prospects. And to his legal studies he diligently applied himself. "But God," he says, "by the secret guidance of his providence, at length gave a different direction to my course." He explains how as a young man he was "obstinately addicted to the superstitions of popery," but that "by a sudden conversion" God subdued his mind and made him teachable. "Having thus acquired a taste of true godliness," he continues, "I was inflamed with so intense a desire to make progress in it that, though not abandoning my other studies, I now pursued them with less ardour. And a year had not elapsed before all who had a desire for purer doctrine were continually coming to me, as yet a mere novice and tyro, in order to learn. Being by nature reserved, and a lover of peace and retirement, I then began to seek some seclusion; but so far from being granted this, all my retreats were like public classes. Indeed, while my one purpose was to live unmolested and unknown, God led me by a variety of turnings in such a way that He permitted me no rest in any place until, contrary to my natural disposition, I was driven into the public light."

This alone is sufficient to show how baseless is the calumny that he was impelled by megalomania to seek power and play the tyrant. Further evidence of his unassuming character is the fact that when his famous *Institutes of the Christian Religion* first appeared, he did not disclose that he was its author. Again, writing to Cardinal Sadoleto a few years later, he declared that, leaving out of account his Christian vocation, the summit of his wishes would have been "the enjoyment of literary ease with something of a free and honourable station."

It was in fact with the intention of settling down quietly in Strasbourg that he decided to leave Basle after the publication of the first edition of the *Institutes* in 1534. The war then being waged between Francis I and Charles V, however, compelled him to take a roundabout route, and this brought him to Geneva. There he expected to spend no more than a single night. But his arrival was reported to his compatriot, the fiery William Farel ("with what incredible zeal for promoting the gospel he burned!"), who sought him out at his lodgings. "When he understood that I had set my heart on private and unseen studies," records Calvin, "and finding that he gained nothing by entreaties, he proceeded to utter an imprecation that God would curse my retirement, if I should withhold my assistance when the need was so urgent. I was struck with such terror that I desisted from the journey which I had undertaken; but, conscious of my bashfulness and timidity, I would not bind myself by a promise to discharge any particular (ministerial) office!" Thus Calvin's famous association with the city of Geneva began—an association which was relentlessly to deny him the scholarly leisure and detachment which he so strongly desired.

But his longing for a peaceful withdrawn existence was not extinguished; for when in 1538 he was forced to leave Geneva, the fact gave him satisfaction rather than grief, since he now felt himself released from the cares and responsibilities of a public charge. Accordingly, therefore, he resolved once more to seek for himself the privacy of a scholar's retreat. But in Strasbourg, to which he now went, no less than in Geneva, there was a man waiting to pronounce an imprecation upon him for his unwillingness to accept a public pastorate. This time it was Martin Bucer; he threatened Calvin with the example of the prophet Jonah, who had turned away from obedience to the will of God.

Three years later the way was open for him to return to Geneva. To retrace his steps would, as Calvin knew, involve him in the tangle and turmoil of public affairs, and he sought every excuse to avoid making the move. This reluctance was due to his

250 ∾ P. E. HUGHES

natural timidity, not to cowardice (which is a very different thing), nor to disregard for the welfare of the church at Geneva. Indeed, the well-being of this church meant so much to him that he would not, he asserts, have hesitated to lay down his life for its sake. No, Calvin was never a coward, least of all at this juncture, when a solemn and conscientious regard to duty prevailed upon him to return to the flock from which he had been driven. But he did so "with grief, many tears, and great anxiety," for he foresaw something of the severe trials and labours which awaited him in that city and from which, from then onwards, he was never to be free.

Two things should be borne in mind as we contemplate the fifty-nine volumes in the *Corpus Reformatorum* which contain his writings, They were not the work of a man whose literary activities were prosecuted in the sequestered solitude of some cloister or academy, with daily leisure for uninterrupted meditation. On the contrary, these writings flowed from his pen (or were dictated) in the midst of, indeed it must be said in spite of, the almost overwhelming pressure of a multitude of other demands upon his time and energy, not to mention the assortment of maladies which frequently assailed his frail physical frame. Writing to Farel in February 1550, he complains of a great deal of time, which should have been employed in useful labours, being taken up with illnesses—a fatiguing cough, severe catarrh, the tortures of migraine, gastritis.

But, just as Calvin was no coward, so he was no hypochondriac. He never behaved like an invalid, but drove himself unsparingly and without proper regard for his health. His close friend Theodore Beza recalls how even when, in 1558, serious illness had made it imperative for him to cease from preaching and lecturing, and from his other pastoral and civic duties, he spent days and nights in dictating and writing letters. "He had no expression more frequently on his lips," says Beza, "than that life would be bitter to him if spent in indolence." When his friends entreated him while sick to spare himself the labour of composition, Calvin would say, "What, would you have the Lord find me idle?" In 1563, the year before his death, "Calvin's diseases had so much increased," Beza writes, "and were so numerous as to make it almost impossible to believe that so strong and noble a mind could any longer be confined in a body so fragile, so exhausted by labour, and so broken down by suffering. But even then he could not be persuaded to spare himself. On the contrary, if at any time he abstained from public duty (and he never did so without the greatest reluctance) he still at home gave answers to those who consulted him or wore out his secretaries by dictating to them, though indefatigable himself."

One of those secretaries, Nicholas de Gallars, who for sixteen years enjoyed the immediate friendship of the Reformer, speaks of him as follows (in his epistolary dedication of Calvin's commentary on Isaiah to the printer John Crispin): "I certainly cannot find words to express what labours, what watchings and solicitudes he endured, with what faithfulness and wisdom he attended to the interests of all, with what frankness and courtesy he received those who visited him, how ready and clear were his replies to those who consulted him even on the weightiest matters, how learnedly, both in private and in public, he solved the difficult and perplexing questions which were proposed to him, with what gentleness he comforted the afflicted and cheered those who were faint and sorrowful, with what firmness he resisted adversaries and with what energy he was accustomed to restrain the haughty and obstinate, with what strength of mind he bore adversity, what moderation he exercised in prosperity; in short, with what ability and cheerfulness he performed all the duties of a faithful servant of God."

His first book, a commentary on Seneca's *De Clementia*, written and published before he was twenty-three, and before his "sudden conversion," was no more than a cool academic exercise in humanist scholarship. All his later writings, however, were the work, not of Calvin the humanist, but of Calvin the Reformer and passionate champion of evangelical truth, and breathe a very different spirit. There were the successive editions of the *Institutes*, the finest *Summa* of Christian theology ever to have been written, a magnificent monument of devotion and industry, and the most important single work that he gave to the world. There was the great series of commentaries, covering almost all the books of the Bible—the supreme examples of the Reformation ideal of a sane, practical, and straightforward exegesis, in which proper respect is had to the plain meaning of words and to the literary form in which they are cast. And there were many other writings—Tracts, as they are called, though they differ infinitely from the flimsy, fluffy opuscules that go by that name today!—which are both voluminous and valuable. All these published works fitted into the single-minded purpose of his life, being intended either for the instruction and edification of Christ's flock, or for the statement and defence of the truth against those by whose teaching it was threatened. Then, too, he was a voluminous correspondent; and the steady stream of letters that issued from his pen, addressed to friends, to civic and ecclesiastical leaders, to churches, to kings, princes, and nobles, and, not least, to humble souls who were suffering persecution for the sake of the gospel, reveal not only how conscientious he was as a correspondent, but also the loving constancy of his friendship, the clear vision of a master strategist, and a deep compassion and noble concern for fellow Christians whose faith was being tested by torture, imprisonment, and the prospect of cruel deaths.

It is difficult to realize that this prolific author was also daily occupied in a multiplicity of other duties—preaching each day of every other week, lecturing three times a week in theology, always in his place at sessions of the Consistory, instructing the clergy, addressing the Council and keeping a guiding hand on the government of his city, visiting the sick, counselling the troubled, receiving the numerous callers from near and far who sought him out, and giving himself wholeheartedly to his friends in a fellowship that meant much to himself as well as to them. No wonder Wolfgang Musculus spoke of him as a bow always strung! How could a single man with so frail a physical frame achieve such prodigious results? The answer is found in the words of the apostle Paul: "We have this treasure in earthen vessels, that the excellency of the power may be of God, and not of us . . . For which cause we faint not; but though our outward man perish, yet the inward man is renewed day by day" (2 Corinthians 4:7, 16). "He took little sleep," says Beza of Calvin, "and he had such an astonishing memory that any person whom he had once seen he instantly recognized at the distance of years, and when, in the course of dictating he chanced to be interrupted for several hours as often happened, as soon as he returned he commenced at once to dictate where he had left off. Whatever he required to know for the performance of his duty, though involved in a multitude of other affairs, he never forgot. On whatever subject he was consulted, his judgment was so clear and correct that he often seemed almost to prophesy; nor do I recollect any person having been led into error through following his advice. He despised mere eloquence, and was sparing in the use of words, but he was by no means a careless writer. No theologian of this period wrote more purely, weightily, and judiciously, though he wrote more than any other individual either in our recollection or that of our fathers. For, by the hard studies of his youth and a certain acuteness of judgment, confirmed by practice in dictating, he was never at a loss for an appropriate and weighty expression, and wrote very much as he spoke. In the doctrine which he delivered at the first he persisted steadily to the last, scarcely making any change." Of the slanders which Calvin's enemies so industriously propagated against his character, Beza remarks that "no refutation is required by those who knew this great man when he was alive, nor by posterity, who will judge him by his works." By his works, indeed, let him be judged afresh today, and it will be found how insubstantial are the many prejudices that still cluster about his name.

Finally, let us hear Calvin's last will and testament, dictated by him on April 25, 1564, just over a month before his death. "In the name of God," he says, "I, John Calvin, servant of the Word of God in the church of Geneva, weakened by many illnesses . . . thank God that he has not only shown mercy toward me, His poor creature, and . . . has suffered me in all sins and weaknesses, but, what is much more, that He has made me a partaker of His grace to serve Him through my work . . . I confess to live and die in this faith which he has given me, inasmuch as I have no other hope or refuge than His predestination, upon which my entire salvation is grounded. I embrace the grace which He has offered me in our Lord Jesus Christ and accept the merits of His suffering and dying, that through them all my sins are buried; and I humbly beg Him to wash and cleanse me with the blood of our great Redeemer, as it was shed for all poor sinners, so that I, when I shall appear before His face, may bear His likeness. Moreover, I declare that I endeavoured to teach His Word undefiled and to expound Holy Scripture faithfully, according to the measure of grace which He has given me. In all the disputations which I led against the enemies of the truth I employed no cunning or any sophistry, but have fought His cause honestly. But, oh, my will, my zeal, were so cold and sluggish that I know myself guilty in every respect. Without His infinite goodness all my passionate striving would only be smoke; indeed, the grace itself which He gave me would make me even more guilty. Thus my only confidence is that he is the Father of Mercy, who as such desires to reveal Himself to so miserable a sinner. As for the rest, I desire that after my passing my body be buried according to the customary form in expectancy of the day of the blessed resurrection."

And so this man whom God subdued died as he had always lived: humbly and unassumingly, in complete faith and obedience to the word and will of Almighty God. At his funeral, despite the presence of a vast and sorrowing crowd of friends and citizens, there was no pomp or ceremony. His body was buried in a coffin of common pine wood, and there was not even a stone or inscription to mark the place where he was laid to rest.

"If any man will come after me, let him say No to self, and take up his cross daily, and follow me." "And where I am, there shall also my servant be: if any man serve me, him will my Father honour."

To God alone be the glory! Amen.

2

THE PURITAN VIEW OF
PREACHING THE GOSPEL

J. I. Packer

I

Those who have followed these conferences over the years will be aware that in this paper I am returning to a subject on which I have spoken before.

In 1955, I gave a paper entitled "Puritan Evangelism." It was meant as a contribution to the current debate on evangelistic methods. In it, I showed how the Puritan approach to the task of winning souls was controlled by the knowledge that fallen men cannot turn to God by their own strength, nor is it in the power of evangelists to make them do so. The Puritan position was that only God, by His Spirit, through His word, can bring sinners to faith, and that He does this, not to our order, but according to His own free purpose. Our evangelistic practice, the Puritans would say, must be in accord with this

255

256 ~ J. I. Packer

truth. Modes of action which imply another doctrine cannot
be approved.

The Puritan position seems indubitably biblical, and, as I
partly showed in the paper, its implications are of great importance for the reforming of inherited evangelistic traditions today.
It implies, to start with, that all devices for exerting psychological
pressure in order to precipitate "decisions" must be eschewed, as
being in truth presumptuous attempts to intrude into the
province of the Holy Ghost. It means, further, that to abjure such
devices is no loss, since their use can contribute nothing whatever
to the effectiveness of evangelistic preaching. Indeed, it will in
the long run detract from it; for while psychological pressures,
skilfully handled, may produce the outward form of "decision,"
they cannot bring about regeneration and a change of heart, and
when the "decisions" wear off those who registered them will be
found "gospel-hardened" and antagonistic. Such forcing tactics
can only do damage, perhaps incalculable damage, to men's
souls. It follows, therefore, that high-speed evangelism is not a
valid option. Evangelism must rather be conceived as a long-term
enterprise of patient teaching and instruction, in which God's
servants seek simply to be faithful in delivering the gospel message and applying it to human lives, and leave it to God's Spirit to
draw men to faith through this message in His own way and at His
own speed.

But this raises a further question: What is the message; how
much is involved in declaring the gospel?

This question is rarely raised in evangelical circles; we assume—too readily—that we all know the answer. But it needs raising; two factors in our situation compel us to face it.

The first is a *minimizing approach to the task of teaching Christian
truth*. This has infected Protestant clergy very widely. The modern
minister does not usually ask, How much ought I to teach? but
rather, How little need I teach? What is the minimum of doctrine
that will do? One reason for this, no doubt, is the reluctance of
those in the pews to learn. But this is no new thing. Baxter met it
three centuries ago in his working-class congregation at Kidderminster, and gave it short shrift. "Were you but as willing to get the

knowledge of God and heavenly things as you are to know how to work in your trade, you would have set yourself to it before this day, and you would have spared no cost or pains till you had got it. But you account seven years little enough to learn your trade, and will not bestow one day in seven in diligent learning the matters of your salvation."[1] Baxter did not humour this ungodly unwillingness; but the modern minister often does, and when he finds that some aspect of biblical truth arouses no immediate interest or approval in his congregation his instinct is to jettison it. And the tendency today is to encourage him to do so. Thus, for instance, some will assure us that it is a waste of time preaching to modern hearers about the law and sin, for (it is said) such things mean nothing to them. Instead (it is suggested) we should appeal to the needs which they feel already, and present Christ to them simply as One who gives peace, power, and purpose to the neurotic and frustrated—a super-psychiatrist, in fact.

Now, this suggestion excellently illustrates the danger of the minimizing approach. If we do not preach about sin and God's judgment on it, we cannot present Christ as a Saviour from sin and the wrath of God. And if we are silent about these things, and preach a Christ who saves only from self and the sorrows of this world, we are not preaching the Christ of the Bible. We are, in effect, bearing false witness and preaching a false Christ. Our message is "another gospel, which is not another." Such preaching may soothe some, but it will help nobody; for a Christ who is not seen and sought as a Saviour from sin will not be found to save from self or from anything else. An imaginary Christ will not bring a real salvation. The minimizing approach leads us to deal in half-truths about salvation; and a half-truth presented as the whole truth is a complete untruth. Thus the minimizing approach threatens to falsify the gospel by emptying it of doctrinal elements that are essential to it. In face of this prevalent habit of mind, it is vital that we raise the question: *How much* does preaching the gospel involve?

The second factor in our situation is *a widespread uncertainty about the evangelistic implications of the Reformed faith.* Many today see the scripturalness of the doctrine of grace set out in the so-called "five points of Calvinism," but do not see how on this basis one can preach evangelistically. If the doctrines of total inability, unconditional election, and effectual calling are true—if, that is, sinners cannot of themselves turn to God, and faith and repentance are graces given only to the elect—what sense does it make to command all men indiscriminately to repent and believe? If the doctrine of particular redemption is true—if, that is, Christ died to win salvation, not for all men inclusively (and for many ineffectively), but for the elect only—we can never tell an unconverted man that Christ died for him; on what grounds, therefore, can we exhort him to trust the Saviour? Are we indeed entitled to make a "free offer" of Christ to sinners at all? Some, perplexed by these questions, feel themselves shut up to a choice between either preaching the gospel like Arminians—addressing the unconverted, that is, as if it were in their own power to receive Christ, and God were simply waiting for them to do so—or else not preaching evangelistically at all. It would be tragic if the current return to Reformed theology, instead of invigorating evangelism, as it should, had the effect of strangling it; but it seems clear that many today have ceased to preach evangelistically because they do not see how an evangelistic application of this theology can be made. Thus, as the minimizing approach leads some to empty the gospel of its doctrinal content, so this perplexity causes others to empty it of its practical application. And either mode of evisceration nullifies the gospel as effectively as the other.

In this situation, we return to the Puritans for further guidance. How much, we ask them, needs saying, by way of both information and application, if the gospel is to be truly proclaimed? What are the essential ingredients in evangelistic preaching?

Only one aspect of this subject—the need to preach the law when proclaiming Christ—received formal discussion in the Puritan period; but there is ample evidence to show how they would answer our question.

A word about this evidence. It consists of printed sermons. The Puritans did not regard evangelistic sermons as a special class of sermons, having their own peculiar style and conventions; the Puritan position was, rather, that, since all Scripture bears witness to Christ, and all sermons should aim to expound and apply what is in the Bible, all proper sermons would of necessity declare Christ and so be to some extent evangelistic. The Lord Jesus Christ, said Robert Bolton, is "offered most freely, and without exception of any person, every Sabbath, every Sermon, either in plaine, and direct termes, or implyedly, at the least."[2] The only difference was that some sermons aimed more narrowly and exclusively at converting sinners than did others. Such were those published in Richard Baxter's *A Call to the Unconverted, A Treatise on Conversion,* and *Directions and Persuasions to a Sound Conversion,* and in Joseph Alleine's, *An Alarme to the Unconverted.* But there are five further classes of Puritan sermons and expositions which are equally relevant, being just as directly, if less exclusively, evangelistic in intent.

i. **Treatises on sin:** e.g., Edward Reynolds, *The Sinfulnesse of Sin;* Thomas Goodwin, *Aggravation of Sin* and *An Unregenerate Man's Guiltiness before God;* Jeremiah Burroughs, *The Evil of Evils, or the Exceeding Sinfulness of Sin.* ("Wherein is shewed," continues the title page, "1. There is more Evil in the least Sin, than there is in the greatest Affliction. 2. Sin is most opposite to God. 3. Sin is most opposite to Man's Good. 4. Sin is opposite to all Good in general. 5. Sin is the Poyson, or Evil of all other Evils. 6. Sin hath a kind of Infiniteness in it. 7. Sin makes a man conformable to the Devil. *All these several Heads are branched out into very many Particulars.*" The work is 537 pages long.)

ii. **Treatises on the office and work of Christ:** e.g., Thomas Goodwin, *Christ set Forth; Of Christ the Mediator; The Heart of Christ in Heaven towards Sinners on Earth; The Knowledge of God the Father and His Son Jesus Christ;* Bunyan, *The Work of Christ as an Advocate; Christ a Complete Saviour;* Philip Henry, *Christ is All;* John Owen, *The Glory of Christ.*

iii. **Treatises on faith and conversion:** e.g., Ezekiel Culver-
well and John Ball each wrote *A Treatise of Faith;* John
Rogers, *The Doctrine of Faith:* William Whately, *The New
Birth;* Thomas Hooker, *The Application of Redemption* (and
many more works on the same subject); Thomas Shepard, *The Sound Believer;* Giles Firmin, *The Real Christian;*
John Flavel, *The Method of Grace.*

iv. **Treatises on the covenant of grace,** exploring the riches
of the relationship with God into which Christ brings believers: e.g., John Preston, *The New Covenant;* Richard
Alleine, *Heaven Opened;* E. F(isher), *The Marrow of Modern Divinity.*

v. **Treatises on hypocrisy and nominal Christianity:** e.g.,
Daniel Dyke, *The Mystery of Selfe-Deceiving;* Shepard, *The
Parable of the Ten Virgins;* Matthew Meade, *The Almost
Christian; or, the False-Professor Tried and Cast.*

Nearly all these works began life as courses of sermons. They
bear the marks that distinguish Puritan sermons; they are textual
and expository, practical and applicatory, analytical and thorough. They are uniformly doctrinal—that is to say, their real subject is always God and His ways, even when the formal object of
consideration is man. And together they show clearly what the
Puritans took to be involved in preaching the gospel.

II

Note, first, *the comprehensiveness of the gospel* as the Puritans understood it. Observe how much they took the word "gospel" to
cover. It denoted to them the whole doctrine of the covenant of
grace. Sometimes they included as part of it the preparatory message of sin and judgment as well. Thus, to preach the gospel
meant to them nothing less than declaring the entire economy of
redemption, the saving work of all three members of the Trinity.
This appears from the following words of Thomas Manton: "The
sum of the gospel is this, that all who, by true repentance and

faith, do forsake the flesh, the world, and the devil, and give themselves up to God the Father, Son, and Holy Spirit, as their creator, redeemer, and sanctifier, shall find God as a father, taking them for his reconciled children, and for Christ's sake pardoning their sin, and by his Spirit giving them his grace; and, if they persevere in this course, will finally glorify them, and bestow upon them everlasting happiness; but will condemn the unbelievers, impenitent, and ungodly to everlasting punishment. That this is the sum of the gospel appeareth by Mark 15:15–16: 'Go, preach the gospel to every creature. He that believeth, and is baptized, shall be saved; but he that believeth not shall be damned';—where you have all the Christian religion laid before you in one short view and prospect."[3]

"The sum of the gospel"—"all the Christian religion . . . in one short view and prospect." We are doing something less than preaching the gospel, the Puritans would tell us, if our preaching contains less than this.

Their view of the comprehensiveness of the gospel comes out in many different connections. We give three further examples. Here, first, is Goodwin, telling us how much is involved in relating the gospel story.

"As there are three persons . . . who have a joint hand in that work of salvation, the subject of the gospel, so the whole story of the gospel hath three parts also, in every of which some one of them bears an especial part.

"The *first* part God the Father had the chiefest hand in, who drew the platform of this great work, contrived it, made the motion first to his Son . . .

"The *second*, God the Son, when he came down and took flesh and . . . transacted the redemption of the world according to that draft.

"As after him, when he was off the stage, came the Spirit, to apply what he had done, and all the benefits of it, whose work makes up the *third* part."[4] And all three parts must receive mention if the gospel story is to be told properly.

Here, again, is John Owen, showing us how much is involved in declaring the promises of the gospel.

"Gospel promises then are: 1. The free and gracious dispensations; and, 2. discoveries of God's good-will and love; to, 3. sinners; 4. through Christ; 5. in a covenant of grace; 6. wherein, upon his truth and faithfulness, he engageth himself to be their God, to give His Son unto them, and for them, and his Holy Spirit to abide with them, with all things that are either required in them, or are necessary for them, to make them accepted before him, and to bring them to an enjoyment of him."[5] And proclaiming the gospel in its character as God's word of promise involves elucidating all this.

Here, finally, is Richard Baxter, giving his first three "directions . . . to a sound conversion"—directions designed to lay the foundation for an intelligent and responsible commitment to Christ.

First, "labour after a right understanding of the true nature of Christianity, and the meaning of the gospel"; begin by clarifying your mind about the Christian message as a whole. Second, study the Scriptures for this purpose. Third, "be much in the serious consideration of the truths which you understand"—that you were made to serve God; that you have fallen short of this end; that you are now in a wretched state, for "you have made God your enemy"; how happy the converted are; how adequate Christ's redemption is; how disastrous it will be to reject redemption; and—before any of the rest—"the nature of that God with whom ye have to do." "If he be good, and infinitely good, there is all the reason in the world that you should love him; and there is no show of reason that you should love the world or sin before him. If he be faithful and true, his threatenings must be feared, and his promises must not be distrusted; and there is no reason that you should make any question of his word. If he be holy . . . then he must be an enemy to sin, and to all that are unholy, because they are contrary to his nature. Consider that he is almighty, and there is no resisting him . . . in the twink of an eye can he snatch thy guilty soul from thy body, and cast it where sin is better known. A word of his mouth can set all the world against thee, and set thine own conscience against thee too . . . and if he be thine enemy, it is no matter who is thy friend; for all the world cannot save thee, if he do but condemn thee . . . He was from eternity, and thou art but as it were of yesterday: thy being is from him; thy life is always in his hands, thou canst not live an hour without him, thou canst not fetch a breath without him, nor think a thought, nor speak a word, nor stir a foot or a hand without him . . . no love can be great enough, and no praises can be high enough, and no service can be holy and good enough for such a God . . . this is not a God to be neglected, or dallied with; nor a God to be resisted, nor provoked by the wilful breaking of his laws . . . O therefore dwell on the meditations of the almighty!"[6] This knowledge of God, Baxter insists, is fundamental to a sound conversion. Evidently, therefore, it too must find its place in the preaching of the gospel.

The importance of all this is that it challenges our modern idea that preaching "gospel sermons" means just harping on a few great truths—guilt, and atonement, and forgiveness—set virtually in a theological vacuum. The Puritan view was that preaching "gospel sermons" meant teaching the whole Christian system—the character of God, the Trinity, the plan of salvation, the entire work of grace. To preach Christ, they held, involved preaching all this. Preach less, they would tell us, and what you do preach will not be properly grasped. What the good news of a restored relationship with God through Christ means for religion cannot be understood further than it is seen in this comprehensive context. Gospel preaching centres always upon the theme of man's relationship to God, but around that centre it must range throughout the whole sphere of revealed truth, viewing the centre from every angle of vision that the Bible provides. In this way, they would say, preaching the gospel involves preaching the whole counsel of God. Nor should the preaching of the gospel be thought of as something confined to set evangelistic occasions, as if at other times we should preach something else. If one preaches the Bible biblically, one cannot help preaching the gospel all the time, and every sermon will be, as Bolton said, at least by implication evangelistic.

And we must not be afraid to start with the basic facts about God the Creator. Revealed truth has a structure, and this is its foundation. When Paul preached to the pagan Athenians, he laid this foundation before going further. He had to, or else the point of his witness to our Lord would not have been grasped. For knowledge of sin and salvation presupposes some knowledge of the Creator; nobody can see what sin is till he has learned what God is. That is why Baxter directed the seeking soul to fix his mind first and foremost on the nature and majesty of God. In pagan England today, we need to lay the same foundation as Paul laid at Athens. We complain that our "gospel preaching" (in the modern sense) does not register with those who hear it. May not this be in the first instance because they know nothing about the God with whom they have to do? Have we taken pains to teach them who God is? The irony of our situation is that if we spend time preaching to modern pagans about the character of God we shall be told that we are not preaching the gospel. But the Puritans would not tell us that; nor would Paul.

III

Note, second, *the emphases of the gospel* as the Puritans preached it. We note a few of the major points.

i. They diagnosed *the plight of man* as one, not merely of guilt for sins, but also of pollution in sin and bondage to sin. And by bondage to sin they meant, not bondage to *sins*—particular weaknesses of character and bad habits—but the state of being wholly dominated by an inbred attitude of enmity to God. They sought to expose the sinfulness that underlies sins, and convince men of their own utter corruption and inability to improve themselves in God's sight. This, they held, was a vital part of the work of a gospel preacher; for the index of the soundness of a man's faith in Christ is the genuineness of the self-despair from which it springs.

ii. They analysed *the issue of sin* in terms of God's hostility in the present, as well as His condemnation in the future. Their constant aim was to make men feel that to be in a wrong relationship with God was intolerable here and now; hence, contrary to common belief, they made even more of the first thought than they did of the second.

iii. They stressed that *the goal of grace* is the glory and praise of God, and our salvation is a means to this end. God, they said, has chosen to redeem us, not for our sakes, but for His own name's sake.

iv. They stressed *the sufficiency of Christ*. They did not teach men to trust a theory of the atonement, but a living Redeemer, the perfect adequacy of whose saving work they never tired of extolling.

v. They stressed *the condescension of Christ*. He was never to them less than the Divine Son, and they measured His mercy by His majesty. They magnified the love of the cross by dwelling on the greatness of the glory which He left for it. They dwelt on the patience and forbearance expressed in His invitations to sinners as further revealing His kindness. And when they applied Revelation 3:20 evangelistically (as on occasion they did), they took the words "Behold, I stand at the door and knock" as disclosing, not the impotence of His grace apart from man's cooperation (the too-prevalent modern interpretation), but rather the grace of His omnipotence in freely offering Himself to needy souls.

These were the emphases which characterized the Puritan preaching of the gospel, and indeed all preaching of it by evangelicals from Puritan times onward till some eighty years ago.

IV

Note, third, *the demands of the gospel* as the Puritans presented them.

The gospel, they said, summons sinners to faith in Christ. Faith means assent to the good news as divine truth and consent to receive Jesus Christ as a Divine Saviour. Faith is not a meritorious work, but the stretching out of an empty hand to lay hold of a Saviour and with Him a salvation. "What doth the Lord offer in the gospel?" asks Thomas Shepard. "Is it not first Christ, and then all the benefits of Christ?"[7] The Lord Jesus Christ must be received in His whole mediatorial office, as Saviour and Lord, as Prophet, Priest, and King; for "never did any man take Jesus Christ savingly, who took him not for a Husband and a Lord, to serve, love and obey him for ever after, as well as a Saviour to disburden him of his sinnes; as a King to govern him by his Word and Spirit, as well as a Priest to wash him in his Blood."[8] To accept Jesus Christ as Saviour and Priest is evangelical faith; to enthrone Him as Lord and King is evangelical repentance.

The persons invited and commanded to believe are sinners, as such. The Saviour is freely offered in the gospel to all who need Him. The question of the extent of the atonement does not therefore arise in evangelism, for what the gospel commands the unconverted man to believe is not that Christ died with the specific intention of securing his individual salvation, but that here and now the Christ who died for sinners offers Himself to this individual sinner, saying to him personally, "Come unto me . . . and I will give you rest" (Matthew 11: 28). The whole warrant of faith—the ground, that is, on which believing becomes permissible and obligatory—is found in this invitation and command of the Father and the Son.

The above assertion, however, has been disputed. C. H. Spurgeon, in a sermon on 1 John 3:23, entitled "The Warrant of Faith," which he preached in 1863, affirmed that some of the Puritans, like the opponents of the Marrowmen in eighteenth-century Scotland and the hypercalvinistic Baptists of Spurgeon's own day, taught that the ground on which believing became permissible was a preliminary work of grace, convicting of sin.

"Some preachers in the Puritanic times," Spurgeon declared, "erred much in this matter . . . Alleine and Baxter . . . Rogers of Dedham, Shepherd (Shepard), the author of *The Sound Believer,* and especially the American, Thomas Hooker, who has written a book upon qualifications for coming to Christ. These excellent men had a fear of preaching the gospel to any except those whom they styled as 'sensible sinners' . . . They preached repentance and hatred of sin as the warrant of a sinner's trusting to Christ. According to them, a sinner might reason thus—'I possess such-and-such a degree of sensibility on account of sin, therefore

I have a right to trust in Christ.' Now, I venture to affirm that such reasoning is seasoned with fatal error . . . "[9]

Spurgeon's theological judgment is surely sound; but equally surely he has put the wrong people in the dock. One wonders whether he had read the authors to whom he refers (after all, he was only twenty-nine at the time); certainly, he misrepresents their teaching. To state the facts correctly, we must distinguish two questions: that of the *warrant of faith*, and that of the *way to faith*.

All the Puritans agreed that the way by which God brings sinners to faith is through a "preparatory work," longer or shorter, of contrition and humbling for sin. This is not repentance (actual turning from sin, which follows faith), but the soil out of which, upon their believing, repentance will spring. The reason why they held this preparatory work to be necessary has nothing to do with the question of the warrant of faith; it is simply because fallen man is naturally in love with sin, and it is a psychological impossibility for him to close whole-heartedly with Christ as a Saviour from sin until he has come to hate sin and long to be delivered from it.

Now, three of the authors whom Spurgeon names—John Rogers (in *The Doctrine of Faith*, 1627), Thomas Hooker (in *The Soul's Preparation For Christ*, 1632, and other books), and Thomas Shepard (in *The Sound Believer*, 1645)—delineated the stages of this preparatory work in great detail; and their writings on the subject may justly be criticized on three counts.

a. They gave the impression (despite parenthetical disclaimers) that God's work of humbling men for sin invariably followed the same course, in every detail of the process, and if you had not experienced it all you must be a stranger to true grace. In his teens, Richard Baxter went through much fear and distress, because, examine himself as he might, "I could not distinctly trace the Workings of the Spirit upon my heart in that method which . . . *Mr. Hooker, Mr. Rogers,* and other Divines describe." Later, however, he realized "that God breaketh not all Men's hearts alike," and escaped from the pietistic strait-jacket which these giants of experimental religion had forged.[10]

b. Hooker and Shepard went beyond Scripture in teaching that the sign of true humiliation for sin was that the sinner, acknowledging his guilt, should be content to be damned for the glory of God. Baxter and, later, Giles Firmin (in *The Real Christian*, 1670) took them to task for this, arguing that it was not required by God nor psychologically possible for any man ever to be content to be damned.

c. By concentrating attention on this preliminary work of grace, and harping on the need for it to be done thoroughly, these writers effectively discouraged seeking souls from going straight to Christ in their despair. "If you that are now converted had lived in our younger days," wrote Goodwin in later life, "you would have seen that we were held long under John Baptist's water, of being humbled for sin."[11] This naturally led to much morbidity.

But on the question of the warrant of faith, these authors are not open to criticism; when they speak of it, their doctrine is exactly Spurgeon's, that the warrant of faith is the command and promise of God to sinners, and that faith is required of everyone who hears the gospel. Firmin spoke for the entire Puritan school when he laid it down that "it is the duty of all the sons and daughters of Adam, who hear the gospel preached, and Christ offered to them, to believe in, or receive, Christ, whether they be prepared or not prepared," and quoted 1 John 3:23 and John 6:29 as proof.[12] John Rogers, discussing the warrant of faith, quotes the same two texts in support of the statement that "faith is one of the commandments of the gospel."[13] Shepard speaks of the "commandment to receive Christ" in 1 John 3:23 which "binds conscience to believe, as you will answer for the contempt of this rich grace at the great day of account,"[14] If any hearer of the gospel does not believe, it is not for want of being divinely directed and laid under obligation to do so. The truth is that to all the Puritans it was one of the wonders of free grace that the Lord Jesus Christ invites sinners, just as they are, in all their filthy rags, to receive Him and find life, and they never waxed more impassioned and powerful than when dilating on what John Owen, in his stately way, calls "the infinite condescension, grace and love of Christ, in

His invitations of sinners to come unto him, that they may be saved."[15]

V

Thus the Puritans preached the gospel of free and sovereign grace. Like Baxter, they were motivated by "a thirsty desire of Men's Conversion and Salvation."[16] But two other motives weighed with them also, both greater even than this; the double desire to glorify God, and to magnify Christ. The latter point is, perhaps, the one that at present we most need to apply to ourselves. All of us who preach the gospel, I suppose, desire men's conversion. Many, no doubt, are concerned also to glorify God by a faithful declaration of His truth. But how many, when preaching the gospel, are consumed by the longing to magnify Christ— to extol the richness, and freedom, and glory of His grace, and the perfection of His saving work? The cheap and perfunctory way in which the person of the Saviour is sometimes dealt with in modern evangelistic preaching forces this question upon us. Puritan gospel preaching was concerned above all things to *honour Christ:* to show His glory to needy men and women. It is much to be wished that we who preach the gospel in these days might recover the same overmastering concern to exalt this mighty Saviour.

(1) *Works* (1838 ed.), 2:482. (2) *Instructions for a Right Comforting Afflicted Consciences* (3rd ed., 1640), p. 185, (3) *Works* (1870 ed.) 2:102 (4) *Works* (1862 ed.), 3:483. (5) *Works* (ed. Goold), 11:227. (6) 2:.589 (7) *The Sound Believer* (1849 ed.), p. 217. (8) Bolton, op. cit., p. 186. (9) *Sermons by Rev. C. H. Spurgeon*, ed. Nicoll, p. 112. (10) *Reliquiae Baxterianae*, 1:7. (11) 4:346. (12) *The Real Christian*, p. 2. (13) *The Doctrine of Faith*, p .502. (14) op. cit., p. 238 (15) 1:422. (16) *Rel. Bax.* 1:12.

3

ANDREW FULLER'S CONFLICT
WITH HYPERCALVINISM

T. E. Watson

I

From the act of uniformity in 1662 to the Glorious Revolution of 1688 the nonconforming Puritans held their ground without flinching in the face of fierce persecution, but the Toleration Act of 1689 ushered in an era of ease which for a time almost killed them. With ease came error, and Presbyterians, Independents, and Baptists were all affected. Those not swept away by the flood of rationalism into Unitarianism were blown by the ill wind of over-emphasis into Hypercalvinism.

Of no one was this more true than the Particular Baptists. The recently reprinted 1689 London Confession of Faith shows that the Puritan Baptists who drew it up were orthodox Calvinists. So were their successors; but as the years passed their Calvinism lost its savour, and while they still lived lives of sincere piety, their zeal for the salvation of the unconverted waned. They seemed to think that this was God's concern, not theirs. Their preaching altered accordingly. "Undue prominence was given in their discourses to the teaching of Scripture respecting the Divine purposes. They were satisfied with stating men's danger, and assuring them that they were on the high road to perdition. But they did not call on them to repent and believe the gospel. They did not entreat them to be reconciled to God. They did not warn every man and teach every man in all wisdom. And the churches did not, could not, under their instruction, engage in efforts for the conversion of souls. They were so afraid of intruding on God's work that they neglected to do what He had commanded them. They seem to have supposed that *preservation* was all they should aim at; they had not heart enough to seek *for extension*. No wonder the cause declined" (Cramp, *Baptist History*).

It was this kind of preaching that Andrew Fuller heard in his youth. Born in 1754 at Wicken in Cambridgeshire, he was nearly fourteen years old before he thought seriously on spiritual issues. He writes: "The preaching upon which I attended was not adapted to awaken my conscience, as the minister had seldom anything to say except to believers, and what believing was I neither knew, nor was I greatly concerned to know." Aged fifteen, he came under great conviction of sin, but still his minister had nothing to say to him except, "Attend the means of grace, and may the Lord call you by it in due time." As a result Fuller underwent a Bunyan-like agony of soul which only ended when he went to Christ in much the same way as Esther went to King Ahasuerus, saying, "If I perish, I perish." Recounting this, Fuller writes, "I now found rest for my troubled soul; and I reckon that I should have found it sooner, if I had not entertained the notion of my having no warrant to come to Christ without some previous qualification."

In 1770 he was baptized and joined the Particular Baptist Church at Soham. Eighteen months later a painful experience set him investigating the problem of human responsibility. "One of the members having been guilty of drinking to excess, I was one of the first who knew of it. I immediately went and talked to him, as well as I could, on the evil of his conduct. His answer was, he could not keep himself; and that though I bore so hard on him, I was not my own keeper. At this I felt indignant, considering it as a base excuse. I therefore told him that he *could* keep himself from such sins as these, and that his way of talking was merely to excuse what was inexcusable. He, however, was offended, and told me that I was young and did not know the deceitfulness of my own heart. Well, I went and told my pastor, who highly commended me, and said, we certainly could keep ourselves from open sins. We had not power, he observed, to do things spiritually good; but as to outward acts, we had power to obey the will of God and to disobey it."

This set the whole church debating the question of ability and accountability. Since most did not agree with their pastor's explanation, they subsequently called upon him to resign. As for Fuller, the more he thought the more puzzled he became. He writes, "I perceived that some kind of power was necessary to render us accountable beings. If we were like stocks and stones, or literally dead, like men in a burying-ground, we could with no more propriety than they be commanded to perform any duty; if we were mere machines, there could be no sin chargeable upon us. Yet, on the other hand, the Scriptures represent the godly as crying to Heaven for preservation from evil, and ascribing all that good that was in them to Him who worketh in us to will and to do of his own good pleasure. I prayed much, and laboured hard to solve this difficulty."

Three years later he was called to the ministry, and began by preaching in the same way as other Calvinistic Baptists did. He had great respect for his elder brethren in the ministry, and for the writings of John Gill and John Brine, and was very slow to differ from them. Yet he did not forget that great men may make great blunders, as may be seen from the following covenant prayer recorded in his journal:

"O Lord God, I find myself in a world where thousands profess thy name. All profess to be searching after the truth; to have Christ and the inspired writers on their side. I am afraid lest I should be turned aside from the simplicity of the gospel. I feel my understanding full of darkness, my reason exceedingly imperfect, my will ready to start aside, and my passions strangely volatile. O illumine my understanding, teach my reason reason, my will rectitude, and let every faculty of which I am possessed be kept within the bounds of thy service.

O let not the sleight of wicked men, who lie in wait to deceive, nor ever the pious character of great men (who yet may be under great mistakes) draw me aside. Nor do thou suffer my own fancy to misguide me. Lord, thou hast given me a determination to take no principle at second-hand; but to search for everything at the pure fountain of thy word. Yet, Lord, I am afraid, seeing I am as liable to err as other men, lest I should be led aside from the truth by mine own imagination.

I pray that I may not only be kept from erroneous principles, but may so love the truth, as never to keep it back. O Lord, if thou wilt open mine eyes to behold the wonders of thy Word, and give me to feel their transforming tendency, then shall the Lord be my God; then let my tongue cleave to the roof of my mouth, if I shun to declare, to the best of my knowledge, the whole counsel of God."

Of his early reading, Fuller writes, "The principal writings with which I was first acquainted were those of Bunyan, Brine and Gill. I had read pretty much of Dr. Gill's *Body of Divinity,* and from many parts of it had received considerable instruction. I perceived, however, that the system of Bunyan was not the same with his; for that, while he (i.e. Bunyan) maintained the doctrines of election and predestination, he nevertheless held with the free offer of salvation to sinners without distinction. These were things which I then could not reconcile, and therefore supposed that Bunyan, though a great and good man, was not so *clear* in his views of the doctrines of the gospel as the writers who succeeded him. I found, indeed, the same things in all the old writers of the sixteenth and seventeenth century that came my way. They all dealt, as Bunyan did, in free invitations to sinners to come to Christ and be saved; the consistency of which with personal election I could not understand."

After some years of prayer and study Fuller became convinced that Bunyan was right after all, and in 1776 he began to exhort the unconverted to repent and believe in Christ. The change that came over his preaching was not appreciated by all his flock, and this was one of the reasons why he eventually left Soham for Kettering, where he worked for the remaining thrity-three years of his life.

The results of his investigation he wrote down for his own benefit, but when friends saw the manuscript they persuaded him to publish it. This he reluctantly did, in 1784, under the title, *The Gospel Worthy of All Acceptation*. As he had feared, its publication launched him into a sea of controversy through which he had to sail for the rest of his life. His broadside against Hypercalvinism was answered by a certain Mr. Button. Fuller countered with A *Reply to Mr. Button*. Meanwhile, into the fight came the General Baptists, who fired on Fuller from behind, thinking he was half way to becoming an Arminian. To their surprise they found Fuller as much opposed to Arminianism as he was to Hypercalvinism. Thus, in 1803 we find Fuller writing to Dr. Ryland, "Baxter considers Calvinists and Arminians as reconcilable, making the difference between them of but small account. I have no such idea: and if, on account of what I have here and elsewhere avowed, I were disowned by my present connexion (the Particular Baptists) I should rather choose to go through the world alone than be connected with them (the Arminian Baptists). Their scheme appears to me to undermine the doctrine of salvation of grace only, and to resolve the difference between one sinner and another into the will of man, which is directly opposite to all my views and experience."

Fuller did not spend all his life writing against Hypercalvinism. A lover of truth, he hated all kinds of error, and from his indefatigable pen came learned treatises opposing Deism, Unitarianism, Sandemanianism, and Universalism. He also published expositions of Genesis and Revelation. C. H. Spurgeon calls the former "one of the very best series of discourses extant upon Genesis." Altogether his complete works run to over a thousand double-columned pages of microscopic print, and they earned for him the offer of two D.D.'s, both of which, however, he declined. Perhaps his greatest work was as secretary of the Particular Baptist Missionary Society from its formation in 1792 to the day of his death in 1815. This was Britain's first proper missionary society, and the exploits of Carey abroad, supported by Fuller's extensive deputation work at home, inspired others to do likewise; so began the great missionary movement. It is no exaggeration to say that Carey's going to India was the logical outcome of Fuller's emancipation from Hypercalvinism. Fuller maintained that the gospel was worthy of *all* acceptation, from which Carey deduced that its acceptance ought to be pressed on *all* mankind.

II

What was the substance of Fuller's case against Hypercalvinism? We may most conveniently answer this question by setting out a summary of his original treatise on the subject. Its full title is *The Gospel Worthy of All Acceptation, or, the Duty of Sinners to Believe in Jesus Christ.* (His later arguments against Arminianism may be seen in his *Reply to Philanthropos* and *The Efficacy of Divine Grace.*)

Preface (defining the matter at issue): "There is no dispute about the doctrine of election, or any of the discriminating doctrines of grace. The question does not turn upon what are the causes of salvation, but rather upon what are the causes of damnation."

Part I: Fuller here states his own thesis. Our proposition, he writes, is that it is the duty of all who hear the gospel to believe in Christ with such a faith as issues in salvation. What is this saving faith? It is a real belief of God's report or record concerning His

Son (Mark 16:15–16; John 20:31) which includes personal trust in Christ's promises. (In an appendix, Fuller answers the Sandemanian view that saving faith is an act of the intellect alone.)

Part II is entitled: ARGUMENTS TO PROVE THAT FAITH IN CHRIST IS THE DUTY OF ALL WHO HEAR . . . THE GOSPEL.

Fuller's main points are as follows:

i. *Unconverted sinners are commanded, exhorted, and invited to believe in Christ for salvation.* John 12:36: "While ye have the light, believe in the light, that ye may be the children of light." Christ exhorts unbelievers (v. 37) to believe in the light (Himself, v. 46) so as to be children of light (i.e. true believers, cf. v. 46). Fuller also quotes John 6:29; Psalm 2:11–12; Isaiah 55:1–7; Jeremiah 6:10, 16 to prove this point.

ii. *The gospel requires obedience, and such an obedience as includes saving faith.* The end of preaching the gospel is "for obedience to the faith among all nations" (Romans 1:5). Obedience supposes previous obligation. If repentance towards God, and faith towards our Lord Jesus Christ, were not duties required of us, it would be incongruous to speak of them as exercises of obedience. Nor would it be less so to describe the impenitence and unbelief which expose men to everlasting destruction from the presence of the Lord, as "not *obeying* the gospel" (2 Thessalonians 1:8–9).

Fuller quotes John Owen: "When the apostle beseecheth us to be reconciled to God, I would know whether it be not a part of our duty to yield obedience? If not, the exhortation is frivolous and vain."

It should be noted, Fuller adds, that, though believing in Christ is compliance with a duty, yet it is not *as a duty* that we are said to be justified by it; otherwise justification by faith could not be, as it is, opposed to justification by works.

iii. *Scripture ascribes the want of faith in Christ to men's depravity.* Wilful ignorance (Romans 10:3), pride (Psalm 10:4), dishonesty (Luke 8:15), aversion of heart (John 5:40), are the reasons why men do not believe. Moreover, unbelief itself is expressly declared to be a sin of which the Spirit of truth has to convince the world (John 16:8–9). But unbelief cannot be a sin if faith is not a duty.

iv. *God has threatened and inflicted the most awful punishments on sinners for their not believing on the Lord Jesus Christ.* Fuller quotes Mark 16:16: "He that believeth and is baptized shall be saved; but he that believeth not shall be damned." It is saving faith to which salvation is promised, and to the want of this that damnation is threatened. Christ's words in John 3:18 similarly show that the want of such faith is a sin (though not the only sin) on account of which the unbeliever stands condemned. Observe also 2 Thessalonians 2:10–12, Fuller adds: note there the "because" and "for this cause." He goes on,

"In order to evade the arguments arising from the addresses of John the Baptist, of Christ and His apostles, who called upon the Jewish people to repent and believe the gospel it has been alleged that it was only an *outward* repentance and acknowledgment of the truth to which they were exhorted, and not that which is spiritual, or which has the promise of spiritual blessings. But an outward repentance and reformation of manners, as distinguished from that which consists in godly sorrow, NEEDS TO BE REPENTED OF. But that which requires to be repented of cannot be commanded of God, or constitute any part of a sinner's duty. The duty of every transgressor is to be *sorry at heart* for having sinned." Unfeigned repentance, like saving faith, is the sinner's duty.

Part III consists of ANSWERS AND OBJECTIONS.

i. *Concerning election.* The Hypercalvinist, says Fuller, argues that God's decree cancels man's duty (Romans

9:19), and the Arminian vice versa. Both agree in holding divine sovereignty and human responsibility to be incompatible with each other. But not so the Scriptures. After all that Paul writes in Romans 9 about God's electing some and rejecting others, in the very same chapter he assigns the Jews' failure to their seeking justification, not by faith in Christ, but by the works of the law, and holds them guilty for it (vv. 31–33).

ii. *Concerning particular redemption.* Fuller accepts the particularity of redemption as a revealed truth. But, he argues, there is no inconsistency between particular redemption and general invitations if the particularity of Christ's atonement lies, not in its insufficiency to save more than are saved, but in the sovereignty of its application. The application of redemption, which is directed solely by sovereign wisdom, is the result of previous design. That which is actually done was intended to be done. Hence the salvation of those that are saved is described as the end which the Saviour had in view in dying (Titus 2:14).

Now, if the gospel required each hearer to believe that Christ in dying had a particular purpose to save him, an inconsistency would arise at once. But in fact what the gospel commands men to believe is just the revealed fact that Christ offers Himself as a perfect Saviour to every last sinner who needs Him; and this will prove true, whether those who hear it believe it or not.

iii. *Concerning human inability.* Scripture declares that no man can come to Christ except the Father draw him, and the natural man *cannot* know the things of the Spirit of God. But now, Fuller asks, what kind of inability is this? Is it of such a kind as to destroy the sinner's obligation to believe the gospel?

Certain kinds of inability render a person excusable. God will not judge an insane man as if he had been a responsible being, nor will He reprove a blind man for not having read the Scriptures, nor will he condemn a heathen who has never heard the gospel for not having believed on Christ. The want of rational faculties, bodily powers, and external privileges, are cases of a kind of inability which frees a person from blame. This inability Fuller terms *natural* or *physical.*

Now, he argues, if the inability of sinners to believe in Christ were of this kind, justice would not hold them accountable for their unbelief and it would be as absurd to exhort them to believe as to exhort the (physically) blind to look, the deaf to hear, or the dead to walk. But, as we have seen, God does hold sinners responsible for their unbelief. Moreover, the blind are admonished to look, the deaf to hear, and the dead to arise (Isaiah 42:18; Ephesians 5:14). This fact alone should assure us that the blindness, deafness, and deadness of sinners to that which is spiritually good is not of the physical kind. These exhortations prove that the inability lies in the sinner's *disinclination,* and this disinclination Fuller terms *moral* inability.

The distinction between natural and moral inability is recognized in ordinary life. When charged with neglecting our duty to a parent or master, if we can say that we were unable to do it at the time no matter how much we wanted to, we never fail to say so. And should a master or parent reply suggesting that our want of ability really arose from want of inclination, we understand this to be the language of reproach, and are very earnest to maintain the contrary.

But if this moral inability (which *presupposes* natural ability) resolves itself solely into the sinner's disinclination to do what is commanded, why use the term "cannot?" Because it is just as impossible for anyone to do that which he has no mind to do, as to perform that which surpasses his natural power. Hence we read that Joseph's brethren *could not* speak peaceably unto him (Genesis 37:4). (Elsewhere Fuller shows that this moral disinclination is so strong that only the almighty operation of the Spirit can remove it.)

The Hypercalvinist, says Fuller, glories in the fact that he lays man much *lower* than other Calvinists do, but see how he does it.

"It is not in the character of a *sinner,* but of a *creature* of God; not on account of what he has made himself, but on account of what God has made him: and if this is the way in which we are to be humbled, it might be done still more effectually if we were reduced to the condition of a stock or a stone."

Last came, CONCLUDING REFLECTIONS.

i. *The warrant of faith.* If faith in Christ is the duty of the ungodly, it follows that every sinner, whatever his character, is completely warranted to trust in Christ for the salvation of his soul. It is not a question merely of "may," but of "must."

ii. *The sinfulness of unbelief.* If we disregard the offer of salvation, in the day of judgment it will be found that a price was in our hands to get wisdom, but that we had "no heart to it," and that herein consists our sin, and hence proceeds our ruin. God called, and we would not hearken; and it is for this reason—not because we were not offered life, but because we refused it—that we are now doomed to an eternity without it.

iii. *The duty of preachers.* "I believe it is the duty of every minister of Christ plainly and faithfully to preach the gospel to all who will hear it; and as I believe the inability of men to do spiritually good things to be wholly of the moral, and therefore of the criminal kind, and that it is their duty to love the Lord Jesus Christ and trust in Him for salvation, though they do not; I therefore believe free and solemn addresses, invitations, calls and warnings to them to be not only consistent, but directly adapted, as means, in the hand of the Spirit of God, to bring them to Christ. I consider it as part of my duty which I could not omit without being guilty of the blood of souls."

We end our review of Fuller's conflict with Hypercalvinism with some application to the present. We live in days when the pendulum is beginning to swing from Arminianism to Calvinism, for which we thank God. But the pendulum may swing too far, and Arminian "activitis" may give way to Hypercalvinistic paralysis. Can we observe in ourselves any symptoms of this disease? Are we less concerned for the salvation of souls than we once were? Do we still think it our duty to get the gospel to every creature? Have we the same zeal for missionary work? Have we grown slack in our use of tracts? Perhaps some of us are reacting too much against the Arminianism from which we have been rescued. Let us beware. Let us take heed to ourselves and to our doctrine for the sake of them that hear us. Whether or not we agree with Fuller at every point, may God give us Fuller's "determination to take no principle at second-hand, but to search for everything at the pure fountain of God's Word."

4

DISCIPLINE IN THE PURITAN CONGREGATION

D. Downham

Today, the question of the right administration of church discipline is both pressing and perplexing. A review of sixteenth- and seventeenth-century opinion on the subject may help us to get our bearings with regard to it.

The Necessity of Discipline

Both Continental and English Reformers were unanimous on this point. Calvin says, "As the doctrine of Christ is the life of the church, so discipline is, as it were, its sinews, for on it depends the adhering together of the members of the body, each in its own place." Discipline is "a kind of curb to restrain and lame those who war against the doctrine of Christ . . . a sort of stimulus by which the indifferent are aroused." Calvin's practice at Geneva was one with his teaching. During his early ministry there he refused to dispense the Lord's Supper because of the city's vice. Lewd citizens reacted to his uncompromising zeal by naming their dogs after him, and for three years he was expelled. On his return, he established a church court, composed of the six city ministers and twelve elders from their congregations, who met each Thursday to put under discipline "without respect of persons, every sort of evil-doer."

Calvin's influence upon the British Reformers in this matter was great. Knox's Book of Discipline, Cranmer's Prayer Books and Articles, and later the Canons Ecclesiastical of 1603, show our divines agreeing with those abroad that a more general form of discipline must replace auricular confession and penance, and that such discipline, along with the preaching of the word and administration of the sacraments, was a true mark of the church.

In England, however, the Reformers' desires were largely frustrated. The inherited relationship between church and state was a major reason for this. By the common law, only civil courts could enforce penalties on the excommunicated. (Today "it is doubtful how far an ecclesiastical court can pronounce sentence on a lay-person in any case whatever" [Boultbee, *The Thirty-nine Articles*, p. 278]). This meant that the established church, while clear in its principles, was from the first very much restrained in its practice.

The Elizabethan Puritans were devout churchmen who demanded a system of discipline that should work on a parochial basis. Hence they were sometimes called Disciplinarians. Only discipline, they held, could preserve church life from ruin through congregational disorders. Later, Baxter testified of his work at Kidderminster, "The exercise of church discipline was no small furtherance of the people's good: for I found plainly that without it I could not have kept the religious sort from separations and divisions." The disciplinarian instinct was evidently a sound one. But the demand for discipline was based on more than a judgment of expediency; what disturbed these men most was the fact that an essential element in the New Testament pattern for the ordering of congregations was being neglected.

The Objects of Discipline

These, to the Puritans, were three.

i. *To glorify God by obeying His word.* He had spoken and pre-scribed discipline; therefore they must obey. As ever, the Puritans were more concerned about obedience than about the consequences of obedience.

ii. *To safeguard the purity of the church's faith and life,* which were it not for discipline would be lost. "Christ," says Thomas Goodwin, speaking of Revelation 2–3, "calls upon the churches to imitate the first pattern given them, and wherein they or any swerved, he reduceth them to what they had first received and learned from the apostles, as containing an immutable rule not to be swerved from. Now, if they had not liberty to swerve from them, then not we: Revelation 3:3 'Remember . . . how thou hast received . . . and hold fast, and repent.' Those epistles to the seven churches do as much concern discipline as matters of doctrine; for the chief fault he doth find with them still [= always] is slackness of discipline, whereby they suffered men to teach or practice amiss." Baxter in his *Reformed Pastor* accused his fellow ministers of drawing the guilt of swearing, drunkenness, fornication, and other crimes upon their own heads by neglecting to use this ordinance, which God had given "for the cure of sinners." (No wonder his colleagues desired him to publish the book in Latin!).

Discipline was also needed to protect the weaker members of the congregation against harmful influences; for "evil company is very infectious. Wicked men, like the crocodile, slime the way to make thee fall, and when thou art down, suck out, as it were, thy blood" (Swinnock). Therefore, for the sake of the babe in Christ, a wicked man must be expelled from the congregation.

iii. *To reform and recover the erring member,* as we shall see more fully later.

Occasions for Disciplinary Action

Persons guilty of flagrant sins such as fornication or theft or of heresy were to be censured and excommunicated at once, unless they showed definite signs of repentance. In the system which the Puritans developed under the Commonwealth and the Nonconformists retained after the Restoration, lesser delinquencies also came under censure. Here are some examples of twentieth century relevance:

i. "Neglecting of public ordinances" was considered to be the first outward sign of backsliding. The church member was expected to be present at all functions; "oncers" were immediately suspect. In a case of persistent absenteeism, a fellow member would be appointed to look after the truant's movements and try to bring him back.

ii. Choosing the company of persons outside the Christian fellowship was regarded as matter for censure, especially when it concerned the opposite sex and resulted in marriage with an unbeliever. "Oh the sorrow, the grief, the perplexity, the holy passion . . . that this abomination had on the good heart of Ezra!" exclaims Brooks. "If thou art a man of holiness, thou must look more for a portion of grace in thy wife, than a portion of gold with a wife: thou must look more after righteousness than riches; more after piety than money; more after the inheritance she hath in heaven than the inheritance she hath on earth; more at her being new born, than at her being high born . . . Do you think that God, that would not have an ass and an ox plough together, that he will be yoked to such wretches, may I say to such asses, whose ungodliness hath debased them below the very ox and ass?" One Baptist was suspended, if not excommunicated, from his church for thirty-six years for such a lapse. Some Puritan pastors found a remedy against mixed marriages by adopting the role of matchmaker themselves!

iii. The Puritan Christian might, moreover, be admonished for the way he (or she) dressed. One of the many reasons why God visited London with the plague and the Great Fire, according to Brooks, was this: "There was (in) many professors of the gospel in London too great a conformity to the fashions of the world." Commenting on Ezekial 23:15, he says, "They that borrow the fashions of the Egyptians may get their boils and their blotches. Certainly such as fear the Lord should go in no apparel but first, such as they are willing to die in: secondly, to appear before the Ancient of Days in; thirdly, to stand before the judgment seat in." No doubt one reason why Charles II considered Presbyterianism "not the religion of a gentleman" was that Presbyterians judged his flamboyant royal attire unworthy of a monarch!

"Almost any fault to which frail human nature is subject," writes G. R. Cragg, "was considered a suitable pretext for admonishing a member and exhorting him to walk more worthily. Strong passions, backbiting or railing, anger ('without provocation'), a peevish and contentious spirit, insubordination, borrowing and not repaying, harsh treatment of fellow-members, idleness—these and many others were listed as just ground for discipline."

The Models of Discipline

Discipline was both *preventative and corrective.*

Preventative discipline was exercised, first, in the careful examination of adult applicants for reception into the church. "In many congregations, reception was neither prompt nor automatic," writes Cragg; "delay was customary, and careful scrutiny of each case the rule." The candidates had to exhibit signs of regeneration, to be willing to make open profession as to God's dealings with them, and ready to yield full obedience to Christ and His commands. Sometimes they would be asked to sign a form of covenant. I quote from one drawn up by Oliver Heywood: "I do also consent to be a member of the particular church whereof Mr. O. Heywood is teacher and overseer, and to submit to his teaching, his ministerial guidance and oversight according to God's Word: to hold communion with that church in the public worship of God, and to submit to brotherly admonition of fellow-members, that so we may be built up in knowledge and holiness."

In Scotland, the next stage in preventative discipline was "fencing the tables." This was done by means of an "action sermon" (or sermons), preached before the sacrament was administered, warning those who were living in known sin not to approach the Lord's Board. The Book of Common Prayer contains a strongly worded admonition to the same effect, to be read to would-be communicants: "If any of you be a blasphemer of God, an hinderer or slanderer of his Word, an adulterer, or be in malice, or envy, or in any other grievous crime, repent you of your sins, or else come not to that Holy Table; lest, after the taking of that Holy Sacrament, the devil enter into you, as he entered into Judas, and fill you full of all iniquities, and bring you to destruction both of body and soul." "Take care," says John Owen, "that these holy things be administered only to those who are meet and worthy, according unto the rule of the gospel. Those who impose on pastors the promiscuous administration of these divine ordinances, or the application of the seals unto all without difference, do deprive them of one-half of their ministerial office and duty."

The stages in *corrective* discipline are set out in the Westminster Confession, 3.4. The offender is to be admonished, privately and, if need be, publicly. If he disregards this, he should be suspended from the Lord's Table. This was sometimes called "lesser excommunication." The last stage is complete excommunication from the congregation. This solemn step must not be taken hastily or frivolously; since, writes Owen, "the great rule of every church society should be, that men observe and do whatsoever the Lord Christ hath commanded, none can be justly ejected out of the society but upon wilful disobedience to His commands. And therefore the casting of men out of church-communions on light and trivial occasions . . . is contrary unto natural light and the reason of things in themselves." Only when the offender's guilt has been established beyond doubt and everything possible has been done to persuade him to amend his ways is he to be thus cut off from the church's life.

Speaking of the consequences of full excommunication, Goodwin writes, "The proper inward effect that accompanies this ordinance is inward affliction and distress of conscience by Satan, which of all afflictions is the greatest punishment . . . This we see in the excommunication of the Corinthian; whose excommunication is said to be a delivering up unto Satan in the name of the Lord Jesus (1 Corinthians 5:4f.). He was to be cast out by a commission from Christ, which going forth in His name, when they published it on earth, He signed it in heaven." Further comment on the solemnity of the act would be superfluous. In a much-used seventeenth-century phrase, it was "with lamentation and sore trouble" that this sentence was passed on offenders.

Baxter recommended a three-day period of prayer to precede it; then the congregation was to assemble. Prayer would again be offered on behalf of the impenitent; Scriptures such as Leviticus 8 and 1 Corinthians 5 would be read and commented on. After a detailed statement of the offender's sins and the means vainly used to reclaim him, it would be declared that "he was from henceforth to be no longer a member of this congregation, but must be cast out into the world, and no longer be partaker with us in the holy mysteries of the Lord, nor in fellowship with us, nor enjoy the privileges of God's House;—and may the Lord have mercy on his soul" (Cragg). The congregation would be admonished to treat him as "an heathen and a publican" till he should be received back, and meanwhile to pray for his soul. Sometimes this act would be accompanied by a congregational fast.

The spirit of the act must be right; the extremes of carelessness on one side, and legalistic, censorious harshness on the other, must equally be avoided. When Puritan leaders dealt with this subject, Paul's tears were often mentioned. Pastors and their flocks were reminded that Paul had warned the Ephesians "day and night with tears," and written to the Corinthians "out of much affliction and anguish of heart . . . with many tears" (Acts 20:19, 31; 2 Corinthians 2:4). A century before, Calvin had remarked that church censure must be "aimed at curing the disease and not destroying the sinner," and that "the rod that is used for chastening must be a fatherly rod." Owen makes the same point: "the nature and end of this judgment or sentence must be corrective, not vindictive; for healing, not destruction." Baxter concurs: "prudence must be exercised in the proceeding, lest we do more hurt than good . . . we should deal humbly, even when we deal sharply, and make it appear that it is not from any ill will nor any lordly disposition, nor from revenge, but a necessary duty which we cannot conscientiously neglect." The temptation to tyrannize is real, but must be resisted. Owen gives principles by which motives may be tried:

1. No excommunication is to be allowed in dubious cases.
2. All prejudices, all partiality, all provocations, all haste and precipitation, are most carefully to be avoided in this administration, for the judgment is the Lord's.
3. There is also required herein a constant remembrance that we also are in the flesh and liable to temptation; which may restrain and keep in awe that forwardness and confidence which some are apt to manifest in such cases.

Since discipline is intended to reclaim the offender, nothing must be done in a spirit that puts needless obstacles in the way of his eventual restoration.

The Restoration of the Sinner

The Puritans were cautious of welcoming back the excommunicate on the first profession of penitence. They remembered that the risen Lord had subjected the erring Peter to careful cross-examination before restoring him to favour (John 11:15ff.); and they kept in view the distinction between the "godly sorrow that worketh repentance to salvation" and the "sorrow of the world" which "worketh death" (2 Corinthians 7:10). The marks of truth and sincerity in penitential confession, for which they looked in such cases, are set out by Brooks as follows:

1. True penitence is free and voluntary, not forced, nor reluctantly squeezed out, like Pharaoh's and Saul's confessions of sin.
2. True penitential confession is full and complete. Contrast that of Judas, who confessed his betrayal of innocent blood but not his covetousness.

3. True penitential confession is sincere, springing from the impressions of grace on the soul.
4. True penitential confession is distinct and not confused; in it offenders confess their sins wholesale and in detail, as David confessed his particular sins of adultery and blood-guiltiness.
5. The true penitent confesses the circumstances and aggravations of his lapse.
6. The true penitent is sorrowful, coming before God as Benhadad's servants came, with ropes about their necks. "Penitential tears are undeniable ambassadors."
7. True penitential confession is always mixed with faith, though not always with strong faith.
8. True penitence is accompanied by reformation of life.

Confession, of course, was to be made to God alone; but where these signs of "godly sorrow" were absent the applicant's request for restoration must be viewed with suspicion.

The mode of reinstatement varied, in different congregations, but was generally simple, consisting mainly of praise and prayer that the restored member might henceforth be kept in the Way. This might be accompanied at times by the laying on of hands. In some congregations, the restored penitent was expected to express sorrow for both public and private sins in the presence of the church, and to ask public forgiveness of those he had wronged.

The "Power of the Keys"

The subject of the authority exercised in discipline was very fully discussed in the seventeenth century. The Puritan position was that the power to excommunicate and restore lodged in the word, and consequently in the church insofar as the church rightly applied the word through its duly authorized representatives.

"This excommunication," says Owen, "is an act of church authority exerted in the name of our Lord Jesus Christ; and if so, then it is an act of the officers of the church . . . for there is no authority in the church, properly so called, but what resides in the officers of it . . . And there are two reasons which prove that the power of excommunication, as to the authoritative exercise of it, is in the elders of the church:

1. Because the apostles, by virtue of their office-power in every church, did join in the authoritative excommunication, as is plain in the case insisted on, 1 Corinthians 5; and there is no office-power remaining but what is in the elders of the church.
2. It is an act of rule; but all rule, properly so called, is in the hands of rulers only. We may add hereunto, that the care of the preservation of the church in its purity, of the vindication of its honour, of the edification of all its members, of the correction and salvation of offenders, is principally incumbent on them, or committed unto them."

However, as a safeguard against misunderstanding, Owen hastens to add that excommunication is the elders' act only "in point of power; for the execration of this sentence is committed unto . . . the body of the church. According as they concur and practise, so it is put into execution; for it is they who withdraw from them (the excommunicated); or the sentence is of no use or validity. The punishment must be inflicted by the 'many' (2 Corinthians 2:6); who are able also to restore him who is rebuked. Wherefore, excommunication without consent of the church is a mere nullity."

The above quotation reflects the Puritan pastor's consciousness that he had received power to exercise rule and discipline from the great Head of the church Himself. Today this consciousness has largely been lost, and a low view of the Christian ministry prevails. This is doubtless one reason why ecclesiastical discipline has fallen into disrepute.

Some Practical Implications

It is clear that both Reformers and Puritans regarded discipline as one of the marks of the well-ordered church. Calvin emphatically repudiated the anti-disciplinarian attitude when he said, "All who wish that discipline were abolished, or who impede its restoration, whether by thoughtlessness or design, certainly are aiming at the complete devastation of the church." If this is right, and discipline is one of the marks by which the true church is distinguished from the false, then such twentieth-century practices as indiscriminate baptism, open invitations to the Lord's Table, remarriage of divorced persons without enquiry into their circumstances, and receiving candidates for membership unexamined, demand serious scrutiny. What of the hearty welcome so often given to lapsed members from the church next door? What of the non-church-attenders, who, to ensure "post-mortem rewards," have had their names on our electoral rolls (or communion rolls) for years past? Are we by thoughtlessness aiming at the complete devastation of the church? If we stand convicted on this matter, are we willing to make positive efforts to amend our ways and restore the ordinance of discipline to its proper place?

Let Baxter close: "If ministers would be conscientious in performing this duty entirely and self-denyingly, they might make something of it, and expect a blessing upon it; but when we shrink from all that is dangerous or ungrateful in our work, and shift off all that is costly or troublesome, we cannot expect that any great good should be effected by such a carnal use of means; we cannot look that the gospel should run, and be glorified, when we do our duty so lamely and so defectively." May God help us to take these words to our hearts.

FOR FURTHER READING. *The Autobiography of Richard Baxter* (ed. J. M. Lloyd-Thomas; an abridgement of *Reliquiae Baxterianae*); *Oliver Heywood's Diaries, etc.* (ed. J. Horsfall Turner); Richard Baxter, *The Reformed Pastor, The Christian Directory*; John Owen, *The True Nature of a Gospel Church*; Thomas Goodwin, *On the Constitution, Right Order, and Government of the Churches*; Confessions of the Reformed churches; H. H. Rowdon, *Puritan Church Discipline*.

5

Revival: An Historical and Theological Survey

D. M. Lloyd-Jones

We are dealing with this subject because this year is the exact centenary of the revival of 1859 which took place, as you know, in various countries. But, still more important, we are calling attention to it because of the present state of the world. It is a good thing that at the end of our Conference we should be looking at a subject such as this, because the ultimate object of this Conference is not mere intellectual stimulation, it is that we may have a true and deep concern about the state of the church. If that is not our main object, then our study becomes just a sort of Puritan scholasticism, a mere barren intellectualism which, though interesting and entertaining, will finally prove to be of no value at all.

Let me make it clear before I go any further that I am not going to give what may be regarded as a formal address on "revival" as such. For twenty-six Sunday mornings this year I have tried to preach on "revival." I am not going to do that this evening. I am speaking primarily to ministers and ministerial students, and my purpose is not to give an address on "revival," but to attempt to face some of the problems and difficulties which seem to surround this whole subject.

I

There is no need to take any time in giving a definition of what is meant by revival. It is an experience in the life of the church when the Holy Spirit does an unusual work. He does that work, primarily, amongst the members of the church; it is a reviving of the believers. You cannot revive something that has never had life, so revival, by definition, is first of all an enlivening and quickening and awakening of lethargic, sleeping, almost moribund church members. Suddenly the power of the Spirit comes upon them and they are brought into a new and more profound awareness of the truths that they had previously held intellectually, and perhaps at a deeper level too. They are humbled, they are convicted of sin, they are terrified at themselves. Many of them feel that they had never been Christians. And then they come to see the great salvation of God in all its glory and to feel its power. Then, as the result of their quickening and enlivening, they begin to pray. New power comes into the preaching of the ministers, and the result of this is that large numbers who were previously outside the church are converted and brought in. So the two main characteristics of revival are, first, this extraordinary enlivening of the members of the church, and, second, the conversion of masses of people who hitherto have been outside in indifference and in sin. (There are many other consequences which I do not stay to mention, such as the needed provision of larger church buildings, the establishing of new causes, large numbers of men offering themselves for the ministry and beginning to train, and so on.) Here, then, in its essence is a definition of what we mean by revival.

II

Having said that, our best approach perhaps is to start with the actual historical facts. The title of this address states that it is to be partly an historical survey. And the first thing I would mention is this. There has never been a revival in the Roman Catholic Church. That is a significant fact as a starting point. Individuals in that church have known and experienced what can be called revival, but the church as such has never known revival. Why? I would say that the main explanation is this—it is a direct consequence of their whole doctrine of the Holy Spirit. They confine the Holy Spirit to the church and the priesthood, and particularly to the sacraments, and more particularly still to that of baptism. So, dealing with the Holy Spirit and His operations in that way, they leave no room for revival at all, and the result is that they never have revival.

In the same way there has never been revival in the Unitarian Church. I am simply stating facts.

The next observation I would make—and here I would be very careful to indicate that I am in no sense concerned to offer criticisms, I am simply trying to face facts—is that on the whole it is true to say that the Anglican Church has not known much about revival. There have been occasions when men in her ministry have undoubtedly been part and parcel of a revival, and greatly used, as we shall see, but, looking at her history, there has been no such thing as a general revival in the Anglican Church. That again is surely a fact of great significance. There was a little experience of revival in the Anglican body in Ireland a hundred years ago, but very little as far as I can find out anywhere else in the Anglican communion. Now why is this? Is it possible that there is something in her form of service that militates against the freedom of the operation of the Spirit? Is it also possible, perhaps, that her association with the state operates in the same direction, and that the whole character of the church and her view of herself and her parochial system tend to discourage the phenomenon of revival within her ranks? There, at any rate, is a big fact which stands out in the history of the Anglican Church.

298 ∽ D. M. LLOYD-JONES

Looking at it now a little more in terms of the centuries, and leaving the Reformation out of account for a moment because I shall come back to it in a later section, we find that in the seventeenth century there was a remarkable revival, or, indeed, series of revivals in Northern Ireland. This was in the 1620s. There were similar sporadic revivals in different churches in Scotland under the ministry of people like Welsh and Bruce and Livingston and David Dickson and Rutherford and Blair. And surely we must agree that in England in the case of Rogers of Dedham, and Baxter at Kidderminster, we are entitled to speak of revival. Then when you come to the eighteenth century there was that remarkable revival that took place about 1727 in the Moravian community at Herrnhut in Germany. That amazing movement of the Spirit is graphically described in the early part of the Journals of John Wesley, and of course in many manuals on the history of the Moravian Brethren. Then in the United states of America you have Jonathan Edwards and the "Great Awakening," in which George Whitefield also took such a prominent part. In England under the ministry of Whitefield, again, and of the Wesleys and various other men, almost right up to 1790, there were clear outpourings of the Spirit in revival. Indeed, this whole period, in a sense, and looked at broadly, can be described as an age of revival.

Exactly the same thing was true of Wales from 1735 onwards. Both Howell Harris and Daniel Rowlands received their "baptism of power," as they would put it, and a great revival broke out. It lasted a number of years, then it began to wane, then it came back again. There was a succession of revival after revival; it came in several waves right up to the end of the life of Rowlands and even beyond that. There were periodic revivals right through to the end of the century. The same thing, of course, was true of Scotland. All who know the story of the eighteenth century have heard about Cambuslang and what happened there on the occasion of that famous communion service, and later at Kilsyth and various other places.

Then when we come to the nineteenth century we find that a notable revival broke out in Northern Ireland in 1858 (though it is generally called the '59 Revival), and this spread later to Scotland. There was a similar movement of revival in Wales lasting right throughout that year. And the same thing had happened, as you know, in America, starting in 1857.

It would be very interesting to stop with these revivals and to give an account of them. There is, however, no need to do so, as excellent books giving an account of them have appeared recently. Two, for instance, have been published on the revival in Ireland, and one has just come off the press about the revival in Wales in 1859.[1] There are various other older books covering the same ground, but in all cases they are simply accounts of the happenings and events. They do not, therefore, deal with our particular difficulties. Even a book like Sprague's *Lectures on Revivals,* recently re-published,[2] is too general in its treatment to do that. However, there is the history, right up until 1860. It is a story of over a century of recurrent revival. I cannot but be interested in this fact, that between 1760 and 1860 there were at least fifteen major revivals in Wales alone.

We now come to the striking fact that there seems to have been a great change in people's outlook on this whole matter after about 1860, or 1870. There seems to be a kind of dividing line at that historical juncture. Before that, we find that people thought in terms of revival, and we hear of frequent revivals in the history of the church; but after that, revivals become rather exceptional phenomena. By now, I believe, we have reached an age in which the vast majority of church members have almost ceased to think in terms of revival at all. Up until 1860 it was the instinctive thing to think in terms of revival. If there had been a period of spiritual drought, if things were not going well in the church, the first thing they thought of was this—"should not we have a time of confession and humiliation and prayer to God to visit us again?" They did it almost instinctively. But we do not do that. Why not? What is the explanation of this change that seems to have come into the thinking of the church? I think I can suggest some of the factors.

The first factor, beyond any doubt, is the decline in Reformed theology. The whole modernist movement that had started in the forties of the last century gained great momentum in the sixties.

It increased at an alarming speed and the Reformed theology in particular fell into the background. Until that date—speaking at any rate for Nonconformity—the prevailing theology was almost entirely Calvinistic, apart from that of the Methodist bodies. But there was a very sad decline and sudden waning of all that. The change took place very rapidly, and those who are familiar with the life of Charles Haddon Spurgeon will know how he not only saw the fact but deeply regretted it and bemoaned it.

Second, there was the influence of the writings of Charles G. Finney. Because of the numerical success of his campaigns and his meetings, his work attracted great attention, and his volume of lectures, *Revivals of Religion,* soon became very popular and almost a best-seller. Finney's whole outlook and teaching seems to have become a governing factor in the outlook of the church. It has led to the notion of what we call "evangelistic campaigns." Finney is the man of all men who is responsible for the current confusion with regard to this matter. Our American brethren even get confused about the very terms. They talk about "holding a revival meeting"; they mean, of course, an evangelistic campaign. That is the result of Finney's influence, and it has really befogged the whole situation. The influence of Finney's teaching upon the outlook of the church has been quite extraordinary. People now, instead of thinking instinctively about turning to God and praying for revival when they see that the church is languishing, decide rather to call a committee, to organize an evangelistic campaign, and work out and plan an advertising programme to "launch" it, as they say. The whole outlook and mentality has entirely changed.

Third, we come to a matter which is a little controversial. I am not certain about it myself—but increasingly I feel that this is a very important factor. I am still dealing, remember, with the change that took place about 1860, and I cannot but feel that theological seminaries have been an important factor in the change. Here is an attempt to explain how it worked. Up until, say, the 1830s the position was something like this. At first the preaching was done by clergy and ministers who had themselves been revived. Numbers of men who had been converted then began to feel a call to preach, or it was suggested to them by some of these leaders that they had a preaching gift. They had manifested it in prayer or in taking part in a class meeting or in a discussion, and now they were encouraged to preach. These men were farmers, workers, manual workers, and so on. They had not been to a theological seminary. They were men who had a living experience of God in their hearts, who read and studied their Bibles and books about the Bible. They were men of strong natural talents and were very largely self-taught. This was the class of men who largely became the preachers after the death of the first great leaders. But then, the idea came in that as education had spread among the masses and the congregations were now more sophisticated and more learned, the ministry of these simple ordinary men was no longer adequate. (I am not criticizing that attitude; I am trying to put the actual facts before you.) It was felt that there was a need for training and that you must have learned men in the ministry. This started with an undoubtedly good and right motive. Nor is there any *a priori* reason why spirituality and learning should be incompatible; but nevertheless it does seem to be the case in practice that as men become more and more learned they tend to pay less and less attention to the spiritual side of things. Now this is almost inevitable, of course, for we are yet in the flesh, and are still imperfect. Whether a man wants to or not, he gradually finds himself becoming more and more interested in things in a purely intellectual manner. I have known this very thing in my own life. Unconsciously one can become so interested in the purely intellectual aspect of Christianity, and in learning and understanding and knowledge, as to forget the Spirit. I am therefore putting it simply as a possibility for consideration that perhaps the increase in theological seminaries may have been a factor in discouraging people from thinking about revival. The more learned we become, the more respectable we tend to become. As we become "men of weight" and important, we feel that we have to be very careful as to what we do or allow to happen to us. It is extremely difficult for such men to maintain that "simplicity which is in Christ Jesus"; certainly more difficult than for the other type of man whom I have just been describing. I do not want to exaggerate this, but I am suggesting that it may very well have been a serious factor.

Whatever the explanation, we have come now to this extraordinary position that, unless I am greatly mistaken, there is a lack of interest today in this question of revival. I am speaking out of knowledge. I am interested in discussions, and I frequent certain circles where men meet for discussion. I suggest on the basis of such experience that there is not only a lack of interest in revival but also an antagonism to the idea. I am told by the publishers that the book on the subject which I commended, Sprague's *Lectures on Revival*, has not been selling too well. I am amazed at that, but it is a fact. Why is there this lack of interest in revival? Why has the subject dropped out of the minds of people? And this is the interesting thing: what I am saying is not only true of the Arminian brethren, it is equally true of the Calvinistic brethren. Let us be clear about this. If you examine the books on the Holy Spirit, published during the past fifty years by men of all schools, you will find that they do not even mention revival at all. One is not surprised at this in some instances, because the writers' particular outlook is one which, though it pays lip-service to the work of the Holy Spirit, really pins its faith on what man does himself, on what man organizes. That whole outlook expresses itself through evangelistic campaigns and their appendages. You first of all get your men to go to the evangelistic campaign to get them saved. Then you take them to another place where they get a further desired blessing. That is the outlook. I am not poking fun at it; I am simply describing what is actually the controlling thought: that you take them to the right places and the results can be expected to follow. "What more do you need?" say such people. "Why are you talking about revival? Things are going well. Look at the crowds, look at the masses of people who are coming; isn't this enough? Why go any further?" Their attitude is perfectly logical if you grant its initial premise.

But that the same thing should be true of Reformed people—this is to me not only surprising but tragic. It is not only the books by Arminians which omit all reference to revival, the same is true of those by Calvinists. Dr. Lewis Sperry Chafer, for instance, in his great volume on pneumatology, does not mention revivals at all. Here is an example of a Calvinist who had on this point become infected by this general climate of opinion. But here is a still more tragic fact. As I was preparing this lecture, I turned to Charles Hodge, but I got no help. Charles Hodge does not seem to have been interested in revival. Why not? I would say it is for the reasons I have already been giving. A man like Charles Hodge becomes a theologian, and he tends therefore not to think as he should in terms of the church in its local concrete situation, but in terms of great abstract systems of truth. He lives in that realm of comparisons and arguments and contrasts, of systems and especially of philosophy, and almost inevitably he ceases to think as he should about revival and the immediate operations of the Spirit.

There is one very interesting point just here. I would say that this change of outlook on the part of Calvinists came in the U.S.A. somewhere between Archibald Alexander and Charles Hodge. Charles Hodge, as you know, was the successor of Archibald Alexander in the theological seminary at Princeton. Now Archibald Alexander had had experience of revival in his early days. Charles Hodge knew something about it, but not to the same extent as Alexander, who was an older man and who belonged partly to the previous century. It is just there that this change seems to me to have taken place.

Another interesting point to observe is that if you want any help at all on the subject of revival you are more or less driven back to books on the Holy Spirit and His work that were written before 1860. There are, for instance, *The Doctrine of the Holy Spirit,* by George Smeaton, and also Buchanan on the Holy Spirit. They both have a section on revival, but you will observe that they are both prior to the date I mentioned. Is not that an interesting fact? They belonged, you see, to the period when the church instinctively thought in the way I have described.

III

Let us now try to analyse this. Why is it that men belonging to the Reformed tradition, of all traditions, have apparently lost interest in this question of revival? I have already given you one reason, which is the danger of becoming theoretical and intellectual in one's approach. A minister of the gospel is a man who is always fighting on two fronts. He first of all has to urge people to become interested in doctrine and theology, but he will not have been long at that before he will find that he has to open up a second front, and to tell people that it is not enough to be interested only in doctrine and theology, that there is a danger of becoming a mere orthodox intellectualist and of growing negligent about your own spiritual life and the life of the church. This is the besetting danger of people who hold the Reformed position. They are the only people who are really interested in theology, so the devil comes to them and drives them too far along the line of that interest and they tend to become pure theologians and interested in truth only intellectually.

Second, I am sure that this phenomenon was due to the fact that so much energy in the last century had to be given to the fight against modernism. The enemy was attacking along that particular line and all the energy of the orthodox was bent to quell him and to hold him back and to defeat him. Yes, but unconsciously they allowed this conflict to control their entire thinking, and apologetics became the chief thing with them instead of a positive message. The same thing had happened in the early part of the eighteenth century. Rationalism and deism had come in and the church became concerned about it. What did they do? They set up the Boyle Lectures, Butler wrote his "Analogy," and so on. They tried to stem the tide by answering the objections and dealing with the intellectual position. Do not misunderstand me; I am not arguing against the value of apologetics altogether, but I am saying this, that a church which becomes governed by the apologetic interest is a church that is ceasing to function positively. The devil has got her, and she tends to be negative only and to fail to recognize the positive activity of the Holy Spirit. History shows that what the Boyle lecturers and Bishop Butler and others failed to do, God did by pouring out His Spirit upon men like Whitefield and Wesley.

The third reason, I would say, is a natural dislike of too much emotion. The theological thinker tends to be distrustful of emotion. "After all," he argues, "other people can and do display emotion; but we are different." In a most subtle manner such a man develops a dislike of emotion that becomes unhealthy and wrong; he loses his balance, and becomes guilty of quenching the Spirit.

Another closely related reason, which I think operates in particular today, is that there has been an excessive reaction against Pentecostalism and its phenomena. Many are so afraid of Pentecostalism and its excesses and aberrations that they are quenching the Spirit. There is always a danger of such extremes, of overreacting against something and so losing the balance of the Scripture.

There is another factor worthy of careful consideration. I have known a number of men belonging to the Reformed constituency who really seem to be controlled by some such thoughts as this. "After all," they say, "a man like John Wesley had a prominent part in the revival of the eighteenth century." From that they seem to deduce that there is something undesirable and wrong about revival. "Can any good come from such a quarter? If men like Wesley and Finney and other Arminians can be involved in revival and used in it, well, we ought to be suspicious of revival." The mistake here is that we all tend to think in terms of labels and parties, not realizing that God displays His sovereignty often in this way, that though a man may be muddled in his thinking, as John Wesley was at certain points, God may nevertheless bless him and use him. And if He cannot do this, then there is no such thing as the sovereignty of God, and His omnipotence. Thus because of party spirit we can go wrong in our thinking and be guilty of quenching the Spirit of God.

But perhaps the most important and most serious matter is this. The Puritans themselves do not seem to teach us anything about revival. Oh, that I could have quoted copiously and extensively out of the Puritans! But I cannot do so. As far as I can find, they did not write on the subject. Did they even recognize it? John Owen's volumes on the work of the Holy Spirit do not deal with it. Try to discover what John Owen has to say on John 7:37–39, or what he has to tell us on Peter's sermon in Acts 2,

306   D. M. Lloyd-Jones

"this is that which was spoken by the prophet Joel," or on Acts 3:19, "that times of refreshing may come from the presence of the Lord." He just does not deal with the subject of these verses; neither do the others. This undoubtedly creates a very real difficulty for many people. "The Puritans did not deal with revival," they say; "they never talked about it. Can it therefore be right? Is there not something inherently dubious about this whole matter?"

We must address ourselves directly to this question. Why did the Puritans not deal with revival? I would like to suggest some reasons for your consideration. Was it not partly the fact that they lived in a particular age and had to meet a particular need? The Puritans in their day were up-to-date; they were modern men; they lived in their own century and faced realistically the actual conditions which confronted them. They had to fight on many fronts themselves. They had to fight not only the old Roman teaching, and the High Church teaching of Laud and his friends, but also the views of some of the "wilder men" amongst themselves, and of the sects. I do not like this epithet "wilder men," but there were among the Puritans men like Walter Craddock and Morgan Llwyd, who differed in a radical way from men like John Owen and Thomas Goodwin. They were much more directly experimental in the pneumatic sense, and had leanings toward mysticism. This was certainly true of Morgan Llwyd and, of course, the Quakers. The leading Puritans, whose works we have, were fighting such men; they were gravely concerned about these excesses and afraid of them. The result was that much of their writing on the Holy Spirit was determined by this polemical interest, and hence very often they are too negative in their approach. I believe that is a partial explanation.

Dare I also hazard the opinion that the fact that some of these leading Puritans were brought up in a certain communion and carried over certain ideas and traditions with them may have had an inhibiting effect upon them? At any rate they were very concerned about order—perhaps too much so. So anxious were they that everything should be done "decently and in order" that I find it very difficult at times to acquit them of the charge of quenching the Spirit.

I am tempted to add another note. I wonder whether even temperament enters into this matter? I announced that I would speak on revival from an historical and theological standpoint. I very nearly added the word "geographical," and even a further word, "ethnological"! I am not sure whether this comes in, but I think it does. Every man has a fight to wage; we are all temperamentally different, and we all have particular weaknesses of temperament to fight against. I wonder whether it is not true to say that the Englishman has a particular fight just here, and that he should be aware of it? Is it just an accident that these revivals in the history of the church have generally been outside England? Not, of course, entirely. The eighteenth century stands out, as I have reminded you, and there were those odd sporadic instances in the seventeenth century. But is there not a real danger that unconsciously, because of temperament and make-up, one man may be more prone to the sin of quenching the Spirit than others of different temperaments?

Whatever may be the true explanation, we can certainly agree about this as regards the Puritans—their primary interest was pastoral and experiential in a personal sense. That was their genius; and it was this that fitted them for the peculiar work that they were called upon to do—the analysis of cases of conscience, the resolution of doubts, and helping people who were in trouble. They excelled at that, and there can be no doubt that this was the thing that was needed particularly in their day and generation.

There, then, are some, at any rate, of the reasons as I see things for the lack of interest in revival amongst those who belong to the Reformed tradition.

IV

Let us come now to another section—difficulties and objections to the idea of revival. An obvious general objection (with which I unfortunately have not the time to deal at length) is the dislike of phenomena. Some people are so appalled and alarmed at the phenomena that sometimes occur in revival that they dismiss the whole subject. The answer is, of course, that you can have, and have had, revivals where there have been no such phenomena at all. Revivals differ greatly from time to time and from age to age and from place to place. I leave it at that.

Here is another particular difficulty. I do not know exactly what is believed by present-day Plymouth Brethren but I do know that the early Brethren taught, and taught very strongly, that it was wrong to pray for revival because, they said, the Holy Ghost had been given once for all on the Day of Pentecost. (In view of that, what right have you to ask Him to come now?) That was their teaching, and I believe it has had a very pervasive effect and has influenced large numbers who do not belong to that section of the church. The argument is, "Why do you pray for the coming of the Spirit—for an outpouring of the Spirit? He was outpoured on the Day of Pentecost. How can He be poured out again?" Such teaching actively discourages prayer for revival.

Another objection sometimes alleged is that nowhere in the New Testament are we taught to pray for revival. Here we come to a subject which might well occupy the whole of our time. There is an abundant answer to this objection. The main point of it is this—that the New Testament church was not exhorted to pray for revival because it was in the midst of a revival. What we read about the church in the New Testament is an account of revival. The New Testament church was full of the power of the Spirit. When you read the history of revivals, are you not reminded at once of the book of the Acts of the Apostles? The church always looks like the church in the New Testament when she is in the midst of revival. The New Testament period was a period of revival; the great outpouring on the Day of Pentecost was continued. The church of the New Testament was a pneumatic church, filled with the Spirit. I have often put the argument like this. Take 1 Corinthians 14, where Paul has to write to the church about speaking in tongues and speaking one at a time, and how, if a man is prophesying and sees another wanting to speak, he should stop, and so on. Would you need to write that chapter to the church today? Of course not! Why? Because the church today is not in this pneumatic condition. The New Testament church was a church that was filled and baptized with the Spirit. (Let me add here another controversial remark. It seems to me that the societies that were started in England and Wales by the Methodist fathers of both schools of thought in the eighteenth century were much nearer to the New Testament church than were the Puritan churches of the seventeenth century. There was more of the freedom of the Spirit, more spontaneity, more taking part by the mass of the people. I think that is something which is worthy of our consideration.)

That, then, provides a part of the answer to the objection that we are not told to pray for revival in the New Testament. But there is much more along the same line. I know that the exegesis of Acts 3:19 is somewhat doubtful. Buchanan and Smeaton, however, seem to be in no doubt as to the exegesis; they say it refers to revival, and I tend to agree with them. These "times of refreshing . . . from the presence of the Lord," they say, are periods of revival, as if Peter's message was this: "Well now, here you have had the first great sample of the Spirit's power and blessing. This is going to keep on recurring until the time of the restitution of all things." Again, in order to prove that the New Testament church was a church in revival, look at this further evidence. In 1 Thessalonians 1:5, Paul says, "Our gospel came unto you not only in word, but in power and in the Holy Ghost, and with much assurance." What was it that turned the ancient world upside down? Was it just theological teaching? Was it mere enunciation of correct doctrine? Over and above that, there was this mighty "demonstration of the Spirit and of power." How did those people turn the world upside down? The answer is that in the book of Acts we have an account of a great revival, of the Spirit outpoured. What happened could not have happened otherwise. How did all these churches come into being? Was it merely that the apostles taught correct doctrine? Of course not! It was the Spirit's demonstration and power which accompanied the correct doctrine. Correct doctrine can leave the church dead; you can have dead orthodoxy; you can have a church that is perfectly orthodox but perfectly useless. Over and above, there was this demonstration, this unction, this authority, this outpouring of the Spirit's power. It is the only explanation of the astonishing things that happened.

That brings us to the next difficulty, about which we are hearing a good deal at the present time. We are told that we must not talk about revival because we need reformation first. You cannot have revival, it is said, without prior reformation. You must be right with respect to your doctrine before you have a right to pray for revival. So we must concentrate on reformation alone. I grant that the relationship between these two things is an extremely difficult question, but I hold that the line is not quite as clear-cut as some would have us think. What happened in the Reformation of the sixteenth century? To start with, of course, there was this unique factor, that not only was the teaching of the church of Rome wrong, her entire church system was wrong too. We called what happened "the Reformation" largely because of the revolution that took place in men's thoughts about the nature of the church and consequently in its organization. It was not only a change in doctrine. And let us never forget this, that there was a great revival in the period of the Reformation. You cannot read the account of a man like Latimer without realizing that obviously the man was being used as a revival preacher. Is it a feasible suggestion that the common people of England were influenced by a mere change of doctrinal teaching? Could that ever lead to such results? Can any examples of that be found? Of course not. No, no, there was a genuine revival then; the presence and the power of the Spirit were undoubtedly there. It is the only adequate explanation of what really took place in the sixteenth century.

Now let me say this on the other side. It is a fact of history that in Northern Ireland, before the revival of 1859, there had been a great period of doctrinal controversy. The Presbyterian Church had become very largely Arian, and the great and famous Henry Cooke had fought and won the great battle against Arianism well before the revival came. Actually, about thirty years before. That time interval is not without significance. To be fair, however, I have to recall these facts.

But now I want to put a fact on the other side again. There are people who say, "You have no right to talk about revival, you have no right to expect revival until people become Reformed in their doctrine." The simple answer to that is that George White-field received his baptism of power in 1737, but did not become a Calvinist in his theology until about 1739, when he was out in America. Revival had come to him, and through him to many others, before his doctrine became right. Exactly the same thing is true of Howell Harris in Wales. He had his great baptism of power in 1735, and it was only two or three years later that he came to see the truth doctrinally. Once more, therefore, I would use this argument. If you say that God cannot give revival until first of all we have had a reformation, you are speaking like an Arminian, you are saying that God cannot do this until we our-selves have first done something. That is to put a limit upon God. It is to lapse into Arminian terminology and thinking, and to deny the fundamental tenet of the Reformed position. If you truly believe in the sovereignty of God, you must believe that whatever the state of the church, God can send revival. As a sheer matter of fact, that is what God did in the eighteenth century. There was the church under the blight of deism and rationalism, and generally dissolute in her living. That was true of the clergy and the leaders; and among the Nonconformists there was a deadness resulting from the Arianism that had even infected a man like Isaac Watts. In the midst of such conditions God did this amazing and astonishing thing, even while some of the men He used were still confused in their doctrinal views. It is amazing that any man holding the Reformed position can be guilty of such a contradiction as to say that you cannot have revival unless you have reformation first. Such a man should never speak like that; he has no right to put in conditions. Revival is something that is wrought by God in sovereign freedom, often in spite of men.

V

Let me now attempt to summarize and assess the position. The result of all this confusion is that the church seems to be di-vided at the present time into two main groups. There is a group of people that always talk about revival and only about revival. They are only interested in the exceptional and unusual, and they tend to "despise the days of small things," the regular work of the church and the regular work of the Spirit in the church. The other group so emphasizes the ordinary, regular work of the church and of the Spirit in the church, that they distrust the whole notion of the unusual and exceptional. The answer is, of course, that both are wrong. Let me quote from Buchanan on the Holy Spirit. Buchanan was a professor in the Free Church College in Edinburgh, and this is what he wrote in 1856. "The Holy Spirit is not limited to any one mode of operation in the execution of His glorious work; and His sovereignty ought ever to be remembered when we are considering a subject of this nature. It has, unfortunately, been too much overlooked, when, on the one hand, some have insisted, as we think, with undue partiality and confidence, on a general and remarkable revival, as being in itself the best manifestation of the Spirit's grace, and as being, in all cases, a matter of promise to believing prayer; and when, on the other hand, not a few have looked to the quiet and gradual success of the Gospel ministry, to the exclusion, or at least disparagement, of any more sudden and remarkable work of grace." (Do you not know the two groups today?) "The former have given a too exclusive preference to what is extraordinary and striking; while the latter have fallen into the opposite error, of preferring what is more usual and quiet. We think it were better to admit of both methods of conversion, and to leave the choice to the sovereign wisdom and grace of the Spirit. It is equally possible for Him to convert souls successively or simultaneously; and in adopting either course doubtless He has wise ends in view. We have no sympathy with those who, overlooking the steady progress of the great work of conversion under a stated ministry, make no account of the multitudes who are added, one by one, to the church of the living God, merely because their conversion has not been attended with the outward manifestations of a great religious revival; nor can we agree with them in thinking, that the church has any sure warrant to expect that the Spirit will be bestowed, in every instance, in that particular way. But as little have

we any sympathy with those who, rejecting all revivals as unscrip-
tural delusions, profess to look exclusively to the gradual progress
of divine truth, and the slow advance of individual conversion under a stated ministry. Both methods—the simultaneous and the
successive conversion of souls—are equally within the power of
the Spirit; and there may exist wise reasons why, in certain cases,
the first should be chosen, while, in other cases, the second is pre-
ferred." There, I believe, you have a remarkable statement syn-
thesizing the characteristic experiences of the seventeenth and
eighteenth centuries, and God forbid that we should ever pit the
one way of divine working against the other. Both happen, in the
providence and wisdom of God.

What then is my final answer to all this? Once more, I can do
nothing better than quote to you out of Buchanan. "We have
been so much accustomed to look to the more slow, and quiet,
and gradual method of maintaining and extending the Kingdom
of Christ, that we are apt to be startled, and even to listen with
some degree of incredulous surprise, when we hear of any sudden and general work of the Spirit of God,—nay, we cease even
to expect and to pray for any more remarkable or more rapid
change in the state of the church and world, than what is usually
observed under her regular ministry." I wonder how many are
guilty of that today? "But God's 'ways are not as our ways, neither
are His thoughts as our thoughts'; and often, in the history of His
church, He has been pleased, for wise reasons, to manifest His
grace and power in a very extraordinary and remarkable manner; partly to awaken and arouse a slumbering church; partly
also, to alarm and convince gainsayers; and most of all, to teach
them at once the sovereignty and the power of that grace which
they are too prone to despise."

Then listen to a quotation from Jonathan Edwards in
Smeaton's book where the same point is made again in a remarkable manner. "It may be observed that from the fall of man
to our day, the work of Redemption in its effect has mainly been
carried on by remarkable communications of the Spirit of God."
Notice that. He continues, "Though there be a more constant influence of God's Spirit always in some degree attending His ordi-

nances, yet the way in which the greatest things have been done towards carrying on this work always has been by remarkable effusions at special seasons of mercy." Any impartial reading of church history must surely lead us to substantiate and to agree with the dictum of Jonathan Edwards. Surely the history of the progress and development of the church is largely a history of revivals, of these mighty exceptional effusions of the Spirit of God. There is no question that God has really kept His work alive and has advanced it most of all by these unusual, exceptional, signal manifestations of His glory and of His power. I am asserting that history alone proves that beyond any peradventure.

VI

I close by putting this question. Why should Reformed people, above everybody else, be interested in the subject of revival? Surely, for the following reasons. First, nothing so proves that the church is the church of God. The graph of the church's history is one of up and down, up and down. That in itself proves that the church is not a human institution. If it were, it would long since have perished and disappeared. It is the church of the living God. It is solely due to the fact that she is His and that He has graciously intervened from time to time for her preservation that she is alive.

Second, I would say this—that this history above everything shows man's impotence when left to himself. However great a defender of the faith he may be, however doughty a champion of orthodoxy, he can fight and sweat and pray and write and do all things, but he is of no avail, he is impotent, he cannot stem the tide. We persist in thinking that we can set the situation right. We start a new society, we write a book, we organize a campaign, and we are convinced that we are going to hold back the tide. But we cannot. When the enemy comes in like a flood, it is the Lord Who will raise and does raise the banner. The fact of revival proves, I say, so clearly again and again the impotence and the smallness of man left to himself.

Here is another important point. What so proves that the work of salvation is the work of the Holy Spirit, and not a mere matter of moral suasion or argumentation, as revival? How? Well, by the very suddenness of revival. If salvation is the result of argumentation and moral suasion, then you need to engage in it for some time. That was the whole fallacy in the thinking of a man like Charles G. Finney. Though he pays lip service to the Holy Spirit, he virtually excludes the Spirit. The work of conversion is achieved by a rational argument. That has always been the position of Arminianism, ultimately. But the Reformed man says, "No, no, it is the work of the Holy Spirit, the direct operation of the Spirit upon the man in his mind and heart and will, in illumination and renewing." And when and where is that seen more clearly than in a revival? Look at the suddenness of the conversions; yes, look especially at the fact which is found so abundantly in the history of revivals, that many people have been converted even before they reached the meeting or heard the preacher. They were converted on the road; conviction suddenly came upon them. You cannot say that is moral suasion. They had not even heard the sermon; there had been no preliminary argumentation whatsoever. Revival thus establishes and proves the great point which was in a sense *the* point of contention at the Synod of Dort—in conversion where does the Holy Spirit come in? The ultimate defect and error in the Arminian argument and all that has emanated from it is that it excludes the Holy Spirit from the real decision, and asserts that man is able to convert himself. Revival demonstrates the contrary contention that this is always and invariably the work of the Holy Spirit. In revivals you see that on a big and dramatic scale, and so attention is called to that truth.

In the fourth place, I would ask, Is there anything that so demonstrates the sovereignty of God as revival? Think of it in terms of the timing of revival. When does revival come? The answer is not that it is when we have produced certain preliminary conditions, as Finney taught. No, God does it at most unexpected times. You never know when He is going to do it; there is always a suddenness and an unexpectedness about it. It is Arminian thinking that teaches in some shape or form, "If only we do certain things then . . ." No, the history of revivals proves the exact opposite, both as regards the beginning, and equally with respect to the ending. This is something which is most glorious. Man not only cannot start a revival, he cannot stop it either. Nor can he keep it going when it has stopped. Men have tried to do all these things, but they have never succeeded. The sovereignty of God appears in the timing. Yes, and also the sovereignty of God appears in the place where revival starts. I do not understand Christian people who are not thrilled by the whole idea of revival. If there is one respect in which God confounds the wisdom of the wise more than in any other it is in revival. Look at the places in which He starts revival—little villages, hamlets, places you have never heard of. It is men who start their movements in London, in St. Paul's Cathedral, or in some great hotel. But God does not do that. He ridicules the wisdom of man and the cleverness and the importance of man both in the matter of time and in the matter of place, and also in the matter of the men used. Look at the men He has used. If you want a perfect exposition of 1 Corinthians 1:25–31, read books on revival. "Not many wise men after the flesh, not many noble," but the foolish, the nobodies, the unwise—God ridiculing, turning upside down the wisdom of men and exposing it. The sovereignty of God is seen in revival above everything.

Last, nothing so shows the irresistible character of grace as revival. This is seen, of course, in every true conversion, but it is in revival that it is seen on the grand scale, and unmistakably. Men who went to the meetings to upset them and to destroy them are suddenly struck, thrown down, their eyes are opened, and they are given life. There is nothing that is so obvious in a revival as just this irresistibility of the grace of God. Not only "the fools who came to scoff," but the enemies, the arrogant, are humbled, subdued, converted, and born again. Revival thus underlines and emphasizes this particular biblical doctrine in a striking manner.

The conclusion of the whole matter is this: that we are called at this moment above everything else to pray for revival. God forbid that we should become a body of people who just denounce activism and do nothing. That is what is said about some of us. God forbid it should be true. Are we to be merely negative, merely to point at the faults of others, to point out the holes in their system and to be always denouncing negatively and ridiculing them? Of course not. What then are we called upon to do? We are called upon to go on with our regular work of preaching the gospel in all its fulness, in all its wholeness, after the manner of the Puritan preaching that we were told about yesterday afternoon. Let us do everything we can by every biblical and legitimate means to propagate and to defend the faith. Let us use our apologetics in their right sphere. Let us do all that, and let us go on with the work of reformation in which we are engaged; but let us at the same time maintain the balance of which we were reminded by Buchanan. Let us pray for revival, because nothing else will avail us in the fight in which we are engaged. Thank God our efforts are producing results, and far be it from any of us to despise them or to underestimate them; but it is not enough. The age in which we are living and the condition of the church, not to mention the world, call for a mighty conviction of the sovereignty of God, the absolute necessity of the work of the Spirit, and these various other points I have been trying to emphasize. And that means that nothing less than revival is needed.

VII

Very well then; let us pledge ourselves to pray for an outpouring of the Spirit of God, and let me put the appeal to you to do so first of all in these words taken from Smeaton. "As to the peculiar mode of praying, we may say that in every season of general awakening the Christian community waits just as they waited for the effusion of the Spirit, with one accord in prayer and supplication in the interval between the Ascension and Pentecost. No other course has been prescribed; and the church of the present has all the warrant she ever had to wait, expect, and pray. The first disciples waited in the youthfulness of simple hope, not for a spirit which they had not, but for more of the Spirit which they had; and Christianity has not outlived itself. Ten days they waited with one accord in prayer, when of a sudden the Spirit came to give them spiritual eyes to apprehend divine things as they never knew them before, and to impart a joy which no man could take from them. It was prayer in the Spirit (Ephesians 6:18) and prayer for the Spirit, the great 'promise of the Father.' But the prayer which brought down the Holy Ghost was not that style of petition which ceases if it is not heard at once, or if the heart is out of tune. The prayer which prevails with Him Who gives the Spirit is that which will not let Him go without the blessing. When the spirit of extraordinary supplication is poured out from on high,—when an urgent desire is cherished for the Holy Ghost,— when the Church asks according to God's riches in glory, and expects such great things as God's promises warrant and Christ's merits can procure,—the time to favour Zion, the set time, is come (Psalms 102:16–18). When we look at the prayers in Scripture, we find that God's glory, the Church's growth and welfare, her holiness and progress, were ever highest in the thoughts and breathings of the saints than personal considerations. And if we are animated with any other frame of mind, it is not prayer taught by the Spirit, nor offered up in the Name of Christ. The praying attitude of the Church in the first days after the Ascension, when the disciples waited for the Spirit, should be the Church's attitude still. I need not refer to the copious references of the Apostles to the urgent duty of praying 'in the Spirit' and praying 'for the Spirit,' nor shall I refer at large to the habits of all true labourers, such as Luther, Welsh, Whitefield, and others, in proof of the great truth that prayer is the main work of the ministry. And no more mischievous and misleading theory could be propounded, nor any one more dishonouring to the Holy Spirit, than the principle adopted by the Plymouth Brethren, that because the Spirit was poured out at Pentecost, the Church has no need, and no warrant, to pray any more for the effusion of the Spirit of God. On the contrary, the more the Church asks the Spirit and waits for His communication, the more she receives. The prayer of faith in one incessant cry comes up from the earth in support of the efforts put forth for the conversion of a people ready to perish. This prayer goes before and follows after all the calls to repentance."

There is nothing better that one can do, therefore, in the light of that than to suggest that the urgent call that comes to us at this moment is to offer unceasingly the prayer that was offered up by Isaiah in the terrible day in which he found himself living. Listen:

> "Look down from heaven, and behold from the habitation of thy holiness and of thy glory: where is thy zeal and thy strength, the sounding of thy bowels and of thy mercies toward me? are they restrained? Doubtless thou art our father, though Abraham be ignorant of us, and Israel acknowledges us not: Thou, O Lord, art our father, our redeemer, thy name is from everlasting. O Lord, why hast thou made us to err from thy ways, and hardened our heart from thy fear? Return for thy servants' sake, the tribes of thine inheritance. The people of thy holiness have possessed it but a little while: our adversaries have trodden down thy sanctuary. We are thine: thou never barest rule over them; they were not called by thy name."

And then having asked God to look down he goes further.

> "Oh that thou wouldest rend the heavens, that thou wouldest come down, that the mountains might flow down at thy presence. As when the melting fire burneth, the fire causeth the waters to boil, to make thy name known to thine adversaries, that the nations may tremble at thy presence! When thou didst terrible things which we looked not for, thou camest down, the mountains flowed down at thy presence. For since the beginning of the world men have not heard, nor perceived by the ear, neither hath the eye seen, O God, beside thee, what he hath prepared for him that waiteth for him. Thou meetest him that rejoiceth and worketh righteousness, all that remember thee in thy ways: behold thou art wroth: for we have

sinned: in those is continuance, and we shall be saved. But we are all as an unclean thing, and all our righteous-nesses are as filthy rags; and we all do fade as a leaf; and our iniquities, like the wind, have taken us away. There is none that calleth upon thy name, that stirreth up himself to take hold of thee; for thou hast hid thy face from us, and hast consumed us, because of our iniquities. But now, O Lord, thou art our father; we are the clay, and thou art our potter; and we are all the work of thy hands" (Isaiah 63:15–64:8).

How many of us have stirred ourselves up to take hold of God? How many? This is typical biblical teaching; this was also the teaching of our fathers. They waited upon God and cried and cried until He did rend the heavens and come down. Let us lay hold upon Him and plead with Him to vindicate His own truth and the doctrines which are so dear to our hearts, that the church may be revived and masses of people may be saved.

[1] Ian R. K. Paisley, The "Fifty Nine" Revival; John T. Carson, God's River in Spate; Eifion Evans, When He is Come.

[2] By the Banner of Truth Trust.